V

# Chick Flicks

From *An Affair to Remember* to *Legally Blonde*, "chick flicks" have long been both championed and vilified by women and men, scholars and popular audiences. Like other forms of "chick culture, " which the editors define as a group of mostly American and British popular culture media forms focused primarily on twenty- to thirtysomething, middle-class—and frequently college-educated—women, chick flicks have been accused of reinscribing traditional attitudes and reactionary roles for women. On the other hand, they have been embraced as pleasurable and potentially liberating entertainments, assisting women in negotiating the challenges of contemporary life.

A companion to the successful anthology *Chick Lit: The New Woman's Fiction*, this edited volume consists of eleven original essays, prefaced by an introduction situating chick flicks within the larger context of chick culture as well as women's cinema. The essays consider chick flicks from a variety of angles, touching on issues of film history, female sexuality (heterosexual and homosexual), femininity, female friendship, age, race, ethnicity, class, consumerism, spectatorship, pleasure and gender definition. An afterword by feminist film theorist Karen Hollinger considers the chick flick's transformation from the woman's films of the 1940s to the friend- ship films of the 1980s and those of the "return to the classics" trend of the 1990s, while highlighting the value of the volume's contributions to contemporary debates and sketching possibilities for further study.

Contributors: Deborah Barker, Carol M. Dole, Suzanne Ferriss, Holly Hassel, Lisa Henderson, Karen Hollinger, Myra Mendible, Lisa M. Rüll, Margaret Tally, Maureen Turim, Kate Waites, Mallory Young.

**Suzanne Ferriss** is Professor of English at Nova Southeastern University. She has co-edited two volumes on the cultural study of fashion: *On Fashion* and *Footnotes: On Shoes*. She is also co-author of *A Handbook of Literary Feminisms*. Most recently, she co-edited, with Mallory Young, *Chick Lit: The New Woman's Fiction*, also published by Routledge.

**Mallory Young** is Professor of English and French at Tarleton State University. She has published on a variety of topics, from the *Odyssey* to Texas women's literature and, with Suzanne Ferriss, has co-authored several articles on chick culture. She co-edited, with Suzanne Ferriss, *Chick Lit: The New Woman's Fiction*, also published by Routledge.

# Chick Flicks

## Contemporary women at the movies

## Edited by Suzanne Ferriss and Mallory Young

 Routledge
Taylor & Francis Group

NEW YORK AND LONDON

First published 2008
by Routledge
270 Madison Ave, New York, NY 10016

Simultaneously published in the UK
by Routledge
2 Park Square, Milton Park, Abingdon, Oxon OX14 4RN

*Routledge is an imprint of the Taylor & Francis Group, an informa business*

© 2008 Taylor & Francis

Typeset in Sabon by
Keystroke, 28 High Street, Tettenhall, Wolverhampton, UK
Printed and bound in the United States of America
on acid-free paper by
Edwards Brothers, Inc., Lillington, NC

*Library of Congress Cataloging in Publication Data*
A catalog record has been requested for this book

ISBN10: 0–415–96255–2 (hbk)
ISBN10: 0–415–96256–0 (pbk)
ISBN10: 0–203–93555–1 (ebk)

ISBN13: 978–0–415–96255–1 (hbk)
ISBN13: 978–0–415–96256–8 (pbk)
ISBN13: 978–0–203–93555–2 (ebk)

For Steven and Craig

# Contents

# Images

# Acknowledgments

Once again we want to thank Matthew Byrnie, our editor at Routledge, for supporting our work on "chick culture." Our thanks go as well to Stan Spring for assistance in preparing the manuscript. We are also grateful for the supportive university environments that made our research possible. Suzanne thanks the Farquhar College of Arts and Sciences at Nova Southeastern University and the University of Trier, Germany. Mallory acknowledges the support of the Department of English and Languages and the Center for Instructional Technology at Tarleton State University; she also benefited from release time provided by Tarleton State University Organized Research Grants.

We also express our gratitude to the contributors to this volume. We greatly appreciate their patience, their loyalty, and their fine essays.

Special thanks go to our friends, colleagues, students, and family members who have shared with us their love for movies. Above all, our gratitude goes to our life partners and devoted movie companions who are always beside us, ready to watch, listen, discuss, and support—even when the movie is a chick flick. We dedicate this book to them.

# Chapter 1

# Introduction

## Chick flicks and chick culture

*Suzanne Ferriss and Mallory Young*

In this volume of essays, we consider chick flicks, a subject that inspires highly polarized and ambivalent responses. Chick flicks have been both championed and vilified by women and men, scholars and popular audiences. Like other forms of "chick culture," chick flicks have been accused of reinscribing traditional attitudes and reactionary roles for women. On the other hand, they have been embraced as pleasurable and potentially liberating entertainments, assisting women in negotiating the challenges of contemporary life.

We contend that the most valuable and productive consideration of chick flicks requires looking at them neither in isolation nor as simply one area of film studies. Rather, chick flicks are best addressed as one form of a prominent popular cultural phenomenon that can be termed *chick culture*.[1] In addressing chick flicks then, our book has a threefold purpose:

- To situate chick flicks in a larger context of chick cultural studies;
- To consider the place of chick flicks in film history and current film; and
- To consider various definitions, approaches, and responses to chick flicks without privileging any particular point of view.

Our collection seeks to examine the polarized responses and the range of positions in between, not advocating a single position but seeking to complicate and explore the questions chick forms, especially films, inevitably raise.

### Chick culture

While we hesitate to pin it down to a single, possibly reductive definition, chick culture can be productively viewed as a group of mostly American and British popular culture media forms focused primarily on twenty- to thirtysomething middle-class women. Along with chick flicks, the most prominent chick cultural forms are chick lit and chick TV programming, although other pop culture manifestations such as magazines, blogs, music—even car designs and energy drinks[2]—can be included in the chick line-up. The dawn of chick lit, the wildly popular body of literature largely spawned by British author Helen Fielding's 1996 novel *Bridget Jones's Diary*, provides a fairly clear starting point for the chick cultural explosion.[3] The TV series *Sex and the City*, based on the book by Candace Bushnell, appearing at the same time, provides another clue to its origins. As a phenomenon dating from the mid-1990s, the chick culture boom both reflected and promoted the new visibility of women in popular culture. What links the products of chick culture is, above all, "the contemporary media's heightened address to women" (Ashby). This deliberate address to female audiences suggested a growing recognition of women's significance in contemporary culture. The media reflected and even shaped women's complex social positioning—with its continued restrictions and its new freedoms—and their aspirations. At the same time, however, the rise of chick culture provided evidence of newly concerted efforts to manipulate and influence the spending habits of young women, whom marketers had at last identified as a huge force in an economy based on consumption.

The moniker *chick flick* dates back considerably further than the mid-1990s. Although impossible to trace definitively, its original use was surely as a derisive term—most commonly applied by unwilling male theatergoers to their girlfriends' film choices. One problem in any consideration of such films is that unlike *chick lit* which has a precise historical meaning,[4] the *chick flick* has yet to be clearly defined—even though Merriam-Webster has at last included it in the eminent dictionary's most recent update. Once we move beyond the, perhaps original, derogatory meaning—a sappy movie for women that men don't like—which films are we referring to? What, precisely, is a chick flick? We might be tempted to answer that we know one when we see one. But it is helpful to make some effort at definition. In the simplest, broadest sense, chick flicks are commercial films that appeal to a female audience. Although we are focusing in this discussion on contemporary films, chick flicks can also be seen as a much more inclusive film category. We do not want to suggest that films from other periods cannot be included as chick flicks.

We are most interested, however, in how contemporary movies designated as chick flicks are enmeshed, for good and for ill, with the wide range of responses invoked by chick culture. The term *chick* itself—whether applied to film, literature, or other popular culture forms—invites immediate and conflicting reactions. The term and reactions to it point up some of the larger issues involved in responses to chick culture.[5]

At the height of the women's liberation movement in the 1970s, the word *chick*, along with the word *girl*, was considered an insult, a demeaning diminutive, casting women as childlike, delicate, fluffy creatures in need of protection and guidance or as appendages to hip young males. Rejecting such terms was a declaration of equality and independence. To the feminists harking from this period—those now known as second-wave feminists—the contemporary revival of these terms signals a return to the infantilizing of women and a failure of their efforts to create a society based on gender equality. For many second-wave feminists, the term invokes an immediate negative response.

For women of a younger generation, however, the word *chick*, like *girl* (and even *bitch*), has been wielded knowingly to convey solidarity and signal empowerment. This new generation made up of women who were born with feminism as their heritage—often referred to as a third-wave feminist or postfeminist generation—has rejected or at least questioned some of the central tenets of feminist thought. Part of third-wavers' response to feminism has been the deliberate re-appropriation and re-visioning of terms that make second-wave feminists cringe: *Girlpower*. "You go, *girl*." "*Chicks* rule!" Much as homosexual activists transformed the disparaging term *queer* into a slogan to proclaim solidarity and increase their cultural visibility—"We're here. We're queer. Get used to it"—so the women of the third wave seek to reclaim and refashion their identity through terms considered unacceptable by the previous generation.

Above all, as the term *chick* suggests, chick culture is vitally linked to postfeminism. The split between feminism and postfeminism has largely been viewed as a generational one.[6] That isn't an entirely valid distinction: certainly many women in their twenties and thirties consider themselves feminists while plenty of women over forty indulge in supposedly post-feminist interests and pursuits such as fashion. It's also possible—and perhaps more helpful—to see feminism and postfeminism in terms of a continuity rather than a conflict. While many definitions of postfeminism have been advanced and many types identified, the most pervasive form—which has appropriately been labeled "chick" postfeminism—is the one most relevant to the study of chick culture.[7]

The ideas associated with postfeminism—and the presumed conflict between feminism and postfeminism—are central to any consideration of chick flicks, which can be viewed as the prime postfeminist media texts.[8] At the risk of indulging in reductionism or oversimplification, we do think it's useful to note some of the major feminist/postfeminist distinctions:

*Feminism:*
- Reliance on political action, political movements, and political solutions;
- The primacy of equality; resistance to and critique of the patriarchy;
- Choice is collective—it refers to women's right *not* to have children and to enter careers and professions formerly closed to them;
- A rejection—or at least questioning—of femininity;

- Suspicion of and resistance to media-driven popular culture and the consumerism it supports;
- Humor is based on the disjunction between traditional women's roles and women as powerful, independent people.

*Postfeminism:*
- The personal as political; agenda is replaced by attitude;
- A rejection of second-wave anger and blame against the patriarchy;
- Choice is individual—whether of family, career, cosmetic surgery, or nail color;
- A return to femininity and sexuality;
- Pleasure in media-driven popular culture and an embracing of the joys of consumerism;
- Humor is based on the discrepancy between the ideals put forward by both feminism and the media, and the reality of life in the modern world; as such, the humor of postfeminism is often ironically self-deprecating.

Not surprisingly, then, postfeminists might tend to view feminists as angry, humorless, self-proclaimed victims of patriarchy. Feminists might tend to view postfeminists as shallow, mindless, unconscious victims of media culture and consumerism.[9] Unquestionably film plays a significant role in framing and reflecting women's place in culture, particularly during moments of cultural shift. It is not surprising then that chick flicks raise questions about women's place—their prescribed social and sexual roles, the role of female friendship and camaraderie—and play out the difficulties of negotiating expectations and achieving independence. They do so, however, in complex and often contradictory ways. Chick flicks illustrate, reflect, and present all of the cultural characteristics associated with the chick postfeminist aesthetic: a return to femininity, the primacy of romantic attachments, girlpower, a focus on female pleasure and pleasures, and the value of consumer culture and girlie goods, including designer clothes, expensive and impractical footwear, and trendy accessories.

As a result, chick flicks are often accused of promoting a retreat into pre-feminist concerns and the unthinking embrace of consumerism, of endorsing not true freedom but "the freedom to shop (and to cook)" (Holmlund) through protagonists "whose preoccupations are likely to involve romance, career choices, and hair gels" (Mizejewski). The women who identify with postfeminist films, however, welcome the inclusion of romance and femininity in their lives, and resist reducing femininity, as many critics do, to superficial markers such as high heels and frilly dresses. The admission of girliness, they argue, doesn't mean the loss of female independence and power.

By contrast, defenders of "girlie feminism" view femininity and sexuality as empowering. Many postfeminists seek to reclaim and refashion their sexuality, to unsettle traditional images of feminine virtue by substituting an image of themselves as "lusty feminists of the third-wave" (Stoller 84). This idea clearly applies to a number of women's films as well as to the popular TV series *Sex and the City*, *Bust* magazine, female pop singers, and more. The members of this "New Girl Order," as *Bust* editor Debbie Stoller styled the girlpower rebellion, defiantly embrace sexuality as its means: "Our mission is to seek out pleasure wherever we can find it. In other words, if it feels good, screw it" (79). The title of Stoller's essay, "Sex and the Thinking Girl," obviously plays on *Sex and the Single Girl,* the title of Helen Gurley Brown's 1962 bestseller. At once she embraces the message of sexual liberation first advanced by the creator of *Cosmopolitan,* and distances the "new girls" from the old, implying that young women are consciously seeking pleasure rather than using their bodies as tokens of exchange with men.[10] While second-wave feminists Andrea Dworkin and Catherine MacKinnon argued that pornographic films sexually objectified women, leading directly to sexual harassment, battery and even rape, some contemporary female erotic filmmakers have sought to revolutionize porn by representing women's sexual pleasure in particular. Winner of the first Emma Award for Feminist Porn (named in honor of feminist Emma Goldman) awarded recently at the "Vixens and Visionaries" event in Toronto, Canada, director Tristan Taormino said, "I consciously work to create images that contradict (and hopefully challenge) other porn that represents women only as objects and vehicles for male pleasure." While such films are by no means mainstream, they have been associated with a more pervasive "raunch culture"—from "Cardio Striptease" fitness workouts to Paris Hilton's sex tapes to *Girls Gone Wild!* to the sexually provocative music videos of Madonna, Britney Spears, and Christina Aguilera (Humphrey). Such manifestations can be seen either as allowing women the freedoms of sexual expression and pleasure previously denied them or as demeaning women by exploiting them once again as sex objects, leading them to overvalue appearance and embrace plastic surgery.[11]

Chick flicks do occupy this conflicted territory. While Drew Barrymore does indeed twirl around a pole in *Charlie's Angels: Full Throttle* (2003), she does so in a campy parody of a stripper and, in both films in the series, the Angels are kept far too busy chasing bad guys to engage in actual sex. As a sex worker, Julia Roberts in *Pretty Woman* (1990) spends more time lounging demurely in a tub than in bed. Cher (Alicia Silverstone) in *Clueless* (1995) is "hymenally challenged"—a virgin. Still, while it may not be overtly represented, many chick flick heroines—from Bridget Jones to *Legally Blonde's* Elle—clearly do engage in sex outside of marriage and juggle multiple partners. However, a substantial number of recent chick flicks, in adhering to older generic conventions of romance and comedy

*Image 1.1* Bridget Jones (Renée Zellweger) attracting her boss's attention

and responding to a more conservative political climate, have returned to the subtle promotion of chastity, allowing the heroine only one sexual partner or, in some cases—such as *Just Like Heaven* (2005), *The Family Stone* (2005), and *She's the Man* (2006)—offering the chaste kiss at the end as the only expression of sexuality.

It is equally important to note that many postfeminist chick flicks do continue to address issues and take stands originally considered feminist. To view chick flicks either from an entirely negative or an entirely positive perspective would be to oversimplify both the films and the issues involved.

We agree with Joanne Hollows and Rachel Moseley that "we need new ways of understanding the relationship between feminism and the popular" and "that such an approach need not imply that post-feminism is either a good or a bad thing" (8–9). Indeed recent films identified as chick flicks can be drawn on to provide clear examples of the claims of both attackers and defenders. On the one hand, some films do reinforce traditional gender roles, promoting a kind of ideological retrenchment similar to that promoted by many films of the late 1940s and early 1950s. As women returned to the home from the more challenging venues of wartime activities, Hollywood pointed them in the direction of the suburbs. Films like *Miracle on 34th Street* (1947) and *Funny Face* (1957) ridiculed or undercut women's efforts at intellectual and professional accomplishment. Similarly, some chick flicks from the 1990s and 2000s promote the choice of romance, family, and love over career and independence. Such films as *Kate and Leopold* (2001), *Thirteen Going on Thirty* (2004), *Raising Helen* (2004), and *The Family Stone* (2005) suggest that a career-oriented woman is a lonely and unhappy one.

On the other hand, just as some 1940s and even 1950s films showed women successfully navigating both career and romance, so do many of today's chick flicks. The idea that women can follow professions while wearing pink, have both successful careers and successful relationships— that femininity and feminism aren't mutually exclusive—appears prominently in both mainstream and independent films embraced by female viewers. *Legally Blonde* (2001), *Real Women Have Curves* (2002), *Bend It Like Beckham* (2002), *Mona Lisa Smile* (2003), *The Devil Wears Prada* (2006), and numerous others promote the idea that while it may not be possible to have it all, choosing education and career does not mean abandoning the possibility of happiness.[12] Many of these films also promote the value and benefits of female friendship.[13] Some contemporary chick flicks do focus on (often vicious) competition among women—seen most prominently in teen flicks such as *Mean Girls* (2004). But today's chick flicks far more often put forward a view of female solidarity and support. Even *Legally Blonde*'s Elle, who finds herself clashing with snobbish female students at Harvard, has the support of her former sorority sisters and the down-to-earth women at the local beauty salon.

The same diversity of perspectives appears with respect to the issue of marriage. Even some romantic comedies which, according to expected conventions, lead necessarily to wedding bells, actually question the desirability of marriage. The attraction between the married heroine (Claudette Colbert) and her bachelor rescuer (Clark Gable) in *It Happened One Night* (1934) suggests that romance and marriage are not necessarily linked. Similarly, the 1990s chick flick *Four Weddings and a Funeral* (1994) highlights the relationship between Charles (Hugh Grant) and Carrie (Andie MacDowell) who finally, after her failed marriage and his failed wedding, get together but agree to forgo wedding vows themselves. The primacy of beauty is another issue that chick flicks can be found simultaneously promoting and questioning. While the beauty makeover may be a chick-flick staple, a film like *The Truth about Cats and Dogs* (1996) is able to explore and finally reject the standard ideals of beauty while remaining solidly in chick-flick territory.

Still other films complicate the issues even further, taking an ambivalent position. Such films as *Bridget Jones's Diary* (2001), *The Princess Diaries* (2001), and *In Her Shoes* (2005) raise questions about the choices women confront, the possibility of having it all, and the effects of society's rigorous and capricious standards of beauty. Others combine pre-feminist and feminist ideas, refusing to choose between them. The 2005 film *Just Like Heaven* provides the ideal example of a postfeminist fairy tale. In this modern take on *Sleeping Beauty*, the film's protagonist lies in an accident-induced coma. As in the original pre-feminist tale, she will be awakened by a kiss. In both cases, the heroine will experience a sexual/spiritual awakening as well as a physical one. But in the postfeminist version, our sleeping heroine (played by Reese Witherspoon) will not simply lie around waiting for her prince to come. Rather, her spirit detaches itself and goes out to find him—and she must "wake" him so that he can appear just in time to wake her. As the movie's prince (played by Mark Ruffalo) pointedly claims, "when we first met, I kept saying that you were dead. But it was me that was dead, and you brought me back. You saved me. And now it's my turn to save you." At the film's end, Reese Witherspoon's character has found her prince but lost her chance to be an attending physician at the hospital where she obsessively worked before her accident. The film doesn't let us know whether her future will return her to a (perhaps more balanced) professional role—individual viewers are left to make that decision for themselves.

## The other chick: race, sexuality, age, class

A charge frequently leveled against chick culture and chick flicks relates to their homogeneity. Feminist film scholars, in fact, frequently discuss chick flicks as part of "a white 'chick' backlash that denies class, avoids race, ignores (older) age, and 'straight'-jackets sexuality" (Holmlund). The nature of chick flicks' appeal and their potential value in illuminating women's lives are controversial issues partly because such films have featured protagonists who are overwhelmingly young, heterosexual, white, and middle-class. To at least some extent, this may be an issue of definition. Frequently the designation of *chick flick* has, for example, been automatically avoided in the case of films focused on women of color. Even such films as *The Color Purple* (1985) that clearly exhibit many of the most obvious characteristics and conventions of chick flicks, are rarely included. This may not be surprising. Krin Gabbard points out that many recent scholars in black media studies, while giving black performers credit for strides made in the film industry, are, nonetheless, "just as concerned with how the artists are appropriated by white culture" ("Cinema"). To identify films focused on women of color as chick flicks will strike some viewers and scholars as a move to de-legitimize them or assimilate them into a prevailing white culture.

Still, major elements of chick flicks appear in cinematic offerings focused on women of color and in films produced in other parts of the world. Accusing chick flicks of focusing entirely on "whiteness" risks oversimplifying the issues while ignoring or dismissing the contributions of other ethnicities. Instead, we should be asking how African-American, Latina, Asian, and other non-Anglo ethnic varieties have appropriated and transformed chick-flick conventions while also noting the features shared across ethnic, racial, and national lines. Issues of women's identity, sexuality, generational conflict (particularly between mothers and daughters), and romantic trials are indeed remarkably similar. Do these similarities reflect a similar experience for twenty-first-century women across ethnic boundaries? Or does the form itself—and the politics of production and reception controlling it—enforce artificial similarities? Could the answer be yes to both questions? If we simply dismiss chick flicks for failing to focus on various ethnic groups, we will neglect to ask these questions.

Unquestionably, woman-centered films from a variety of cultures are gaining mainstream recognition and attention. African-American chick flicks include, for example, those based on the novels of Terry McMillan—*Waiting to Exhale* and *How Stella Got Her Groove Back* (1998)—*Love Jones* (2004), and *Beauty Shop* (2005). *Girlfight* (2000), *Tortilla Soup* (2001) (based on the original Chinese *Eat, Drink, Man, Woman* [1994]), *Maid in Manhattan* (2002), and *Real Women Have Curves* qualify as Latina chick flicks.[14] Each film conforms to and significantly transforms what might be seen as prevailing chick conventions. These films and many others should, we believe, be considered in the context of chick culture.

Asian, Indian, and Pakistani cultures have also been prominent in the production of films that can be and have been labeled chick flicks. *Bride and Prejudice* (2004), the Bollywood version of Jane Austen's classic, suggests that the conventions of femininity and romance characteristic of the chick flick are present in Indian culture, despite the persistence of arranged marriages. Directed by Gurinder Chadha on the heels of her wildly successful paean to girlpower, *Bend It Like Beckham*, the film, it's worth noting, was intended not for Indian but Anglo-American audiences. We might suspect then that it makes Indian traditions conform to chick-flick formulas rather than creating a truly indigenous Indian chick flick that captures the complexity of women's position in the developing world. Still, the appearance of chick conventions beyond the borders of

*Image 1.2* In *Bride and Prejudice* Austen's Jane and Elizabeth Bennet are transformed into Jaya and Lalita Bakshi (Namrata Shirodkar and Aishwarya Rai)

the Anglo-American world might suggest their adaptability to diverse cultures, as Mira Nair's film *Monsoon Wedding* (2001) more clearly demonstrates. Several Asian films including *Eat, Drink, Man, Woman* and the original Japanese version of *Shall We Dance?* (1996) also give evidence of the widespread appeal of chick-flick formulas. European filmmakers too, once distinguished by their reliance on dark, naturalistic themes, now participate in chick cultural trends, as evidenced by the enormously popular French film *Amélie* (2001) and the German/Italian *Bella Martha* (2002), among others.

Similar issues arise in considering sexuality in chick flicks. While Chris Holmlund has contended that the chick flick " 'straight'-jackets sexuality" by foregrounding heterosexual romance, others have pointed to possibilities for more complex, even resistant, viewing practices. Patricia White, for example, has argued that "cinema is a public fantasy that engages spectators' particular, private scripts of desire and identification" (xv). While some female viewers may identify with the attractive chick-flick heroine who is the object of male desire on screen, others may see her as an object of desire herself.[15] Lesbian viewers have also seen models of same-sex desire in secondary characters, as in Mrs Danver's worshipful devotion to the first Mrs De Winter in Alfred Hitchcock's classic *Rebecca* (1940).[16]

With the growing visibility of sexual minorities, a contemporary lesbian or "queer chick flick" has arguably emerged. In her study of lesbian representation in film, Shameem Kabir has identified a homoerotic subtext in *The Color Purple*, *Fried Green Tomatoes* (1991), and *Thelma and Louise* (1991). Such films certainly stress female friendship and solidarity. While they may only portray female bonding (or homosociality), it is entirely possible that they convey themes of lesbian desire. (In the case of *Fried Green Tomatoes*, the original novel indicates an underlying homoerotic theme far more strongly than the film, suggesting both its actual presence in the film and the tendency of mainstream films to suppress such elements.) Other recent films such as *Go Fish* (1993), *The Incredibly True Adventure of Two Girls in Love* (1995), *The Watermelon Woman* (1996), *Better than Chocolate* (1999), and *Saving Face* (2005) do address lesbian relationships openly. These explicitly lesbian films lead us to ask if the primacy of romance in the narrative offers a true "queer" alternative to the heterosexual romance or merely shapes lesbian desire to fit a heterosexual romantic model. Either way, it is important to note that the boundaries of the chick flick are being pushed.

In addition to a new lesbian heroine, recent films have offered a strange blend of hyperfemininity and hypermasculinity in the action heroines of films like *Lara Croft: Tomb Raider* (2001) and *Kill Bill, Vol. 1* and *Vol. 2* (2003, 2004). Whether these films offer women a pleasurable fantasy of postfeminist empowerment or rather cater to male fears and fantasies is an issue worth exploring in connection with postfeminist film. Once again, such films certainly stretch the generally perceived limits of chick flicks.

*Image 1.3* The Asian-American romantic comedy *Saving Face* subscribes to and subverts chick-flick conventions

When it comes to the issue of age, woman-centered films have recently made significant strides in expanding their focus. Indeed a whole body of "older bird" films has gained prominence. Some of these—*Unconditional Love* (2002), *Calendar Girls* (2003), *Mrs Henderson Presents* (2005)—are independent or British films, intended for a small, select, non-mainstream audience. Others, however—*The Banger Sisters* (2002), *Something's Gotta Give* (2003), *Under the Tuscan Sun* (2003), and *Because I Said So* (2007)—are big-budget Hollywood star vehicles. In many of these films, women over forty discover—or rediscover—their independence, sexuality, or self-worth. Still, not all critics and viewers are pleased to see such an expansion of chick formulas. Like the films directed at younger women, many of these films, while allowing older women to display and explore sexuality, reinscribe that sexuality safely within the confines of the traditional family.

In *Unconditional Love*, for example, Kathy Bates' character is a fifty-something housewife whose husband walks out on her at the film's beginning. With the help of a handsome, much younger man and her feisty daughter-in-law, she tracks down a killer and finds self-respect. In the end, she is reunited with her repentant and reformed husband—on her terms.[17] In *Something's Gotta Give*, Diane Keaton's character has her confidence in her sexual desirability and desire restored. But, while the film offers the possibility of an older woman–younger man pairing, it doesn't follow through on that option. Keaton opts instead for a commitment-phobic but age-appropriate mate. The film thus manages to indulge middle-aged women's fantasies while allaying middle-aged male fears. Still, the supposedly narrow confines of the chick flick prove to be less narrow than might have been suspected.

Issues of class and consumerism are particularly controversial ones. The critique of the pursuit of status through purchase—and the role of women as the main symbols, if not the main suspects—goes back, of course, to Thorstein Veblen's 1899 *Theory of the Leisure Class*. The prevailing critique today suggests that women who, quite literally, "buy in" to post-feminist consumerist culture are the victims of a patriarchal order and a capitalistic media-driven system seeking to suppress and control them. It is certainly true that chick flicks, like chick culture in general, often uncritically embrace a supposedly feminine delight in consumer goods. The montage of the heroine joyously shopping—often as part of a physical and/or class-status makeover—is a staple of chick flicks including *Moonstruck* (1987), *Pretty Woman*, *Freaky Friday* (2003), and *The Devil Wears Prada*.

To assume that women are the unwilling and unknowing victims of manipulation, however, may be to demean and discredit them—and even to suggest that they are incapable of making choices for themselves. As Hollows and Moseley note, " 'consumption' in these debates frequently becomes reduced to the act of purchase and the reproduction of consumer capitalism, ignoring more extensive understandings of consumption" (11). Recent studies of film spectatorship and stardom complicate such readings, as do studies of women's uses of fashion to shape identity and even undermine gender conventions. The exaggerated presentation of femininity in *Legally Blonde*, for instance, is clearly part of the film's critique of the dumb-blonde stereotype. Elle (Reese Witherspoon) not only manages to graduate from Harvard law school, her success turns on her superior knowledge of perms. Obviously played for laughs, this plot twist does not imply that female viewers should devote more serious attention to hair care; rather, they take pleasure in the revelation that Elle's critics are more overinvested in appearance than she is.

In addition, the relationship between spectatorship and spending may be less clear than critics suggest. Rather than influencing women to spend more on consumer goods, such films—along with chick-lit novels—might just as likely satisfy or replace the desire to consume.[18] Viewers of chick flicks can spend $10 for a movie ticket to enjoy the vicarious screen experience of glamour instead of purchasing pricey Prada outfits or Manolo Blahniks. Chick flicks thus serve as a relatively guiltless pleasure.

While in the 1930s, Hollywood studios did blatantly attempt to forge fashion trends by joining forces with fashion houses, offering inexpensive knock-offs of designer dresses for middle-class consumers,[19] such tactics are relatively rare in today's chick flicks. Nonetheless, although the connection of present-day chick flicks to consumer desire is more complicated, the relationship between chick flicks and consumer culture cannot be denied. Luxury watchmaker Tissot did prominently feature its "Touch" watches on the wrists of Brad Pitt and Angelina Jolie in *Mr & Mrs Smith* (2005) and then featured the stars in print ads and jewelry store window displays. Chanel conscripted *Moulin Rouge!* director Baz Luhrmann to create a television ad for its classic fragrance No. 5 starring Nicole Kidman, a project then documented in the pages of *Vogue*. And the beauty supply chain Sephora launched a campaign based on *The Devil Wears Prada*—unimaginatively titled "The Devil Wears Sephora"—quite obviously trying to capitalize (literally) on the film's setting in the beauty industry.[20] The effects of such strategies are difficult to measure. Did these campaigns actually entice film viewers to buy the products by making glamour appear accessible through purchase? Or, given the campaigns' obvious emphasis on fantasy—particularly in the case of Chanel, which presented Kidman as a ball-gowned and bejeweled starlet—did the ads only reinforce the luxury brands as exclusive and out of reach of the average consumer/viewer? Either way the intent to promote consumerist desire is clear.

Certainly, chick flicks, like other commercial films, are enmeshed in a complex network created by mega corporations to reach a global consumer market.[21] The same corporation may produce and distribute the film featured on the morning programs and late-night talk shows on the network it owns, and reviewed in the pages of the magazine it publishes. And chick flicks, in particular, often intersect with other chick media, such as magazines. Celebrities such as Reese Witherspoon and Kate Hudson grace the covers of fashion magazines and others have been hired to advertise products, from Rachel Welch for hair extensions to Elizabeth Hurley for milk. However, similar strategies are used to reach male consumers, as well, suggesting that the indictment of popular women's media as consumerist may not only miss the complexities of contemporary media culture but unfairly single out female consumers for criticism. [22]

## The pleasure principle: chicks just wanna have fun

Of course, most viewers of chick flicks never consider the political ramifications of postfeminism or the subtle subtexts of female friendship films. For most of the audience, watching chick flicks is a matter of pleasure. In *Chick Flicks: A Movie Lover's Guide to the Movies Women Love*, film critic Jami Bernard claims a chick flick is "any movie that makes a special connection with a female audience" (xii). In their almost identically titled *Chick Flicks: Movies Women Love*, Jo Berry and Angie Errigo define it as "a film made specifically to appeal to a female audience" (1). Rather than perceiving the term *chick* as a disparaging appellation that marginalizes women's films, they have instead embraced it to categorize films on the basis of the pleasure they bring women, emphasizing desire with their repeated use of the phrase "movies women love."

Until recently, most feminist film critics ignored the pleasures women have found in film stressing instead that Hollywood films have marginalized and objectified women, leading them to accept a position as victim. Molly Haskell claimed that the majority of the so-called "woman's films" of the 1930s and 1940s, often cited as precursors to chick flicks, presented the female protagonist as a victim. By identifying with her, the female viewer was led to wallow in self-pity rather than to rebel against unfairness and inequity. At its lowest level, she wrote, the woman's film "fills a masturbatory need, it is soft-core emotional porn for the frustrated housewife" (155). Like Haskell, Mary Ann Doane argued that the only pleasures offered by the woman's film were masochistic. She claimed that the films presented the female protagonist as an object of male desire, promoting the female audience's identification with her as passive objects, rather than active agents, of desire. Jeanine Basinger countered that the woman's film operated out of a paradox: "It both held women in social bondage and released them into a dream of potency and freedom. It drew women in with images of what was lacking in their own lives and sent them home reassured that their own lives were the right thing after all" (6).

More recent writing about the woman's film and its female audience has challenged such views. Pam Cook notes that such arguments "imply that the category of the woman's picture exists in order to dupe female spectators into believing that they are important, while subtly marginalizing and disempowering them" (229). Instead, she and others have suggested that cinema offers women (and men) more complex possibilities for identification. Judith Mayne, for example, has rejected the idea that spectators are seeking to identify with those most like them. Instead, "spectators may experience the thrill of reinventing themselves rather than simply having their social identities or positions bolstered" (Cook 234). It is unlikely, then, that chick-flick viewers presume they are or can become Julia Roberts or Renée Zellweger. In part, they take pleasure in the obvious difference between themselves and the women on the screen, just as women of earlier eras gravitated toward the glamour of Hollywood stars, who served as unreal, transcendent figures of desirability and femininity. In her study of British women's reactions to Hollywood films of the 1940s and 1950s, Jackie Stacey found that "the cinema . . . was remembered as offering spectators the chance to be part of another world and participate in its glamour in contrast to their own lives" (116).

Several recent chick flicks even take an ironic stance on overly simple theories of identification. *Down with Love* (2003), for example, a tongue-in-cheek homage to the films of Doris Day and Rock Hudson, consciously distanced itself from contemporary fashion with its retro 1960s art design, and even from contemporary sexual politics, with its campy send-up of a world of "playboys" and sexy stewardesses. Instead, viewers were invited to revel in the distance, credited perhaps with additional knowledge of Hudson's homosexuality which made any pretense to real romance between the film couple a joke.[23]

The pleasure women take in chick flicks is not, it should also be noted, a purely self-centered or solitary one. Like shopping, going to the movies is often an experience women share, rather than pursue individually. The chick flick *Sleepless in Seattle* (1993) self-reflexively stages a typical chick-flick viewing: Meg Ryan and Rosie O'Donnell cry together over *An Affair to Remember* (1957) while sitting next to each other on a sofa eating popcorn in their pajamas. (In a companion scene, Rita Wilson tells the plot to her male dining companions, who dismiss it as a "chick movie" and mock her own weepy response by claiming to have cried at the end of *The Dirty Dozen*.) The shared experience of chick flicks is surely a major contributor to their appeal.

The principle of pleasure clearly complicates some of the more censorious views of chick flicks. Reactions are polarized and reflect more general and entrenched divisions in response to popular culture. On one side are

Marxists including members of the Frankfurt School, such as Theodor Adorno and Max Horkheimer, who criticized the "culture industry" for cranking out products for profit and inspiring passivity rather than resistance to capitalism. On the other are those such as John Fiske who stress the power of the audience to interpret media texts and create alternative or resistant readings. We would argue that positions in between such readings are not only possible but preferable, given the increased complexity of contemporary culture in a late capitalist society. If chick flicks are influencing female viewers to accept rather than resist the societal conventions that restrict them, then surely such films are open to censure. But given the complexities of spectatorship and psychology found in response to the woman's film, it is just as likely that chick flicks allow women to enjoy imaginative possibilities or to indulge in vicarious experience that assists them in returning to the challenges that face them. In fact, it's only fair to note that in this heyday of postfeminist chick flicks, the number and percentage of women attending college, graduate schools, and professional schools continues to climb.[24]

Women's complex negotiation with film may explain, in part, the range of films commonly designated as chick flicks. Some, such as *Bridget Jones's Diary*, stress the audience's identification with an ordinary working girl, seeking love and companionship in contemporary London while sidestepping the intrusions of her family and relying instead on her friends for support. Others, such as *Gone with the Wind* (1939), present female characters far removed from the daily grind, offering escapist fantasies of fulfillment.

Considering chick flicks as a group emphasizes the fluidity of generic classification. Chick flicks do not clearly align themselves with any particular genre. Certainly some contemporary chick flicks can be traced back to 1930s and 1940s woman's films. Although these films cannot be tied to a single genre themselves, those most often cited as "classic" woman's films—films such as *Dark Victory* (1939), *Rebecca* (1940), *Now, Voyager* (1942), and *Mildred Pierce* (1945)—are all melodramas. The origins, then, of at least one type of chick flick may be found here: the melodramatic woman's film may well be the source of chick-flick "weepies" such as *Terms of Endearment* (1983), *Beaches* (1988), *The Hours* (2002), and *The Notebook* (2004).

The woman's film cannot, on the other hand, be considered the source of chick-flick romantic comedies, such as *Four Weddings and a Funeral* or *French Kiss* (1995). Seeking the roots of these films, we need to look to another early film genre, the screwball comedy. Early romantic comedies such as *It Happened One Night* and *Bringing Up Baby* (1938) although not created for a specifically female audience, did, like the woman's film, feature a female protagonist. As James Harvey has noted, the "screwball comedy . . . was a special kind of woman's game nearly always favoring the heroine to win" (287); it was the "witty heroine who had the edge" (409). These classic comedies also focused on the dynamics of heterosexual romance, treating obstacles and impediments not with sentimentality but as sources of humor. The prevalence of remarriage storylines allowed characters, particularly females, to acknowledge sexual experience.[25] Dialogue in classic remarriage comedies such as *His Girl Friday* (1940) and *The Philadelphia Story* (1940) featured witty banter between the sexes about sexual desire and performance that, while cloaked in innuendo, may prefigure the frankness of contemporary chick-flick comedies from *When Harry Met Sally* (1989) with its fake female orgasm scene to *How to Lose a Guy in 10 Days* (2003), in which Andie (Kate Hudson) deliberately causes an argument by nicknaming her boyfriend's member "Princess Sophia."

Even romantic comedy and melodrama together, however, do not account for the full range of chick flicks, which includes the gun-toting heroines in *Thelma and Louise*, the strange mix of cannibalism and humor in *Fried Green Tomatoes*, the Cinderella story of *Pretty Woman*, the old-world elegance of *Pride and Prejudice* (2005)—and possibly the leather-clad futuristic revenge fantasy of Lara Croft.

As the popular guides referenced earlier suggest, chick flicks can, in the broadest sense, be defined as films that give women pleasure. We would add, as we have above, that they are overtly commercial films tailored to appeal to a female audience. In our view, it is no shame that the films are successful and popular—that doesn't necessarily mean that the women who view them are mindless dupes of the patriarchal Hollywood machine. Instead, we suggest that they are legitimate consumers of film, desirous of entertainment that either speaks to them in ways that they can identify with or that offers them tried and true fantasies. Rather than mindlessly pining after a dream they've been fed to keep them down, they are exercising their imaginations and forging connections, however tenuously, with images of more glamorous femininity and purer, simpler visions of success and independence. Other definitions of chick flicks are put forward by other viewers and scholars. Each, we believe, enriches the discussion in some way. No single definition is finally possible—nor, we contend, is it necessary.

## The essays in this volume

The essays included in this volume are not intended to cover the field of chick flicks nor of postfeminist film theory. Rather we have selected essays that we believe will help situate chick flicks as part of chick culture and initiate a critical discussion. We don't expect readers to accept the ideas in all of the essays presented here—indeed many of the authors disagree among themselves in what we think is a productive and meaningful way.

Just as the films themselves reflect a wide range of views, so do our contributors. We are inviting readers to engage in a similarly beneficial give and take.

While we intend the collection to work as a unified whole, we also hope that individual essays will stand on their own. What follows is a brief note on each essay to help readers choose those they will find most interesting, useful, or challenging.

The first essays in the volume consider the origins and conventions—historical and contemporary—of the chick flick. In the opening essay, "Women's Films: Comedy, Drama, Romance," Maureen Turim considers the historical background of chick flicks. She contends that their origins lie much further back in film history than usually noticed, in films that cross generic boundaries and appeal to audiences of both male and female moviegoers. Citing examples from the teens through the fifties, she argues that the woman-centered film straddles the genres of drama and comedy. Recurrent themes shared by earlier women's films and contemporary chick flicks include girls' coming of age and the travails of shopgirls and female professionals, as well as marriage, divorce, and reconciliation.

Hollywood has produced a long tradition of films featuring a seemingly unattractive girl transformed into an attractive woman. In "Fashioning Femininity in the Makeover Flick," Suzanne Ferriss focuses on makeover films that deliberately highlight fashion not simply as a means of physical transformation but as an essential part of the film narrative. Fashion makeover films, such as *Funny Face* (1957), *Party Girl* (1995), and *The Devil Wears Prada* (2006), raise significant questions regarding the relationship between external beauty and inner worth, as well as fashion's role in feminine self-transformation and display, offering insights into the place of consumer culture in chick flicks, as well as women's lives.

The definition of femininity itself is at stake in Carol Dole's essay. In "The Return of Pink: *Legally Blonde*, Third-Wave Feminism and Having It All," she considers what might be called postfeminist chick flicks advocating "girlpower" for teens and younger girls, and promising unlimited opportunities for females. Focusing on *Legally Blonde* (2001), she explores how costuming—relentlessly pink—augments the film narrative to suggest that femininity and feminism can go hand in hand.

If a true chick flick is designed to appeal to a female audience, can the same be said of the music? In "A Soundtrack for Our Lives: Chick-Flick Music," Lisa Rüll argues that chick flicks have established a more complex relationship between music and movie-making than other films. She explores how music functions to advance the narrative within chick-flick films and also considers how the compilations cash in on the success of films such as *Bridget Jones's Diary* (2001). Chick-flick music, like the movies themselves, valorizes female voices and reinforces narrative concerns with women's empowerment.

Subsequent essays test the boundaries of the chick flick, considering variations in region, age, sexuality, ethnicity, and nationality. While the chick-flick trend has its roots and arguably its greatest influence in mainstream middle-America and Britain, it has inspired translations that challenge thematic and generic boundaries. One such variant appears in regional chick flicks, particularly those set in the South. *Gone with the Wind* (1939), as the South's most famous woman's film, embodies contradictions that persist in what Deborah Barker calls the "Southern-fried chick flick" in her essay of that title. In contemporary films such as *Steel Magnolias* (1989) and *Fried Green Tomatoes* (1991), a spunky, independent working woman is put in her place by a masculine leading man, as Scarlett was by Rhett. The South, according to Barker, functions as an ideal setting for playing out contemporary tensions between feminism and the backlash against it.

While such films have tended to feature a young protagonist, Margaret Tally argues that an "older bird" chick flick exists. Films such as *The Banger Sisters* (2002), *Under the Tuscan Sun* (2003), and *Calendar Girls* (2003) offer more realistic portrayals of middle-aged women than films from the 1950s such as *Sunset Boulevard* (1950) and *All About Eve* (1950) which featured the aging female losing her social powers and sinking into depression and madness. Taking Nancy Meyer's *Something's Gotta Give* (2003) as exemplary, she argues that the films do present an affirmative image of sexually alive older women but still contain their sexual expression within the confines of family. Like other variations from the conventional chick-flick model, they offer conflicted and ambivalent messages about women.

Recognition of lesbian sexuality introduces further complexity into chick-flick formulas. Lisa Henderson's "Simple Pleasures: Lesbian Community and *Go Fish*" considers the issue of film spectatorship and lesbian spectators at a specific moment in the mid-1990s. Henderson argues that the 1994 independent film *Go Fish* functioned as both an example and an anti-example of the Hollywood romantic comedy. Following the standard romantic conventions but dispensing with the typical requirement for heterosexual engagement, *Go Fish* thus provided a new context for its lesbian characters. At the same time, rather than merely influencing or reflecting its audience, the film initiated a dialogue leading to a "communal ethos."

Communities of women united by ethnicity and class appear in chick flicks as well. In "Chica Flicks: Postfeminism, Class, and the Latina American Dream," Myra Mendible considers films such as *I Like It Like That* (1994), *Maid in Manhattan* (2002), and *Real Women Have Curves* (2002). In these films, the ethnic working-class woman poses a triple threat to the social and economic status quo—as lower-class, as female, and as other—but also serves to reaffirm the reliability and value of the American dream. The "chica flicks" surveyed hint at the potential for an oppositional politics and an independent Latina subjectivity. At the same time, they are structured and informed by the grand narrative of American populism—particularly its promise of equal opportunity, upward mobility, and consumerist pleasures.

The final essays in the collection test the generic boundaries of the chick flick. Several recent European filmmakers, for example, have managed to incorporate elements of English-language chick flicks while retaining a darker naturalistic perspective more typical of European films. While some—for instance, the Italian *Bread and Tulips* (2000) and the French *Happenstance* (2000)—merely play out typical romantic-comedy themes in different settings, others offer more distinctly European resistance to romance conventions. In "Chic Flicks: The New European Romance," Mallory Young considers *Amélie* (2001), *The Princess and the Warrior* (2000), and *Mostly Martha* (2001) as "quirkier and edgier than mainstream American romantic movies." Still, she notes that the films refrain from treating romantic love as utterly futile or absurd as European filmmakers of a previous generation would have. As such, they effect a compromise of sorts, fusing naturalism with romanticism.

As Young's essay attests, chick-flick conventions have transformed existing modes of film. The essays that follow ask whether gender-bending versions of the action film might be a form of chick flick as well. An intelligent female—the "babe scientist"—is central to what Holly Hassel identifies as a trend to reshape the American action film, or "male melodrama," into a quasi-chick flick. In "The 'Babe Scientist' Phenomenon: The Illusion of Inclusion in 1990s American Action Films," she traces the decade-long effort to feminize the action-adventure film by incorporating an attractive female collaborator as an antagonist to the male hero.

Kate Waites sees the warrior woman figure, who appears to be the equal of men as she brandishes swords and engages in martial arts combat to overcome villainy, as constructed more to appeal to young male audiences than to young women looking for female models of heroism. In "Babes in Boots: Hollywood's Oxymoronic Warrior Woman," she contends that Lara Croft, Charlie's Angels, and Beatrix Kiddo are constructed to suit extreme notions of conventional femininity even as they go about their business of "kicking enemy butt." While the films she discusses may feature strong female protagonists, by catering to male spectators they cannot truly claim the title *chick flick*.

In her Afterword, Karen Hollinger questions whether contemporary chick flicks can be considered progressive advances over their predecessors, not simply the woman's films of the 1940s but also the friendship films of the 1980s and those of the "return to the classics" trend of the 1990s. She contends that chick flicks present ambiguities and contradictions, raising important questions about women and film that the contributors to this volume have only begun to explore.

Our volume is intended to initiate, not close, discussion on the phenomenon of chick flicks and chick culture. Whatever position scholars, filmgoers, and others might take, chick flicks' prominence as a part of contemporary popular culture makes serious consideration not only worthwhile but essential.

## Notes

We would like to thank Myra Mendible and Karen Hollinger for their insightful comments on earlier drafts of this essay. Our thanks also go to Gerald Duchovnay who included a version of this essay in the Fall 2007 issue of *Post Script: Essays in Film and the Humanities*.

1 Rochelle Mabry, in her essay "About a Girl: Female Subjectivity and Sexuality in Contemporary 'Chick' Culture," was, to our knowledge, the first to use this term in an academic context.
2 Coca-Cola, for instance, advertises its Tab Energy drink as "fuel to be fabulous." Commercials on screen and online describe it as "the deliciously pink 5 calorie energy drink created specifically for women with a sense of style and purpose." The product's interactive website offers music, desktop images, e-greetings and "daily thoughts" with a decidedly feminine appeal, boldly colored pink.
3 See the Introduction to Ferriss and Young, *Chick Lit: The New Woman's Fiction* for information on the genesis and development of chick lit.
4 See Ferriss and Young (Intro.), and Mazza.
5 See Ferriss and Young, "Chicks, Girls and Choice."
6 See Henry.
7 This term is put forward by Chris Holmlund in the October 2005 issue of *Cinema Journal*. Holmlund also identifies two other forms of postfeminism: "grrrl" postfeminism which can be identified with third-wave feminism, and "academic" postfeminism which she uses to refer to academic theorists "steeped in French, British, and American postmodern, postcolonial, post-structural, queer, (etc.), theory." Cris Mazza, by contrast, presents a compelling view of postfeminism as the next phase of feminism, a phase in which women no longer see themselves as victims of patriarchy, blaming and harboring anger towards men. Rather, postfeminist women accept responsibility for their choices and their lives. For further discussion of postfeminism see Baumgardner and Richards, Dicker and Piepmeir, Henry, Modleski, Roiphe, Rowe-Finkbeiner, Walker, and Wolf.
8 For this reason, *Cinema Journal* devoted an "In Focus" section to the subject in Winter 2005. In it, one prominent film scholar defines chick postfeminism as a "backlash against or a dismissal of the desirability for equality between women and men, in the workforce and in the family" (Holmlund). That seems to us a reductive view. Instead, it is more legitimate to note, as Yvonne Tasker and Diane Negra do, that "the continuing contradiction between women's personal and professional lives is more likely to be foregrounded in post-feminist discourse than the failure to eliminate either the pay gap or the burden of care between men and women." Overall, the essays included do a fine job of presenting the issues from feminist film scholars' perspectives.

9  Joanne Hollows and Rachel Moseley argue that such resistance to popular culture on the part of feminists may be disingenuous. They contend that "apart from women actively involved in the second-wave of feminism in the 1960s and 1970s, most people's initial knowledge and understanding of feminism has been formed within the popular and through representation. Rather than coming to consciousness through involvement in feminist movements, most people become conscious of feminism through the way it is represented in popular culture" (2).

10  See Ferriss and Young, "Chicks, Girls and Choice."

11  Madonna's 1980s postfeminist discourse is clearly a precursor to and major influence on the 1990s movement we focus on here. Her later works, however, such as *Erotica* (1992), *Body of Evidence* (1993), and her book *Sex* (1992) provide ideal examples of the 1990s' postfeminist aesthetic. See, for example, Humphrey and Fricke for favorable accounts of Madonna's sexual power politics. On the other hand, both Ariel Levy and Pamela Paul have argued that participants in "raunch culture" mistake sexual power for power itself.

12  Nor does it necessarily mean eschewing domestic pleasures. Joanne Hollows argues that "the domestic can't be simply celebrated as a site of feminine virtue or as a site of pre-feminist subordination. Instead, the meanings of the domestic, and domestic femininities, are contextual and historical and what operates as a site of subordination for some women may operate as the object of fantasy for others" (114).

13  Karen Hollinger's book, *In the Company of Women: Contemporary Female Friendship Films*, explores this issue fully.

14  It is worth noting that the modern ethnic Cinderella story of *Maid in Manhattan*, unlike the other films mentioned here, was clearly aimed not at Latina but at white audiences.

15  Laura Mulvey argued that classic cinema positions the female protagonist as the object of a male gaze, that she embodies "to-be-looked-at ness," and that female spectators find pleasure in narcissistic identification with her, imagining themselves in her position. Recent film theory has criticized this theory for reifying gender stereotypes and presuming an exclusively heterosexual model of desire. For a succinct overview of complications introduced by consideration of lesbian spectatorship, see Hollinger, "Theorizing."

16  See Berenstein.

17  *Unconditional Love*, however, was not successful at the box office.

18  On chick lit's relation to fashion and consumerism, see Van Slooten.

19  See Eckert and Gaines.

20  By contrast, television appears to have more successfully targeted viewers to sell products. The online shopping site SeenON! (www.seenon.com) allows consumers to search for the clothing, furniture, cars and even paint colors featured in their favorite shows, such as *Desperate Housewives* and *Grey's Anatomy*. The film category features only a handful of recent releases, while the TV section organizes dozens of shows by network.

21  See MediaChannel's chart for a compelling visual representation of the six major media corporations and their holdings.

22  It may also be worth observing that at least one recent film, *The Devil Wears Prada*, based on Lauren Weisberger's chick-lit *roman à clef* about her stint working for Anna Wintour at *Vogue*, holds fashionistas up to ridicule.

23  Still, it should be noted that the film was not a box office success, finding its primary audience through a cult appeal to gay men and academic women. The suggestion here may be that the distancing mainstream chick-flick audiences will embrace has a limit.

24  The National Center for Education Statistics in the US reports in *The Condition of Education 2006* that "At the graduate and professional level, as among undergraduates, women are outpacing men, in raw numbers and in particular fields. . . . Women now earn more degrees than do men in a range of fields once overwhelmingly male . . . and women earn as many degrees as men in such previously male-dominated disciplines as medicine and law, the report says. A generation ago, women earned only a quarter to a third of those degrees. And women have maintained their dominance in fields they have long flocked to, such as education" ("Enrollments Keep Rising").

25  The term "remarriage comedy" comes from Stanley Cavell.

## Works cited

Adorno, Theodor W. and Max Horkheimer. *Dialectic of Enlightenment.* 1947. Trans. John Cumming. New York: Verso, 1997.

Ashby, Justine. "Postfeminism in the British Frame." *Cinema Journal* 44.2 (2005): 127–33. <http://muse.jhu.edu/journals/cinema_journal/v044.2ashby.html>.

Basinger, Jeanine. *A Woman's View: How Hollywood Spoke to Women, 1930–1960.* New York: Knopf, 1993.

Baumgardner, Jennifer and Amy Richards. *Manifesta: Young Women, Feminism, and the Future.* New York: Farrar, 2000.

Berenstein, Rhona J. "Adaptation, Censorship, and Audiences of Questionable Type: Lesbian Sightings in *Rebecca* (1940) and *The Uninvited* (1944)." *Cinema Journal* 37.3 (Spring 1998): 16–37.

Bernard, Jami. *Chick Flicks: A Movie Lover's Guide to the Movies Women Love.* New York: Citadel, 1997.

Berry, Jo and Angie Errigo. *Chick Flicks: Movies Women Love.* London: Orion, 2004.

Cavell, Stanley. *Pursuits of Happiness: The Hollywood Comedy of Remarriage.* Cambridge, MA: Harvard University Press, 1981.

Cook, Pam. "No Fixed Address: The Woman's Picture from *Outrage* to *Blue Steel.*" In *Contemporary Hollywood Cinema.* Ed. Steve Neale and Murray Smith. London and New York: Routledge, 1998: 229–46.

Dicker, Rory and Alison Piepmeier. *Catching a Wave: Reclaiming Feminism for the 21st Century.* Boston: Northeastern University Press, 2003.

Doane, Mary Ann. *The Desire to Desire: The Woman's Film of the 1940s.* Bloomington: Indiana University Press, 1987.

Eckert, Charles. "The Carole Lombard in Macy's Window." *Quarterly Review of Film and Video* 3 (1978): 1–21.

"Enrollments Keep Rising, and Most Are by Women, Says Annual Report on Condition of Education." *The Chronicle of Higher Education*, June 2, 2006. <http://chronicle.com/daily/2006/06/2006060205n.htm>.

Ferriss, Suzanne and Mallory Young. "Chicks, Girls and Choice: Redefining Feminism." *Junctures: The Journal for Thematic Dialogue* 6 (2006): 87–97.

——"Introduction." In *Chick Lit: The New Woman's Fiction.* Ed. Suzanne Ferriss and Mallory Young. New York: Routledge, 2006: 1–13.

Fiske, John. *Understanding Popular Culture.* London: Unwin Hyman, 1998.

Fricke, Erika. "Material Girls: Behind the Seams of Beloved Pop Icons Dolly Parton and Madonna." *Bitch: Feminist Response to Pop Culture* 32 (Summer 2006): 62–67.

Gabbard, Krin. *Black Magic: White Hollywood and African American Culture.* New Brunswick, NJ: Rutgers University Press, 2004.

——"Cinema and Media Studies: Snapshot of an Emerging Discipline." *The Chronicle of Higher Education*, Feb. 17, 2006. <http://chronicle.com/weekly/v52/i24/24b01401.htm>.

Gaines, Jane. "War, Women and Lipstick: Fan Mags in the Forties." *Heresies* 18 (1986): 42–47.

——"The Queen Christina Tie-Ups: Convergence of Shop Windows and Screen." *Quarterly Review of Film and Video* 11 (1989): 35–60.

Harvey, James. *Romantic Comedy in Hollywood, from Lubitsch to Sturges.* 1987. New York: Da Capo, 1998.

Haskell, Molly. *From Reverence to Rape: The Treatment of Women in the Movies.* 1973. 2nd ed. Chicago: University of Chicago Press, 1987.

Henry, Astrid. *Not My Mother's Sister: Generational Conflict and Third-Wave Feminism.* Bloomington: Indiana University Press, 2004.

Hollinger, Karen. *In the Company of Women: Contemporary Female Friendship Films.* Minneapolis: University of Minnesota Press, 1998.

——"Theorizing Mainstream Female Spectatorship: The Case of the Popular Lesbian Film." *Cinema Journal* 37.2 (Winter 1998): 3–17.

Hollows, Joanne and Rachel Moseley (eds). *Feminism in Popular Culture.* Oxford: Berg, 2006.

Hollows, Joanne. "Can I Go Home Yet? Feminism, Post-feminism and Domesticity." In *Feminism in Popular Culture.* Ed. Joanne Hollows and Rachel Moseley. Oxford: Berg, 2006: 97–118.

Holmlund, Chris. "Postfeminism from A to G." *Cinema Journal* 44.2 (2005). <http://muse.jhu.edu/journals/cinema_journal/v044.2holmlund.html>.

Humphrey, Michelle. "Bare Necessity: On Porn and Progress with Author Carly Milne." *Bitch: Feminist Response to Pop Culture* 32 (Summer 2006): 58–61.

Just Like Heaven *Script—Dialogue Transcript.* Drew's Script-O-Rama. <http://www.script-o-rama.com/movie_scripts/j/just-like-heaven-script-transcript.html>.

Kabir, Shameem. *Daughters of Desire: Lesbian Representations in Film.* London: Cassell, 1998.

Levy, Ariel. *Female Chauvinist Pigs: Women and the Rise of Raunch Culture.* New York: Free Press, 2005.

Mayne, Judith. *Cinema and Spectatorship.* New York and London: Routledge, 1993.

Mazza, Cris. "Who's Laughing Now? A Short History of Chick Lit and the Perversion of a Genre." In *Chick Lit: The New Woman's Fiction.* Ed. Suzanne Ferriss and Mallory Young. New York: Routledge, 2006: 17–28.

MediaChannel.org. "Ultra Concentrated Media: Top Selling Brands." <http://www.mediachannel.org/ownership/chart.shtml>.

Mizejewski, Linda. "Dressed to Kill: Postfeminist Noir." *Cinema Journal* 44.2 (2005). <http://muse.jhu.edu/journals/cinema_journal/v044.2mizejewski.html>.

Modleski, Tania. *Feminism without Women: Culture and Criticism in a Post-feminist Age*. New York: Routledge, 1991.

Mulvey, Laura. "Visual Pleasure and Narrative Cinema." In *Feminism and Film Theory*. Ed. Constance Penley. New York: Routledge, 1988: 57–68.

Paul, Pamela. *Pornified: How Pornography Is Transforming Our Lives, Our Relationships, and Our Families*. New York: Times Books, 2005.

Roiphe, Katie. *The Morning After: Sex, Fear, and Feminism on Campus*. Boston: Little, Brown, 1993.

Rowe-Finkbeiner, Kristin. *The F-Word: Feminism in Jeopardy: Women, Politics, and the Future*. Emeryville, CA: Seal, 2004.

Stacey, Jackie. *Star Gazing: Hollywood Cinema and Female Spectatorship*. London and New York: Routledge, 1994.

Stoller, Debbie. "Sex and the Thinking Girl." In *The Bust Guide to the New Girl Order*. Ed. Marcelle Karp and Debbie Stoller. New York: Penguin, 1999: 74–84.

Tasker, Yvonne and Diane Negra. "In Focus: Postfeminism and Contemporary Media Studies." *Cinema Journal* 44.2 (2005). <http://muse.jhu.edu/journals/cinema_journal/v044.2tasker.html>.

Taormino, Tristan. "Political Smut Makers: Feminist Porn Takes Center Stage at Historic Event." *The Village Voice*, June 8, 2006. <http://www.villagevoice.com/people/0624,taormino,73480,24.html>.

Van Slooten, Jessica Lyn. "Fashionably Indebted: Conspicuous Consumption, Fashion, and Romance in Sophie Kinsella's Shopaholic Trilogy." In *Chick Lit: The New Woman's Fiction*. Ed. Suzanne Ferriss and Mallory Young. New York: Routledge, 2006: 219–38.

Veblen, Thorstein. *Theory of the Leisure Class*. 1899. Introduction by Robert Lekachman. London: Penguin, 1994.

Walker, Natasha. *The New Feminism*. London: Little, Brown, 1998.

Wolf, Naomi. *Fire With Fire: The New Female Power and How it Will Change the 21st Century*. New York: Random, 1993.

White, Patricia. *unInvited: Classical Hollywood Cinema and Lesbian Representability*. Bloomington and Indianapolis: Indiana University Press, 1999.

# Chapter 2

# Women's films
## Comedy, drama, romance

*Maureen Turim*

Much current discussion of chick flicks briefly mentions their antecedents in earlier film history, while touting the evolution of female lead characters. Clearly, some of today's romantic comedy heroines and the female protagonists of melodrama engage in sexual encounters much more openly and with less direct chastisement for doing so than did some of their predecessors. However, we should not confuse engaging in sex acts or actively pursuing partners outside marriage with all that constitutes a desiring subject. In fact many of today's heroines seem to know or discover less about their desires than some of their ancestors. It is for this reason that we should compare structures, delving beneath certain superficial characteristics and references that differentiate the time periods.

Indeed the antecedents of many of today's chick flicks may be traced far back in film history. As Rochelle Mabry points out, most chick flicks today are either romantic comedies or admixtures of comedy and drama. The woman-centered romance has in fact long been split between the genres of drama and comedy, or has created an amalgam, the dramatic comedy. It investigates girls' coming of age, shopgirls and women workers in relationship to office romance and sexual harassment, relationships with men and with other women, marriage, divorce, and reconciliation. The dramatic comedy and comedic genres such as screwball comedy were considered films with broad-based appeal, directed and advertised to both sexes.

By contrast, women's weepies, tearjerkers, domestic melodramas were, in the vernacular of Hollywood, the generic categories seen as appealing almost exclusively to a female audience. This assumption is in part based on prejudices of male reviewers who wielded great power over exhibition patterns in the pages of the trade press and the major dailies. If both sexes traditionally flocked to melodramas in the Teens and early Twenties, by the Thirties and Forties, reviewers felt the extremes of emotional appeal played out through formulaic narratives were unworthy of their attention. Assigning their continued appeal to a female audience could be read in part as a misogynist act, blaming the sex already seen as more emotional, less educated, and less artistically sophisticated for what may have lingered within mass appeal.

Much of the early theoretical feminist writing on melodrama keenly saw the denigrating of the genre as a male elitist perspective against mass culture itself. Couched as an aesthetic judgment, such masculinist disdain saw as feminine the excess within a melodramatic mode. In fact, some of the disdain may have been riddled with homophobia, in reaction to the gay male following that the woman's films garnered, especially in a time when no decent portrayals of gay men made their way to the screen.

Countering such dismissive critical attitudes, we might note there were no absolute lines between those films dismissed as weepies and those films championed as dramas, just as there is no absolute distinction between the domestic melodrama on stage and the chamber drama. Certainly both explore the impact of jealousies, desires, murders, and departures within the family; however, greater restraint and minimalism marked Ibsen's or Chekhov's expression and staging in their chamber dramas. The legacy of the chamber drama may be felt in the films of Victor Seastrom (Victor Sjöström) and Ingmar Bergman. We should note how popular these influential playwrights and filmmakers were with female audiences, especially in the central focus they sometimes gave to female characters who challenge male authority.

When one thinks of the weepie, one thinks particularly of the ending of *Stella Dallas* first filmed by Henry King in 1925 and remade by King Vidor in 1937 or *Dark Victory* (1939), famed as they are for the pathos of a self-sacrificing mother and a brave bride facing blindness and death. It is worth noting that *Stella Dallas* was adapted from an Olive Higgins Prouty novel, first by Frances Marion; it represents a literature not only written by women, but aimed at a female audience. *Dark Victory*, however, came from the Broadway play by George Emerson Brewer, Jr. and Bertram Bloch, and was hardly confined to a strictly female audience. Consider the praise in Frank S. Nugent's April 21, 1939 review in *The New York Times*, even while he notes the appeal to a female emotionality:

> Casey Robinson's adaptation has distilled the drama of the play; Edmund Goulding's direction has fused it into a deeply moving unity; Miss [Bette] Davis, Geraldine Fitzgerald, and the rest of the players have made it one of the most sensitive and haunting pictures of the season.
>
> It isn't, of course, entirely a happy theatrical occasion. The mascara was running freely at the Music Hall yesterday. For essentially the picture is simply a protracted death scene in which the heroine's doom is sealed almost in the first sequence.

This review demonstrates that the woman's film could be elevated in the eyes of the critics by masterful engagement with the form. The success of these films in the Twenties and Thirties was guaranteed by their appeal to male as well as female audiences.

Certainly the draw of great actresses in the woman's film had much to do with the appeal of this genre to a wide audience. Barbara Stanwyck, Bette Davis, Miriam Hopkins, Merle Oberon, Joan Crawford, and Joan Fontaine lent their considerable talents to fulfilling these demanding parts, tempering the sentimentality of certain scenes with nuanced and varied performances.

Clearly, some women's films approached the drama (psychological or social) as much as they harked back to high melodrama; there was never a sharp distinction between drama and the woman's film, between the plays that were opening on Broadway and the films adapted from them, between appeals to a general public and one to the female gender alone. Consider the adaptation of Lillian Hellman's play, *The Children's Hour*, as *These Three* (1936) directed by William Wyler and starring Miriam Hopkins as Martha Dobie and Merle Oberon as Karen Wright. Joel McCrea appears as Dr Joe Cardin, the man whose friendship with both women generates the evil rumors that Hellman originally presented as accusations by a pupil of a lesbian love between the two teachers. A serious drama, despite the studio self-censorship of this aspect of the play's daring innovation, the film also notably appealed to a female audience with its sharply drawn female protagonists. While it remains accurate to hold that Hollywood not only censored the play, but accentuated its conventional melodrama, this ignores how impressive the film remains as a drama centering on female friendship, unfair charges, and one girl's accusations giving way to mass hysteria.

Only the "romance pix" among the appellations for comedies has a similar pejorative edge, albeit one far less pronounced than the disparagement attached to the weepie. Romantic comedies, screwball comedies, comedies of remarriage were—and are—all seen with more respect by male reviewers, as they heralded the comediennes who held their own in these comic battles of the sexes.

If the chick flick may be seen as a revival or continuation of previously existent genres, how does previous writing on those genres affect the way we regard today's films? Specifically, as much of the best writing on the woman's film genre was historical (informed by critical theory) and theoretical (informed by image theories and psychoanalysis), what tools does a look at the history of the genre provide? Popular reception of chick flicks, even while acknowledging their legacy, often lacks the tools to read these films critically.

Molly Haskell, in *From Reverence to Rape*, was key in critiquing the intense identification accomplished by the genre. Haskell coined an indelible phrase to describe the expenditure of time and emotion spent on woman's films: "wet, wasted afternoons" (154). In fact, Haskell's book devotes a separate chapter to "The Woman's Film" even as most of the rest of the book proceeds through US film, decade by decade, with chapters titled The Big Lie, The Twenties, The Thirties, The Woman's Film, The Forties, The Fifties, The Europeans, The Sixties, and The Age of Ambivalence. This structure isolates the woman's film as a genre limited to the Thirties and Forties. Still, Haskell remains opposed on many levels to the very tradition of singling out a genre aimed at women. Reacting defensively to the pejoratives of other critics, she treats the genre as a marketing ploy by Hollywood that is cynically disrespectful of its target audience. Haskell's approach evidences great antagonism towards popular culture; her book attempts to redeem the films she admires from the more pandering instances of Hollywood production. Subsequently, for her the most unforgivable error of the woman's film remains the excessive play to emotional response, cheaply earned in her estimation.

Mary Ann Doane's exacting definition of the women's picture focuses on these same melodramas, with a significant shift in assessment and methodology. She begins by addressing popular usage: "The label 'woman's film' refers to a genre of Hollywood films produced from the silent era through the 1950s and early '60s but most heavily concentrated and most popular in the 1930s and '40s" (3). She then notes how the films center on women, using terminology that indicates her theoretically informed analysis, telling us that the films' female protagonists have "significant access to point of view structures and the enunciative level of the filmic discourse" (3). It is the women's story the film tells. She also stipulates "the films treat problems defined as 'female' (problems revolving around domestic life, the family, children, self-sacrifice, and the relationship between women and production vs. that between women and reproduction), and, most crucially, are directed toward a female audience" (3). Further, Doane holds that the genre has ideological implications: "The existence of the women's picture both recognizes the importance of women, and marginalizes them. By constructing this different space for women (Haskell's 'wet, wasted afternoons') it performs a vital function in society's ordering of sexual difference" (3).

Her actual corpus in Desire to Desire includes Back Street (1941), Dark Victory (1939), Dark Mirror (1946), The Two Mrs Carrolls (1947), Caught (1949), Rebecca (1940), The Heiress (1949), Gaslight (1944), Now, Voyager (1942), and Secret Beyond the Door (1948). Note that Gothic and domestic melodrama of the early 1940s predominates. Her theoretical parti-pris is richly multiple, but a main argument examines the way this genre addresses but confines female desire, enclosing female identification within a representation marked by limits, reticence, displacements, and fears.

To this same corpus of films, Diane Waldman brings an analysis more centered on historical context, reading the films as emanating from and speaking to homefront anxieties during the war, and Gothic paranoia about husbands and male intentions. Similarly, Andrea Walsh provides a reading that emphasizes historical context, in fact drawing on reflection theory to emphasize, and as a result, perhaps exaggerate their overdetermination by history and the war, as well as their symbolic reading within it.

If the domestic melodrama as it evolves into the woman's picture often eschewed comedy in favor of intense emotional identifications and traumatic turns of events, it may be due to its great affinity for the Gothic. Many of the films labeled woman's pictures were more likely to employ a suspense structure than a comic mode. As Doane, Waldman, and Walsh all point out, this preoccupation with an exclusively dramatic approach to melodrama was conditioned by the external context of the Second World War, and to the sense that these films spoke to deep-seated and displaced anxieties of women on the homefront (though famous exceptions such as Preston Sturges's *The Palm Beach Story*, 1942, gave comedian Claudette Colbert a chance to defy such standards). The height of this sort of woman's film then coincides with the situation of the homefront female audience. Even when a film begins in comedy, as does *Tender Comrade* (1943) based on a bride's quest for her husband's constant attention and her relentless efforts to please him, it is to turn these situational comic interludes into ironic preludes for tragic events to follow. The film, in its transition to a serious mode, implies that the times demand maturity, while comedy is associated with the foibles of a prewar youth.

The theoretical scrutiny to which the woman's film of the war years was subject then posited both psychoanalytic and ideological readings that were in the best instances closely analytic of film form. By limiting their scrutiny to Forties films, however, they could not perform a comparison to the woman's films of other periods, or trace the later development of narratives that lend female characters the enunciative voice Doane finds so crucial in her definition.

What happens to these findings if we go back to the women-centered films of the turn of the twentieth century through the Teens to pose parallel questions? As Shelley Stamp argues in *Movie-Struck Girls: Women and Motion Picture Culture after the Nickelodeon*, serials may be considered the woman's films of their day, so much so that suffragists sought to reach this constituency with a "scenario of thrills and melodrama wrapped around the suffrage crusade" (154). Women-centered films in the short form of 1906–1911 did divide more evenly between dramas and comedies, and addressed both women and men in a variety of ways concerning gender roles, leaving us to theorize retrospectively on how what we know of the Forties woman's film might be applied to this period.

Was there a woman's film before there was the label? We know the domestic melodrama in the early silent period held a general appeal; men made up a large portion of the audience for the films of D. W. Griffith, many of which center on the plights of young women as they find themselves beset by difficulties and often at odds with their communities. Historians have examined the female audience for early film, considering its early composition of workers and immigrants, and efforts to expand filmgoing to greater numbers of middle-class women.[1]

The films themselves serve as evidence of such appeals. *The New York Hat* (1912), directed by Griffith based on a script by Anita Loos, highlights the coming of age of a young girl played by Mary Pickford. Set in a small town, the film opens with the impending death of the girl's mother, her dying wish to leave a modest sum through her minister to her daughter. She designates this gift to purchase some fancy clothing that her daughter would otherwise be denied once left in the care of the woman's miserly and dictatorial husband.

This legacy is remarkable for a number of reasons. Orphan girls were a common trope in stage and screen melodramas, clearly evoking women's empathy. In this case the mother's dying desire takes the form of a gift of a consumer good to be bestowed to ease her daughter's transition to womanhood and to grace her with both dignity and attractiveness.

It is also significant that the bestower of the gift is a minister. First, it sanctifies sartorial decoration as central to self-presentation, whereas certain US Protestants still evidenced the legacy of plain dressing as a sign of virtue. Second, by trusting her clergyman, the woman chooses a man supposedly beyond suspicion, but in fact this study of small-town reactions depicts precisely the preemptory judgment of the populace.

The film cuts to a moment considerably later, as the girl, walking with her clergyman, eyes a "New York" hat at the milliner's. Its purchase on her behalf by the pastor incites the townswomen to gossip. Mary's father rips the hat to shreds. The destruction of the hat immediately seems suggestive of an attack on the pubescent girl's sexuality and her desire for a world larger than the town.

The film can be seen as a symbolic blessing offered to the growth of a female-led consumer economy. It also engages in a discourse similar to Sinclair Lewis's novelistic critiques of small-town mentalities. Even though the gossips are women whose unfair, cruel tongues are renounced by the film's end, this ballad to a mother–daughter legacy, especially considering the charm of Mary Pickford's portrayal of the daughter, had great appeal to a female audience.

Several D. W. Griffith melodramas in particular insist on this woman-centered focus, including *True-Heart Susie* (1919), *Way Down East* (1920), and *The White Rose* (1923). The first is a narrative of self-sacrifice, as a young woman works to pay secretly for a young man's religious training and ordination as a minister, only to lose his affections to another whom the film marks as a thoughtless and unfaithful wife. The film weights all identification with Susie, yet also aligns her choices with extreme selflessness; she never tells the Reverend of her role in providing for his education or of his wife's philandering. Such self-effacement reaps narrative rewards, as the wife dies of illness contracted due to her behavior (pneumonia caught from being locked out in the rain). In other words, the female protagonist's absolute goodness is ultimately rewarded by a redeeming marriage to the man of her desires after the evil or at least morally compromised other woman's convenient death. These melodramatic narrative patterns then align themselves with a strict opposition between good and evil, which more sophisticated melodramas of the time treat with greater nuance and complication.

It is not clear that women spectators, as a group, would identify so completely with such a clear-cut opposition of female behavior. Certainly Lillian Gish's performance is endearing, especially in a comic scene in which she attempts to mimic the fashion of the day for the hobble skirt by tying a string around her own dated outfit. However, the discourse of the film seems aimed at a male-identified and conservative audience wishing to contain female desire and enforce the values of fidelity and female self-sacrifice. Yet, in representing the central male character as making a choice so clearly against his best interest and values as a minister, it is also presenting strong condemnation of such male behavior. This critical depiction of questionable male judgment perhaps could have appealed to female spectators, especially those whose traditional values chafed at modernist consumer culture introducing new tendencies in mate selection. The film becomes in part a parable about the danger of superficial attractions and the "fast" life replacing arranged or carefully considered marriages sanctified by shared religious values.

Gender, then, becomes a complex variable in audience identification, intermixed with reigning value systems on one hand and desires for social change on the other. Clearly, a portion of the audience for Griffith's films saw as outdated the terms in which his melodramas presented choices and channeled resolutions. Impatience with a character like Susie Trueheart and with a form that needs to symbolically name and hammer home her absolute goodness seems likely in audiences that were flocking to see Theda Bara play the evil temptresses that became known as the vamp. Yet cultural moments often juxtapose just such disparate representations, and they can appeal to overlapping audiences, caught in conflicting allegiances during periods of social transformation.

Melodramas of this period do often struggle with issues more immediately open to less problematic female identification. The other two female-centered Griffith melodramas I cited earlier take this tack by exploring the problem of women betrayed by men. *Way Down East* and *The White Rose* both focus on single mothers. Both narratives stage elaborate deceptions to explain how these women ended up in this position of "illegitimacy" owing to men who faked marriages, or took advantage of their naïve trust and genuine love. They also stage equally elaborate circumstances of redemption. The heroine of *Way Down East* earns her purification in a self-punishing brush with death on the ice floes during a storm after being victimized anew by the man and ostracized by the family who had taken her in. *The White Rose* doesn't match this cinematically thrilling symbolic action sequence; its redemption comes through the death for the heroine in childbirth, causing the contrition of the deceptive man. In both cases, women can identify with unfair moral judgments and punishments placed on these working-class heroines whose only flaw seems to be naïve trust. Equally they could vent their anger at male antagonists whose manipulative and dishonest seductions receive the cover of their elevated social standing. More basically, unwed motherhood was a major threat to the well-being of young working women, and these films provided an outlet for exorcizing the fear and anger this part of the audience could experience on this issue. Still these films also function as cautionary tales against elopements that could be deceptions and all possible breaches of promise. While they enforce the necessity for legitimate liaisons by suggesting dire consequences for the alternatives, they nonetheless hold out the possibility of a society more able to forgive and to move beyond simplistic condemnations. In other words, these narratives, read with some subtlety, do complex ideological work that questions fundamentalist and absolute values, suggesting that any morality consider circumstances. These films remain patriarchal in their discourses, but suggest the need to critique abuse of male privilege and condemn hypocrisy within that patriarchy.

Much can be gleaned by examining a leading male critic's response to *Way Down East* at the time of its first release as hopelessly outdated. He cynically wishes that the heroine had drowned in the ice floes. Such a spectator does not have the distance of a contemporary viewer who might find the film quaint, campy, or historically fascinating, and will not be mollified by sheer cinematic bravura and accomplished camerawork and editing. He rejects the usefulness of this heroine's cardboard naïveté and the energy that goes into redeeming her, only necessary if one shares the film's moralistic foundational premises. One can well imagine much of the female audience agreeing consciously or unconsciously with him that such a framed and restricted heroine was simply beside the point at the end of the second decade of the twentieth century.

Melodrama's appeal, as well as its rejection, across gender during this period in which nineteenth-century stage melodrama still had a hold on sectors of twentieth-century film production may be instructive to the study of later women's films. Permutations of the genre become imperative to facilitate a broader appeal. Continued emotional identification, or at least suspension of cynical rejection, will only meet genre demands if the heroines become less virginally naïve and more psychologically rich. In her chapter "The Clinical Gaze," Doane analyzes this preoccupation with the female psyche, a trend that can be coupled with a more general tendency in the Forties and Fifties for American films to use the flashback to more thoroughly engage with character subjectivity (Turim). Janet Walker traces the same issue through a slightly later time period in her *Couching Resistance: Women, Film, and Psychoanalytic Psychiatry from World War II through the mid-1960s*, reading the patients as offering a resistance to normative female roles.

Still, the action melodrama as parable has hardly vanished in favor of the psychological melodrama in our most recent film history. *Titanic* (1997) is perhaps the most direct descendant of the stylistics of *Way Down East*, including parallel endings of lovers on ice floes. *Titanic*, a classic melodrama of a woman caught between lovers of different classes, more often was treated as both romance and disaster film, but it certainly evoked as many audience tears as anything Hollywood ever offered to the matinee audience. Similarly, *Lara Croft, Tomb Raider* (2001) uses the action melodrama to symbolically stage its heroine's Oedipal conflict.

Perhaps part of the reason the woman's film of the Twenties and Thirties was less remarked upon for its gender-specific address was its liaison to melodramas of the Teens and the stage tradition before them that clearly had a broad audience of both sexes. Externalization of emotion as action and symbolic representation may have something to do with that cross-gender appeal, most noticeable in the more action-oriented, historical silent melodramas. As in the serials, emotions and psychology are presented through actions and movement, with a foregrounding of fear and the overcoming of fear as the most primal and central of all emotions. A number of recent action films similarly rely on characteristics of melodrama to secure a broad audience appeal. The George Lucas Star Wars Trilogy (*Star Wars* [1977], *Star Wars: Episode V—The Empire Strikes Back* [1980] and *Star Wars: Episode VI—Return of the Jedi* [1983]), and *Alien* in its many incarnations (*Alien* [1979], *Aliens* [1986], *Alien 3* [1992], and *Alien: Resurrection* [1997]), for example, borrow elements of the melodramatic tradition. Action and special effects, the characteristics of the so-called "testosterone genres," allow for the revival of heroines borrowed from silent melodrama and the serial of the Teens, but tend to deny these women the interiority that the melodramas of family conflict permit.

By contrast, female interiority in everyday life is the focus of *Too Wise Wives* (1921) adapted from a story by Marion Orth. Recent work on Weber by Jennifer Parchesky and Shelley Stamp, particularly on her films *The Blot* and *Shoes*, has highlighted the centrality of Weber to studies of gender in this period. *Too Wise Wives* is a dramatic comedy of newlyweds and infidelity in the upper classes. The "martyred" wife, Mrs David Graham, proves overly fussy in her devoted attention to her husband. His annoyance leads to his flashback memory of contrasting behavior on the part of his old sweetheart now married to a richer man. His memory image of the old flame introduces the parallel story of this woman in her marriage as Mrs John Daly. While she may be a self-acknowledged poor house-keeper (who has a bevy of servants to perform these tasks anyway), her calculated charming sensuality leaves her husband far more contented than his counterpart. Weber then crosses the two narratives as Mrs Daly tries to revive her relationship with her former suitor Mr Graham.

In the central section of the film, Weber depicts the interaction of the two women, as she satirizes the foibles of the upper classes. A meeting of the "Women's Social and Political Club" becomes the occasion, we are told, for Mrs Graham "to torture herself with sight of her husband's old flame." It also gives rise to Weber's satire of Republican wives, as she presents a flirtatious monologue from Mrs Daly, displaying great smugness and ignorance as she discusses a vote on an amendment, which Mrs Graham misreads, admiring her superior cleverness in conversation. This satire is all the more poignant, given the recent ratification of the nineteenth amendment in 1920. Class satire continues in shots that contrast the furs of the two rivals to the cloth coat of an old friend who has not married as well. This contrast carries over to the next scene as Mrs Daly flaunts her extravagant expenditures in a dress salon featuring clothes neither of the others can afford. These sequences also mark the film's attempt to reach a female audience, as both are filled with the display of beautifully designed luxury items, even as the film denounces the class privilege and competitive instincts behind indulgent purchases.

Mrs Daly sends Mr Graham an invitation for a weekend when her husband is gone. As it is delivered by an office clerk, the wife, suspicious of its contents, conceals it from her husband, but when he receives the weekend invitation verbally from the departing Mr Daly himself, she agrees to the weekend as a means of confirming her husband's affair with her rival. The complex device of the purloined letter means that Mr Graham remains ignorant of the private rendezvous proposed by Mrs Daly in her letter, and Mrs Graham feels guilty for having doubted her husband. This results in a scene between the two women in which Mrs Graham confesses her distrust first to Mrs Daly, then to her husband, revealing the purloined letter. With the wife totally abased by these circumstances, resolution comes only as Mrs Daly still urges him to read her letter. Then she is the one who is abased, suffering rejection and humiliation. She renounces the good impulse she temporarily felt in empathy with Mrs Graham's confession. The film ends with each of the couples reconciled.

It is remarkable to see a crusading social realist like Weber, known for her depictions of poverty and factory work, turn to painting the indul-gences of the upper classes. Many viewers today miss the complex social satire, failing to pay attention to the sophisticated authorial voice that, while remaining sympathetic to the women, offers sharp criticism of their class position and both of their concepts of marriage. Calling them simply Mrs John Daly and Mrs David Graham throughout (except in Sara Daly's signing of her rendezvous proposition) becomes one marker of how the roles they play seem overdetermined by the system of matrimony into which they have bought.

While the couriers, letters, and telegrams used in this film would today be replaced by cellphones, instant messaging, answering machines, and email, the basic structure of this dramatic comedy could be reset in a contemporary Beverly Hills or Westchester. Romantic comedy, as well as the dramatic comedy, once established in the Twenties, gives us the basic structures of many chick flicks today, including the tensions between traditional roles and conventional behavior on one hand and women seeking more sexual and intellectual freedom on the other.

The truly "invisible" women's films and strong chick-flick predecessors of the Twenties through the Sixties were films such as *Twentieth Century* (1934), *The Philadelphia Story* (1940), and *Pat and Mike* (1952), all romantic and screwball comedies. These films had broad-based appeal to both genders, and were often advertised as "battles of the sexes." Further, in these battles, the women often capitulated to male anxiety over their careers and independence—but not always. Many had the same gutsy sense of female rebellion that occurs in the best chick flicks, such as *When Harry Met Sally* (1989), *Sleepless in Seattle* (1993), *Bridget Jones's Diary* (2001), *Le Fabuleux destin d'Amélie Poulain* (2001), *Brown Sugar* (2002), *Love Actually* (2003), and *Lost in Translation* (2003).

Addressing, then, the division of male and female genres, one finds the differences are not just ones of subject matter or focus, but rather whether conflicts are explored for their internal ramifications and resonances or acted out externally. However, many of the so-called male genres, such as the war film, detective story or western, in their development across the Thirties, Forties, and Fifties move towards greater concern with interiority. So by the time that the woman's film emerges as a distinct genre, it does so in a context of films in general moving towards the modes associated with it.

Another reason for less focus on the woman's film as a separate address to female audiences in the Twenties and Thirties is that many of the woman's films offered titillating sexuality. Exploitation of the fallen-woman narrative before the Hays Code offered images of this woman as sexually enticing and active. Once the industry adopted the Code under threat of government-imposed censorship, the fallen woman reaped the punishment meted out for ignoring proprieties. Most noticeably, the elaborate costumes of the vamp still linger in these films, cloaking the sexual woman in exotica and finery, first of art nouveau elegance, then of art deco simplicity. The appeal of these films to audiences of both genders for their sexual frankness masked their iteration of the concerns and conflicts of women.

Ultimately the theoretical questions we should pose concern whether current chick flicks have been able to carve out positions for women as desiring subjects all that different from those that marked their predecessors. We may find many a predecessor, for instance, to recent films dealing with women and work across the decades of films devoted to secretaries. Claudette Colbert plays the role for comedy in *She Married Her Boss* (1935), as secretary to a department store manager, who treats her only with respect until she urges romance. Colbert earlier played the secretary for melodrama in *Secrets of a Secretary* (1931). Both films, and innumerable like features, correspond to gender transformations of this niche of the workforce. In the 1930s women dominated the office workforce, moving from the steno pools to the coveted title "secretary" previously reserved for men. Many of these women were graduates of newly emerging secretarial colleges, as trade schools came to be called, while others had college degrees in business. Films worked and reworked the tensions between male office managers and ambitious females, as well as conflicts between the older women workers and the young recruits, often presented as a conflict between propriety and sexuality.

Tone also becomes significant in determining the valence of such films. *Big Business Girl* (1931) directed by William A. Seiter, again explores the secretary's relationship to a male boss, this time keeping up an ironic tone that grants the heroine, Claire McIntyre, self-determination. From the start of the film, she is depicted as above the fray of her environment; at the graduation dance at State University, while other couples head off into the woods "making love," she gently chides her musician boyfriend for his lapses as a student and his lack of ambitions for the future. In contrast, she tells him of the serious debt that motivates her plans to go to work. She takes a job in New York City to pay it off, sending her Johnny off with his swing band to Paris to make his own career. It is rare for a Thirties film to posit its female college graduates as so clearly ambitious. A montage sequence depicts hurdles such a graduate might find in the early 1930s marketplace, showing her difficulties finding a job, chronicled by want ads, and her applications.

This struggle leads her to a deco office waiting room, where she is in the right place at an opportune moment. Advertising executive Clayton returns from a business trip to find his telegram has failed to communicate to his staff the necessity of working this Saturday afternoon. Taking impromptu dictation, she types out his brainstorming revelation that they should advertise a car from a woman's angle.

Her poetic copy for this account ensures her career. This initial success still leaves her with the challenge of overcoming sexist workplace attitudes that are strikingly and critically represented in the film, such as remarks she overhears on an open intercom "that she makes a nice office decoration." Her expert handling of the car account eventually leads to her helping Johnny land a radio gig on a show underwritten by the advertising dollars of the car company. Their reunion disposes of a possible narrative convention—uniting her romantically with the boss who has made moves on her—thus leaving the critique of office sexism to resonate within the light comedic tone of the film.

Contrast this with the treatment of the female businesswoman in a melodrama produced in 1925, *Smouldering Fires*. The trope here concerns the romantic melting of the cold spinster boss, in the arms of an attractive young male employee. Can a romance offer this combination of power, desirability, and fulfillment untroubled by a dampening of possibilities available to women? Here the narrative intervention of an attractive, adored younger sister who apparently has no careerist ambitions acts to diffuse the fantasy that a woman's film might actually allow for fulfillment and empowerment in both the workplace and private life. A film such as *Smouldering Fires* may not constitute the melodrama one normally considers the woman's film, but I would argue that it addressed the horizon that many young women surveyed as they enrolled in business schools and entered commerce, suggesting the inevitable self-sacrifice or compromise such ambitions would necessitate.

Anita Loos wrote the script of another film focused on the work environment, John Emerson's *The Social Secretary* (1916), in which Norma Talmadge plays Mayme who reacts to constant sexual harassment at previous jobs with an inventive strategy. She answers an ad for a society matron's secretary who must be "extremely unattractive to men." In appropriately clever disguise, she lands the job, and her intuition about men saves the daughter of the family grief from a scheming suitor. She reverts to her attractive appearance to elicit the son's attention, a liaison sanctioned by the family's admiration. Fifteen years later, Mary Astor starred in a similar transformation romance, Melville W. Brown's *Behind Office Doors* (1931). A conscientious secretary helps the man she loves become head of the company, but then must struggle to win him from another woman he meets in the society to which he now belongs.

Not many recent chick flicks pay this much attention to female employment and careers. From the prostitute of *Pretty Woman* (1990), to the disenchanted housewife of *Fried Green Tomatoes* (1991), to the small-town inhabitants who assemble in Truvy's Beauty Parlor in *Steel Magnolias* (1989), many women in recent chick flicks markedly are not employed outside the home except in service jobs conventionally assigned women. One has to look back to *Nine to Five* (1980) and *Working Girl* (1988) to find other films centering on secretaries, in contrast with the secretaries and shop clerks who dominated the romance genre of the Thirties. One might think that this reflects female advances in the workplace and in education, but the lives of professional women and businesswomen as bases for narratives are nearly as rare in films as those of secretaries. The few exceptions include *Erin Brockovich* (2000), which focuses on the heroine's midlife move into the job market as prelude to a muckraking legal crusade against corporate corruption and pollution. It follows in a tradition of narratives not actually focused on the work world but on women aroused to political action: *Norma Rae* (1979), *China Syndrome* (1979), and *Silkwood* (1988). One further exception is seen in the films of Barbra Streisand, who, as actress and director, examined professional women in the Nineties: the psychiatrist, Dr Susan Lowenstein, in *The Prince of Tides* (1991) and a Columbia University professor in *The Mirror Has Two Faces* (1996).

While chick flicks continue earlier women's film structures in many ways, then, they seem largely to neglect the trials of female employment so prevalent as a focus in earlier decades. Television, on the other hand, often situates its females as detectives, doctors, nurses, writers, and journalists, making the non-salaried status of some contemporary chick-flick protagonists not only out of step with over half of the women in the audience, but with other media. Thus although films of the Teens through the Forties demonstrate feminist components, today's chick flicks have arguably not kept pace with the advancements made by women since then.

Returning then to my earlier request for a more theoretical approach to the contemporary chick flick, perhaps we need to put aside a tendency to simply champion any films that deviate from the entirely male-centered action heroes to address the female audience. We need to ask much harder questions of how they situate female desire (in both the psychoanalytic and philosophical dimensions of that term), or, to put the same concept differently, how they ascribe subjectivity to females. We should also ask how they situate women in the public sphere, beyond a new myth of a sleeping beauty aroused to political activity. Romance comedies, be they straight, gay, or bi, need to be examined for how they position their contemporary interventions in light of genre conventions, especially since the screwball comedy delighted in a temporary madcap anarchy only to restore order and impose a conservative finality on women's subjectivity. Enjoyment by female audiences or showcasing female actors and comedians should be our cue to pay attention to what structures such enjoyment and showcasing, not so much to judge each film as either entirely retrograde or progressive, but rather to get a more complex reading of our contemporary women's films.

## Note

1   Some of the authors who have addressed gender and class issues in assessing audiences for early cinema include Ewen, Hanson, and Mayne.

## Works cited

Bean, Jennifer M. and Diane Negra (eds). *A Feminist Reader in Early Cinema*. Durham: Duke University Press, 2002.

Doane, Mary Ann. *The Desire to Desire: The Woman's Film of the 1940s*. Bloomington, IN: Indiana University Press, 1987.

Ewen, Elizabeth. "City Lights: Immigrant Women and the Rise of the Movies." *Signs 5* (Spring 1980): S45–66.

Hanson, Miriam. "Early Cinema, Late Cinema: Transformations of the Public Sphere." In *Viewing Positions: Ways of Seeing Film*. Ed. Linda Williams. New Brunswick: Rutgers University Press, 1994: 134–52.

——"Early Cinema: Whose Public Sphere?" In *Early Cinema: Space-Frame-Narrative*. Ed. Thomas Elsaesser. London: British Film Institute, 1990: 228–46.

Haskell, Molly. *From Reverence to Rape: The Treatment of Women in the Movies*. 2nd ed. Chicago: University of Chicago Press, 1987.

Hollinger, Karen. *In the Company of Women: Contemporary Female Friendship Films*. Minneapolis: University of Minnesota Press, 1998.

Mabry, A. Rochelle. "About a Girl: Female Subjectivity and Sexuality in Contemporary 'Chick' Culture." In *Chick Lit: The New Woman's Fiction*. Ed. Suzanne Ferriss and Mallory Young. New York: Routledge, 2006: 191–206.

Mayne, Judith. *Cinema and Spectatorship*. New York: Routledge, 1993.

——"The Two Spheres of Early Cinema." In *Private Novels, Public Films*. Athens: University of Georgia Press, 1988: 68–94.

Parchesky, Jennifer. "Lois Weber's *The Blot*: Rewriting Melodrama, Reproducing the Middle Class." *Cinema Journal* 39 (Autumn 1999): 23–53.

Stamp, Shelley. "Lois Weber, Progressive Cinema, and the Fate of 'The Work-a-Day Girls' in *Shoes*." *Camera Obscura* 56 (2004): 140–69.

——*Movie-Struck Girls: Women and Motion Picture Culture After the Nickelodeon*. Princeton: Princeton University Press, 2000.

Turim, Maureen Cheryn. *Flashbacks in Film: Memory & History*. New York: Routledge, 1989.

Walsh, Andrea S. *Women's Film and Female Experience, 1940–1950*. New York: Praeger, 1984.

Waldman, Diane. "Horror and Domesticity: The Modern Gothic Romance Film of the 1940s." Dissertation, University of Wisconsin-Madison, 1981.

Walker, Janet. *Couching Resistance: Women, Film and Psychoanalytic Psychiatry*. Minneapolis: University of Minnesota Press, 1993.

# Chapter 3

# Fashioning femininity in the makeover flick

*Suzanne Ferriss*

A long tradition of chick flicks features a seemingly unattractive (but secretly talented) girl who, following a transformation into an attractive woman, wins the man she appears to dismiss but secretly pines for. From *Now, Voyager* (1942) to *Funny Face* (1957) to *Moonstruck* (1987) to *She's All That* (1999) to *My Big Fat Greek Wedding* (2002), the so-called "unattractive" girl sports a frumpish wardrobe and bookish glasses that signal her intelligence and independence, but lead men to shun her.[1] In the course of the film, she undergoes a makeover, losing the glasses and gaining fashion sense to attract the man she desires, an attraction that is sealed when, although goggle-eyed at her looks, he realizes that her inner qualities are what make her worthy of his love. Despite its apparent superficiality, the makeover does have high stakes: the woman's life itself is transformed. As such, makeover films are a dependable subgenre of chick flicks, where superficial external changes are signs of an internal moral transformation: the female protagonist admits she needs love and companionship despite her apparent commitment to social and intellectual independence.

The stakes are clearest in makeover films that consciously highlight fashion, not simply as a tool of physical transformation but as a driving force in the character's personal and professional life. Set in the catty world of fashion magazines, the Audrey Hepburn classic *Funny Face* and 2006's *The Devil Wears Prada* test the resolve of intellectual females dismissive of the fashion business as the work of shallow airheads devoted to a frivolous consumer culture rather than the enduring and intangible life of the mind. The independent film *Party Girl* (1995), directed by Daisy von Scherler Mayer and starring Parker Posey, deliberately reverses this plot, as the unabashed fashionista and "party girl" of the title yearns to become a librarian. The glasses go on, not off. Working self-consciously against the mainstream Hollywood tradition, *Party Girl* highlights the gender conventions characteristic of fashion makeover films, such as the objectification of women and the equation of female intelligence with unattractiveness. Ironically, however, the film persists in using the "makeover"—or, in this case, "reverse-makeover"—as the vehicle for the female character's moral development. Taken together, the films raise questions about the connection between fashion and identity, the nature of female agency in feminine self-transformation and display, and the role of consumer culture in chick flicks, as well as women's lives.

## The makeover flick

Critics have argued that the "woman's film"—a variable set of narrative conventions, but most simply defined as movies for women—privileges a female point of view both in terms of narrative and spectatorial position: the female protagonist is the center of the plot and the focus of the cinematic gaze.[2] With its persistent emphasis on appearance and display, the makeover film inevitably and irrefutably puts the woman at the center. As such, it also capitalizes on the role fashion and commodification played in the classic woman's film, where "the film frame [was] a kind of display window" (Doane 26) for the latest styles.[3] If, as Jeanine Basinger has argued, "movies clearly state that fashion and glamour are fundamental to a woman's definition" (114), then the makeover film is the ultimate chick flick, promising self-transformation through shopping.

Justine King has further argued that a recurrent motif of the woman's film is escape (not escapism, as detractors would have it), defined as "a movement through a *liminal* space, a realm of possibility" which results in "a redefining and re-empowering transformation of identity or rite of passage" (220). Often such an escape in contemporary woman's films has been from the confining roles of women in patriarchal society: Shirley Valentine leaves her husband behind in search of sexual fulfillment and personal freedom, Jess defies her Indian parents to pursue a career as a professional soccer player in *Bend It Like Beckham* (2002), and Thelma and Louise drive off a cliff rather than submit to male rule at home or in the courts.

In the makeover film, such self-transformation fuses the external and the internal. It unites physical crossings, such as passages through space or location or alterations of dress and appearance, with interior rites of passage and psychic changes through the medium of the body. The complexity and enduring fascination of such films comes from the problematic extent to which outward transformation of the body affects the character's outlook or behavior. Is Eliza Doolittle still a Cockney flower girl once she becomes Henry Higgins's Fair Lady?

An additional dimension of complexity comes through the nature of display inherent in the makeover film: the woman's transformation has two audiences—one within the film itself and one external to it. Within the film narrative, the transformation typically occurs for a man. While the female protagonist may be the center of attention and story, the secondary male character puts her there, either as the agent of her transformation or its intended object, acting as either Pygmalion or the Prince, depending on the film's allegiances to the two prevailing myths that are staples of the makeover flick: the Pygmalion myth and the Cinderella story.[4] In both variations, physical transformation initiates a secondary, but more significant, transformation of character—generally for the male protagonist, not the female—offering a self-affirming message to viewers. Paradoxically, despite the makeover film's emphasis on transformation, the reassuring message to viewers is that the woman was perfect all along and that the man simply needed to see her.

Both *My Fair Lady* (1964) and *Vertigo* (1958), for instance, feature a male protagonist intent on transforming a woman to suit his ideal image. But, in *My Fair Lady*, Henry Higgins (Rex Harrison) must drop his pretentious upper-class snobbery to win the love of Eliza Doolittle (Audrey Hepburn). In Hitchcock's variation, *Vertigo*, the consequences for the hero Scottie (James Stewart) are far darker. The ex-detective refuses to accept Judy Barton (Kim Novak) as she is—brunette and brassy—but insists on making her over to appear as the idealized Madeleine, the mysterious, sophisticated blonde he was tricked into thinking had plunged to her death from the mission tower. Once he has succeeded—or more properly *she* has by complying to reproduce her previous self-transformation—he loses her as she really falls from the tower.[5] In the modern makeover film narrative the man must realize the impossibility of his ideal and accept "imperfection" as not only real but preferable. He must learn, in short, not to attempt to change women but accept them as they are.

As the almost ludicrous casting choices of most makeover films also suggest, the heroine needs little assistance from a fairy godmother. Unlike the overweight, greasy-haired candidates for television's *E! Fashion Emergency*, the film frump is far from frumpish. In *Pretty Woman*, for instance, Julia Roberts slums briefly as a bubble-bath-taking prostitute before shopping spree turns her back into the winning girl-next-door audiences expect (complete with celebrity Rodeo-Drive wardrobe). Her transformation is merely a means of awakening the man's recognition of her preexisting physical, as well as moral, worth. (Recall that even the footman in *Cinderella* who holds the shoe can see she is "very handsome" [Perrault 303].) The reassuring message to female audiences is that women do not need to change—at least physically.

Thus, crucial to film makeovers is their essential recognition of a female audience. Obviously, the film narratives cater to women's aspirational desires, promising life transformations. As Rachel Moseley has noted, the tools of the contemporary film makeover—costume and makeup—provide another source of audience identification, for "dress and fashion are also part of the connective tissue of the social" (*Growing Up* 6). Women have access to the same tools of transformation and thus can identify not simply with the female film protagonist but the star who plays her. Fashion initiates a complex, doubled identification between the spectator, the film, and its star.

Makeover films that deliberately highlight fashion not merely as a visual component of transformation but as an integral part of film setting and narrative demonstrate that the makeover flick also captures polarized responses to fashion in contemporary culture. Fashion has been demonized as an enterprise emblematic of the worst excesses of capitalism, synonymous with waste and superficiality, at least since Thorstein Veblen argued in *The Theory of the Leisure Class* (1899), that "expenditure for display is more obviously present, and is, perhaps, more universally practiced in the matter of dress than in any other line of consumption" (167). According to this argument, women are its dupes, malleable and subordinate to an industry that preys on their insecurities and creates imagined inadequacies to sell goods of no lasting value. At the other extreme, fashion is championed as a means of self-transformation offering pleasurable possibilities for trying on roles or even forging an identity—individual or collective. Obviously, as fashion theorist Elizabeth Wilson has noted, both are true to some degree: "Fashion *speaks* capitalism. Capitalism maims, kills, appropriates, lays waste. It also creates great wealth and beauty, together with yearning for our lives and opportunities that remain just beyond our reach. It manufactures dreams and images as well as things, and fashion is as much a part of the dream world of capitalism as its economy" (14). As a preeminent manufacturer of dreams and images, commercial film allies itself with fashion, and the fashion makeover films make this emphatically clear. In them, fashion is ambivalently presented as essential to transformation of lives, but, ironically, not bodies. The makeover makes nothing over: it is ultimately unnecessary since the protagonist never really needed to change physically, but only to recognize—and be recognized for—her true worth.

## A not so funny face

One of the most enduring makeover films—*Funny Face*—captures the contradictions of contemporary fashion, cleverly exploiting star Audrey Hepburn's already established links to the fashion world. As Moseley has argued, fashion, "as a narrative device and as visual pleasure, is central to Hepburn's persona" ("Dress" 112). She had an earlier career as a model and served as muse to French designer Hubert de Givenchy (Moseley, *Growing Up* 34). In the film, however, her character, Jo Stockton, represents the antithesis of this world: she is a book clerk in a Greenwich Village bookstore who reads philosophy. (Not accidentally, the bookstore is named Embryo Concept, signaling the transformation to come.) The film manages quite artfully to celebrate the überfeminine world of fashion, particularly in musical numbers and through its use of fashion photojournalism devices, while capturing resistance to it through Jo's disparaging comments and "beatnik" anti-fashion (Moseley, "Dress" 112).

As in all makeover films, the candidate for the transformation is hardly in need of it: Jo's dowdy dress and flat shoes merely disguise the beauty she innately possesses, beauty that simply awaits recognition from a male admirer. Here the ruse is even more transparent for it plays on the audience's knowledge that underneath the tweedy disguise is an ultrafeminine European film star whose own Cinderella story of survival during the German occupation of Holland has become entrenched Hollywood myth.[6]

Enter fashion photographer Dick Avery (Fred Astaire), whose name is quite obviously a play on Richard Avedon, who served as art director on the film and was associated professionally with Hepburn. Avery's editor at *Quality* magazine, Maggie Prescott (Kay Thompson), is seeking "blood, brains and pizzazz" for her next issue. For atmosphere they descend upon the "sinister" Greenwich Village bookstore where Jo works. Barging in with their equipment, Maggie and her minions send Jo, perched on a ladder shelving books, careening along the rails, then rearrange the books since they look "too much alike." Even though Maggie later describes her as "that creature from the bookshop," it does not take the trained eye of the fashion photographer to see that Jo is actually as attractive—or more so—than the vacuous model he is photographing.[7] A close-up shot framed like a fashion portrait signals the "transformation" to come.

Photographer Avery simply needs to cure Jo of her unattractive interest in "epiphenomenalism" and materialist philosophy. He convinces her to become the new *Quality* woman with the promise of a fashion trip to Paris, baiting her with the possibility of meeting Emil Flostra, the "greatest living philosopher and founder of 'empathicalism.'" She justifies her decision as a "means to an end, not a loss of integrity," even though she had earlier dismissed fashion as superficial and criticized Avery for photographing "silly dresses on silly women." At the end of her makeover, she has become the model she once disparaged. As the couturier Paul Duval (a stand-in for Givenchy) announces, the gamine has become a "bird of paradise." Wearing a pink and white gown, she emerges on the fashion house runway. The camera closes in to reveal her face, with dramatically shadowed eyes, heavily penciled eyebrows and the "marvelous mouth" she had earlier claimed had "no functional advantage." She can argue that it is still "not her," because the transformation is at this point merely physical not internal.

As we have seen, the male love interest in the typical makeover film follows a parallel yet inverse trajectory. Initially interested in the woman's transformation for superficial reasons, he eventually realizes the value of looking beyond appearances. In *Funny Face*, Dick seeks Jo's makeover because his photos of her can advance his career as a fashion photographer and enhance his standing with his boss. His flirtatious manner also indicates

*Image 3.1* Before: Dick Avery (Fred Astaire) photographing Jo Stockton
(Audrey Hepburn) and Marion (Dovima) in the Embryo Concepts
bookstore

*Image 3.2* After: the "gamine" turned "bird of paradise"

he's interested in a fling. His editor encapsulates their shared superficiality:
"you belong to the fashion world. Face it: we're a cold lot, artificial and
totally lacking in sentiment." By contrast, Jo—the compassionate intellectual—eventually falls in love. During their week-long photo shoot, he

commands her to imagine herself as part of a romantic narrative as she poses. She lives, rather than acts, the part. Finally, Cinderella-like, posing in a bridal gown outside a church (which looks more like a Disney-esque castle), she confesses her love for him during the dance to "He Loves and She Loves." When he says that they can continue to see each other if she models, she agrees to become one. At least temporarily, she abandons her principles and intellectualism for love.

The madeover Jo nonetheless succumbs to the temptation to meet the philosopher Flostra in a Paris café, only to discover that he is not old, as she'd expected, but young and attractive. Flostra is "enchanted" by her looks rather than her boast to be his most "loyal disciple of empathicalism." Jo's famous interpretative dance in the café in the black turtleneck, slim trousers and ballet flats that become synonymous with Hepburn's classic style further hints that "beatnik" antifashion is itself a fashion,[8] and that, despite claims to the contrary, Flostra is as much a manufacturer of images as Avery. When Avery, apparently jealous, tries to convince her that Flostra is "more man than philosopher," he reveals in a moment of anger that his own feelings for her are far from genuine: "he's about as interested in your intellect as I am." While Dick had earlier declared his love for Jo, he lets slip that his interest in her is as calculated as Flostra's.

The film does conclude happily, however, once both practice "empathicalism": they put themselves in each other's place. She rebuffs Flostra's lewd advances and fulfills her part of the bargain by appearing in the fashion show orchestrated by *Quality* magazine. Her appearance in the bridal gown at the end of the show reminds her of her love for Avery and, tears streaming down her cheeks, she flees the scene, apparently compelled by genuine emotion to dismiss the artifice of the fashion world. Avery does the reverse: initially determined to return to New York, he meets Flostra at the airport and, learning that Jo had violently rejected him, returns to the fashion show, only to discover Jo has left. He puts himself in her place and returns to the church where they had staged the photoshoot in the bridal gown and she had first expressed her love. He recognizes her principles by accepting the genuineness of emotion; she inserts herself in his world, posing once again as the bride in the photoshoot. But this time, it's for real (or within the world of the film narrative, that is).

Note that, while he gains a heart and a bride, she gains a husband while sacrificing her attachment to philosophy. Intellectualism in the film is reduced to a tricked-up form of male come-on, a sexually compromising enterprise for a young woman who would do better to trade books for a bridal gown. Moseley has observed the final wedding scene "is explicitly marked as fantasy through the use of soft focus and contrived iconography" (*Growing Up* 72). As such, it is at odds visually with the rest of the film, perhaps suggesting that Jo's intellect has been uncertainly circumscribed or contained. However, the shift in focus might suggest that Avery no longer sees Jo through the calculating lenses of the ambitious fashion photographer but becomes part of the same Cinderella fantasy he created for her within the film and that is sustained outside the film by Hollywood studios and bridal magazines.

## The geek's revenge

It is clear that *Party Girl* is working deliberately not only against the make-over tradition, but overtly against *Funny Face*, and, as an independent film, against its glossy commercialism. *Party Girl* updates the setting and cultural details, substituting a library for the bookstore and trendy clubs for bohemian cafés. In virtually every respect, *Party Girl* turns *Funny Face* on its head to offer a critique of mainstream fashion and conventional femininity. Our heroine, Mary, is not a dowdy bookstore clerk but a popular "party girl," seen at the opening of the film being arrested at a house party in her apartment, where alcohol and drugs proliferate. Even the morning following an evening in jail, she is decked out in a chic leopard-print coat over a sexy red leather miniskirt with matching fishnet stockings and high heels. In place of fashion icon Hepburn is the "queen of the indies," Parker Posey, credited with fusing "aristocratic hauteur and downtown street style" (Negra 76) not haute couture.

Rather than being "discovered" by a sophisticated but superficial photographer, Mary "discovers" a falafel vender, Mustafa (Omar Townsend), who initially attracts her only because he gives her the chance to flirt in another language. *She* is the superficial sophisticate, while, despite appearances to the contrary, *he* is the intellectual. He was a teacher in Lebanon and sells falafel merely to earn enough money to pay for teacher certification courses in New York.

To earn his love, she needs to find—not lose—her intellect, and abandon —rather than gain—her designer wardrobe. To pay back the bail money her godmother Judy (Sasha von Scherler) had posted on her behalf, Mary seeks a job in the library where her godmother works. There she eventually discovers that a career as a librarian is her true calling. Just as the beauty of the traditional makeover heroine is always evident behind her disguise, so are there early signs that Mary really is not as vacuous as she appears. We can see the inner librarian lurking beneath the surface in her classification of the fashionable items in her wardrobe. She shrieks at a friend who dares to disturb the impeccable order of her countless pairs of jeans, neatly arrayed on hangers.

In place of the fashionable set casting aspersions on the badly dressed bookworm that we find in *Funny Face*, in *Party Girl* the intellectually pretentious librarians, including her heavy-set godmother, heap abuse on Mary, calling her "dyslexic" and "small for her age." They mock her desire to become one of them, reminding her that a librarian is a professional with a degree. When she fails to master the Dewey Decimal System, her god-mother chastises her: "a trained monkey learned this system on PBS in a matter of hours." Undaunted, however, Mary immerses herself in the system, mastering it one drunken, stoned evening after breaking into the empty library. A montage, set to techno repetitions of the empowering plea "believe in me," shows Mary shelving books. One scene parodies a fashion show, as Mary struts down an improvised runway composed of two long tables pushed together to shelve a book high in the stacks. The common iconography of visual display is appropriated to showcase library science.

Note that, as in *Funny Face*, initially the makeover doesn't take, as Mary reverts to superficial self-display. On the night of her library epiphany, self-absorbed in her self-transformation, Mary forgets her first date with Mustafa. Miffed, he shuns her, refusing to succumb as she parades herself before him at his falafel stand in an increasingly elaborate series of outfits. In keeping with the film's indie pedigree, the ensembles are not, however, off-the-rack designs but improvised one-of-a-kind fashions—street couture. Over this montage of fashionable display the lyrics "I know I hurt you, boy. / Can I make it up to you?" play on the soundtrack.

*Image 3.3* Before: Mary (Parker Posey) strutting her stuff on the improvised "runway" in the library

*Image 3.4* After: "Party girl" turned librarian

Only when Mustafa accidentally sees her in the library are they reunited, and only once he has discovered that she's a librarian, does he size her up physically. Their ensuing dalliance among the stacks leads to her being fired when it is discovered that she not only had sex in the library but left the windows open in a rainstorm, destroying dozens of books. In despair, she admits, "Keith Richards would make a better librarian than me." About to be evicted from her apartment, she has to sell her designer clothes to pay the rent. Convinced that she's not good at anything but partying and flirting, she throws a Middle-Eastern-themed party in Mustafa's warehouse, forcing him to man a post as a falafel vendor, making him merely a prop in her spectacle. Insulted, he again abandons Mary, who has reverted to being the drugged-out party girl she was at the start of the film.

The final scene reverses the opening, as Mary appears at her twenty-fourth birthday party dressed not as a rave queen but as a librarian, in a severe, dark suit and nerdy glasses. "You're working a new look," a friend snidely announces. The physical transformation signals a more significant inner change. She is adamant: "I want a career in library science." And the male character undergoes his own transformation: Mustafa acknowledges that his physical desire—not intellectual interest—played a part in Mary's firing, and redeems himself by admitting that she did in fact use her library skills to assist him. "Empathicalism" is again at work here: Mary has become an intellectual while Mustafa joins the party.

*Party Girl*, like *Funny Face*, emphasizes that external changes mirror internal changes but refuses to equate femininity with emotional submission in marriage. Instead, while sustaining the makeover film's fixation on appearance and fashion, the film manages to convey a more optimistic image of female autonomy in a character who finds happiness in the prospect of a career. Rather than the marriage dance that closes *Funny Face*, the librarian dances to her own beat and on her own terms, as her boyfriend looks on. It's hip to be dowdy and trendy to be intelligent.

Thus, the film ultimately manages to fuse fashion and intellectualism. The runway is co-opted as a place to display Mary's cataloguing skills; the librarian can still party with the in-crowd. Her final dance does not mock faddish intellectual trends, as did Jo's dance in the beatnik café, but makes brainy professional achievement stylish. In the closing sequences, a purple feather boa accessorizes her librarian uniform implying that beauty and brains can happily coexist in the same body.

## The devil within

*The Devil Wears Prada* (2006) invokes both films. The film is based on the narrowly disguised *roman à clef* by Lauren Weisberger about her stint as Anna Wintour's assistant at *Vogue* magazine and thus, like *Funny Face*, uses the offices of an iconic but fictional fashion magazine, *Runway*, as its setting. Its protagonist, Andy Sachs (Anne Hathaway), is a recent journalism graduate initially indifferent to, if not dismissive of, what she sees as a frivolous enterprise that offers little opportunity for her to hone her talents.[9] Unlike Jo Stockton, however, she is not conscripted against her will but enters voluntarily, seeking professional advancement. Like *Party Girl*'s Mary, Andy dreams of a real career. She wants to write for a serious magazine, not a fashion rag, and sees her stint as a necessary evil in attaining her ultimate goal. While Weisberger's chick-lit book was commonly seen as an indictment of the grasping and catty fashion world, embodied by the imperious Miranda Priestly, the film departs significantly from the book to offer a more complex and nuanced interrogation of both fashion and female ambition. The devil, as it were, is in the details.

Once again the makeover candidate/star hardly needs assistance. Hathaway is a modern-day Hepburn with her pale skin, dark hair and balletic bearing, recognizable for her appearance in the Cinderella films of the new millennium, the *Princess Diaries* series (2001, 2004) and *Ella Enchanted* (2004). At the opening of the film, she sports a variation of the outfit worn by Hepburn's bookish waif, the costume Hollywood appears to equate with intellectualism—flat shoes and a shapeless sweater-skirt combination—making her, as one real fashion journalist colorfully put it, "about as well suited for her position as Paris Hilton would be for a job as a nanny" (La Ferla). Her hair hangs limply. Although supposedly not model thin—she's a size 6, "the new 14"—she eventually does fit into the designer samples filling the magazine's spacious fashion closet.

Her prince arrives offering Jimmy Choo stilettos. Rather than a photographer, the agent of her transformation is the magazine's art director, Nigel (Stanley Tucci). Unlike in *Funny Face*, however, he is not a potential love interest, but a colleague. (She already has a boyfriend, aspiring chef Nate [Adrian Grenier]). Nigel's interest in her physical transformation is not inspired by a desire to make her over to advance his own ambitions or to suit him, but out of compassion combined with no small measure of his impatience at her inability to do so herself. When Andy initially rejects his assistance, claiming, "Miranda knows what I look like," he retorts, "Do you?" Instead, Andy changes not to please a man, as in *Funny Face*, or herself, as in *Party Girl*, but a woman—or women: Miranda and her fashionista coworkers.

She eventually capitulates not out of desire but ambition. Andy pleads for Nigel's help only when she senses her job, and hence her future career at the *New Yorker*, is at risk. Marshalling the vast and seemingly endless supply of designer clothing at the magazine's disposal, Nigel turns the frumpish Andy into a Glamazon. As in *Party Girl*, a montage shows her arriving at the office in a parade of Gucci, Dolce & Gabbana, Prada and Valentino designs. The climactic moment of her induction into the fashionable world comes, as it does in *Funny Face*, with a coveted trip to Paris, where she proves herself not only useful to her boss but attractive to another man, a Flostra-like phony who lures her with the promise of connections to the serious world of publishing while orchestrating a position for himself with *Runway* as part of a surreptitious takeover plot of the magazine.

In the film, the temptations leading Andy toward sin do not stem from the Devil wearing Prada—Miranda Priestly—or even Prada. The most radical departure from Weisberger's novel is the characterization of Miranda Priestly. In the book, she is a cartoonish harridan, issuing impossible demands, sending employees scurrying on demeaning errands, oblivious to the suffering of her oppressed minions. Played by Meryl Streep with an icy calm, Miranda is revealed to be an overworked mother of two in a demanding job, seeking to placate a disappointed husband while fending off a potential rival for her position within the corporate conglomerate that operates the magazine.

Even the consumerist world of fashion evades critique. In an early scene, Andy is summoned to take notes at a meeting of stylists who are presenting Miranda with their ideas for the issue's feature spread. Their intense debate

*Image 3.5* Before: Andy Sachs (Anne Hathaway) reacts to the first step in her makeover: Jimmy Choo stilettos

*Image 3.6* After: the "fashionista" applies finishing touches

about the subtle differences between two studded turquoise belts, which appear identical to Andy, causes her to snigger derisively. Miranda responds with a withering speech challenging Andy's belief that she exists above and apart from such superficial concerns. Pointing to Andy's blue cable-knit sweater, Miranda identifies its precise shade of blue (cerulean), cites the exact dates that it appeared in a designer's collection and when it was first featured in the magazine, where it was spotted by the mass-market clothing manufacturer that copied it for a season before it was remaindered and then sold at a "tragic Casual Corner clearance bin" to Andy, making her a beneficiary of their work, if not complicit in supporting the very industry she derides. Even Andy's boyfriend objects less to her new look than to her incessant work on Miranda's behalf, questioning not her allegiances to the magazine but her neglect of her friends.

Perhaps this shift in emphasis from book to film derives from its connections to the fashion-centered HBO series, *Sex and the City*. The film was directed by David Frankel, who directed many episodes of the series, and the show's stylist, Patricia Field, assembled the film's pricey accumulation of designer goods. Like the series, beloved by young women internationally, the film shies away from any critique of fashion as either a superficial distraction from real human development, or an insidious capitalist force tricking women into overpriced clothing and out of their disposable income. Like other products of chick culture, the film also questions whether professional ambition can substitute for personal happiness. Note, however, that the end of *The Devil Wears Prada* departs from both *Funny Face* and *Party Girl* in that the protagonist does not find satisfaction in either marriage or a job. Separated from her boyfriend, she is still pursuing a career in publishing, startled to learn that she received a positive recommendation from her former boss. In the final sequence, Andy spots Miranda entering a limousine and, without speaking, they share a knowing look, suggesting mutual respect if not gratitude for each other's assistance.

## Conclusion

Taken together these fashion makeover films offer perhaps unexpected takes on consumer culture and identity. Each highlights a sequence of elaborate dress that, drawing on the visual conventions of fashion shows and photojournalism, makes the film temporarily a moving shop window or a kinetic substitute for flipping through the pages of a magazine. Such sequences do emphasize fashion as a visual treat, offering audiences the vicarious pleasure of sampling artistry in clothing design. But just as window shopping rarely leads to purchase and the average magazine buyer hardly plans her own wardrobe out of the pricey items in the latest copy of *Vogue*, the film's heightened display of fashion is the stuff of fantasy, like Cinderella's transitory experience at the ball. The derogatory comments of industry insiders regarding the clothing choices in *The Devil Wears Prada* emphasize this point. Hal Rubenstein, the fashion director of *InStyle* magazine, complained that the film demonstrated "a weird desire for abundance for the sake of abundance" (qouted in La Ferla). Tiffany Dubin, a former vintage fashion curator at Sotheby's, sniffed, "It's costume." Precisely.

Instead of fashion itself, the films interrogate the intersection of fashion and identity, granting greater weight to the protagonist's internal rather than external changes. Dress serves as a marker of larger transformations, each film reflecting larger debates about women's roles in contemporary society. *Funny Face* ends with Jo Stockton in a wedding gown, capitulating to marriage after abandoning her intellectual desires, in keeping with conventional ideas of femininity in the 1950s. *Party Girl* ends with Mary celebrating her discovery of a satisfying career and a supportive boyfriend, reflecting mid-1990s' expectations that a young woman find both professional and personal success. *The Devil Wears Prada* ends inconclusively with Andy Sachs embarking on a new phase of her professional development after what may have been a false start and without the boyfriend who had previously supported her ambitions. The most recent film captures the uncertainties experienced by a new generation of young women, leery of promises that they can have it all.

Notably, *Party Girl* and *The Devil Wears Prada* make the female protagonist more of an agent in her own transformation. As such, they signal a further transformation in ideas about fashion, moving away from the clichéd notion of the industry as oppressing women. Instead, external transformation through clothing and cosmetics appears as a means of performing identity, of trying on roles, cognizant that, despite naïve expectations to the contrary, there is no way of living outside of contemporary consumer culture. Instead, its tools are harnessed as a means of self-fashioning.

This may explain, in part, the often derided pleasures female viewers take in makeover television shows such as *E! Fashion Emergency* or *What Not to Wear*. Like makeover flicks, they too capitalize on female identification with the protagonist, though the identification is enhanced since the candidate for a makeover is not an already glamorous celebrity, but an "ordinary" woman and, while the tools are the same—makeup, hair styling, and clothing—they do not require big Hollywood budgets. They promise that self-transformation is within the reach of any woman with even modest disposable income. Unlike more ambitious—and controversial —shows such as *The Swan* or *10 Years in 10 Days*, the changes they showcase do not require cosmetic surgery or reconstructive dentistry, procedures which are not simply expensive but permanent. Hair can grow in or be cut, color changed, clothing discarded or tailored, makeup removed. The ephemeral nature of physical change is not lamented but celebrated, as women vicariously experience the joy of playing with a new *look*—not a new "you."

Ultimately, both makeover television and flicks offer the female viewer reassurance. They suggest that external transformation is unnecessary, that she will ultimately be valued for herself, in relationships and at work. But they suggest that the means of gaining recognition are easily within her reach, and, in more recent films, increasingly under her control.

## Notes

1  In *The Makeover in Movies*, Elizabeth Ford and Deborah Mitchell identify *Now, Voyager* as the first major makeover movie (3).
2  See Doane, Haskell, and King.
3  On the connection between the woman's film and fashion, see Bruzzi, Eckert, Gaines, Renov, Turim and the essays in *Fabrications*, as well as Basinger's chapter on "Fashion and Glamour," 114–59.
4  While Ford and Mitchell identify the same literary sources as the foundation of the makeover film, our interpretations differ.
5  As Paula James notes, "The finishing touches to the transformation are provided by the cinematic techniques at Hitchcock's disposal, filming Judy through the soft focus filter used for Madeleine." See her essay for a more detailed analysis of the parallels between the Pygmalion myth and *Vertigo*, as well as their creators Ovid and Hitchcock.
6  The Cinderella parallels in a scene such as this are augmented for viewers familiar with Hepburn's own past. As Moseley notes, "The story of the little girl who survived for weeks in a cellar during the German occupation of Holland, and who carried *Resistance* messages in her dance shoes, later to become one of Hollywood's greatest stars, is perhaps the most powerful Cinderella narrative of all. This key trope, which embodies aspirations of beauty, romance and social mobility and which has been central to feminine popular culture and socialization, is surely at the centre of Hepburn's appeal and address to a female audience, structuring both the star's image and career" ("Trousers," 39). Also see Moseley, "Dress," 116.
7  Moseley has noted the film's exploitation of the "apparent transparency and authenticity of Hepburn's star image—the extreme degree of fit between what is known of the fairytale femininities she embodied in her 'real' life, and her film roles which later played quite self-consciously on this." She had been a model and a dancer before becoming an actress.
8  On Hepburn's recuperation of the "beatnik" look, see Moseley, *Growing Up* 42–45.
9  See Jesella on the place of style writers in the contemporary media.

## Works cited

Basinger, Jeanine. *A Woman's View: How Hollywood Spoke to Women, 1930–1960*. New York: Knopf, 1993.
Bruzzi, Stella. *Undressing Cinema: Clothing and Identity in the Movies*. London: Routledge, 1997.

Doane, Mary Ann. *The Desire to Desire: The Woman's Film of the 1940s.* Bloomington: Indiana University Press, 1987.

Eckert, Charles. "The Carole Lombard in Macy's Window." *Quarterly Review of Film Studies* 3 (Winter 1978): 1–21.

Ford, Elizabeth A. and Deborah C. Mitchell. *The Makeover in Movies: Before and After in Hollywood Films, 1941–2002.* Jefferson, NC: McFarland, 2004.

Gaines, Jane. "The Queen Christina Tie-Ups: Convergence of Show Window and Screen." *Quarterly Review of Film and Video* 11 (1989): 35–60.

Gaines, Jane and Charlotte Herzog (eds). *Fabrications: Costume and the Female Body.* New York: Routledge, 1990.

Haskell, Molly. *From Reverence to Rape: The Treatment of Women in the Movies.* 1973. 2nd ed. Chicago: University of Chicago Press, 1987.

James, Paula. "She's All That: Ovid's Ivory Statue and the Legacy of Pygmalion on Film." *Classical Bulletin* 79 (2003): 63–91. ProQuest.

Jesella, Kara. "Paper Dollhouse: Why Can't Style Writers Get any Respect?" *Bitch: Feminist Response to Pop Culture* 32 (Summer 2006): 40–45.

King, Justine. "Crossing Thresholds: The Contemporary British Woman's Film." In *Dissolving Views: Key Writings on British Cinema.* Ed. Andrew Higson. London: Cassell, 1996: 216–31.

La Ferla, Ruth. "The Duds of 'The Devils Wears Prada.'" *The New York Times*, June 29, 2006. <http://www.nytimes.com/2006/06/29/fashion/thursdaystyles/>.

Moseley, Rachel. "Dress, Class and Audrey Hepburn: The Significance of the Cinderella Story." In *Fashioning Film Stars: Dress, Culture, Identity.* Ed. Rachel Moseley. London: British Film Institute, 2005: 109–20.

——*Growing Up with Audrey Hepburn: Text, Audience, Resonance.* Manchester: Manchester University Press, 2002.

——"Trousers and Tiaras: Audrey Hepburn, a Woman's Star." *Feminist Review* 71 (2002): 37–51.

Negra, Diane. " 'Queen of the Indies': Parker Posey's Niche Stardom and the Taste Cultures of Independent Film." In *Contemporary American Independent Film: From the Margins to the Mainstream.* Ed. Chris Holmlund and Justine Wyatt. London and New York: Routledge, 2005: 72–88.

Ovid. "Pygmalion." *The Metamorphoses of Ovid: A New Verse Translation.* Trans. Allen Mandelbaum. New York: Harcourt, 1993.

Perrault, Charles. "Cinderella, or The Little Glass Slipper." In *Footnotes: On Shoes.* Ed. Shari Benstock and Suzanne Ferriss. New Brunswick, NJ: Rutgers University Press, 2001: 299–304.

Renov, Michael. "Advertising/Photojournalism/Cinema: The Shifting Rhetoric of Forties Female Representation." *Quarterly Review of Film and Video* 11 (1989): 1–21.

Turim, Maureen. "High Angles on Shoes: Cinema, Gender and Footwear." In *Footnotes: On Shoes.* Ed. Shari Benstock and Suzanne Ferriss. New Brunswick, NJ: Rutgers University Press, 2001: 58–90.

——"Seduction and Elegance: The New Woman of Fashion in Silent Cinema." In *On Fashion.* Ed. Shari Benstock and Suzanne Ferriss. New Brunswick, NJ: Rutgers University Press, 1994: 14–58.

Veblen, Thorstein. *The Theory of the Leisure Class.* New York: Macmillan, 1912.

Wilson, Elizabeth. *Adorned in Dreams.* Berkeley: University of California Press, 1985.

# Chapter 4

# The return of pink

## Legally Blonde, third-wave feminism, and having it all

*Carol M. Dole*

In 2001, Nike was advertising women's athletic shoes with a campaign that capitalized on the dissonance of femininity and feminism, but also suggested that it was time to erase that dissonance. Slogans such as "I paint my toenails. I play football" promised that women could be simultaneously sexy and hard core. In television commercials aired during the US Open, tennis powerhouse Venus Williams appeared in Reebok ads attired in a pink princess gown—another visual argument that female strength could coexist with the accoutrements of femininity. Pink had come out of the closet—and not just as a symbol of gay culture.

Suddenly, at the outset of the new millennium, women were ready to reclaim pink. Yes, little girls had dressed in pink for decades, and every toy manufacturer had continued to use pink to market toys designed for girls. Since the feminist movement of the 1960s and 1970s, however, many adult women had shied away from a color that seemed to emphasize their difference from men even while women were demanding equality to men. Feminist writers of the Seventies urged women who wanted to be taken seriously to dress the part, and soon women in corporate culture sported the skirted equivalent of the grey suit with white shirt. During the ensuing decades, colors and more varied styles crept back into women's professional dress; but not until the new century did women's fashion once again embrace the color that had long served as the American cultural sign for femininity.[1] By 2003, marketers were using pink to sell women ballgowns, beachtotes, and books.

The color pink was part of a larger fashion trend toward brighter colors, sexier styles, and longer hair in the early years of the new century— in short, a return to femininity. Of course, this fashion cycle like others is part of the endless search for something new to entice the consumer. But I will argue that it is also a cultural symptom of shifting attitudes to femininity, attitudes explored in both feminist thought and popular culture. This essay will track how women's anxieties about balancing femininity and power play out in mainstream films marketed to American women. My central text will be *Legally Blonde* (2001), the ultimate celebration of the power of pink (and all that pink represents), but I will place it within the broader discourse of early twenty-first-century chick flicks that, within the genre of comedy, explore the current appeal and the current limitations of femininity.

## Femininity and feminism

The return of femininity evident in *Legally Blonde* and other chick flicks, as well as chick lit, is consistent with third-wave feminism's "girlie" strand. Girlie is only one position within third-wave feminism, a loose movement of younger women that originated in the Nineties. Third-wave is less politically active than the second-wave feminism of the Sixties and Seventies, and is expressed more through popular culture than through petitions and marches—a difference that has led some veteran feminists and others to deride it as ineffective. Third-wavers argue that their brand of feminism is spread through popular culture, such as the punk-rock Riot Grrls movement, the hip teen magazine *Sassy* and the feminist magazine *Bust*, or women-centered shows such as *Ally McBeal, Buffy the Vampire Slayer*, or *Sex and the City*. Although some third-wavers urge political action and many share an interest in such issues as child sexual abuse, AIDS awareness, self-mutilation, body image, and eating disorders (Baumgardner and Richards 21), for the most part third-wave feminism is closer to an attitude of confidence than to an agenda.[2] Many young women share the third-wavers' world view that a woman should be whatever she wants to be without labeling that view as feminist or even recognizing the term *third-wave*. For many of their generation, "feminism is like fluoride. We scarcely notice that we have it—it's simply in the water" (Baumgardner and Richards 17). Indeed, the majority of American women in their teens, twenties, and thirties resist calling themselves feminists—making it possible for *Time* to run their 1998 cover story on the death of feminism (Bellafante)—even though a large number of them share the same attitudes, interests, and belief in equality as the women who label themselves third-wave feminists.

Would Elle (Reese Witherspoon), the fashionista heroine of *Legally Blonde*, call herself a feminist? Possibly not. But her attitudes, signaled by her combination of a relentlessly pink wardrobe and an equally relentless drive for success, are textbook "girlie" feminism. In *Manifesta: Young Women, Feminism, and the Future* (2000), Jennifer Baumgardner and Amy Richards explain that "Girlies are adult women, usually in their mid-twenties to late thirties, whose feminist principles are based on a reclaiming of girl culture (or feminine accoutrements that were tossed out with sexism during the Second Wave). [. . .] Girlie encompasses the tabooed symbols of women's feminine enculturation—Barbie dolls, makeup, fashion magazines, high heels—and says using them isn't shorthand for 'we've been duped'" (400, 136). As this passage suggests, third-wave feminists often define themselves in opposition to the second-wave feminists of their mothers' generation, women who worked in the 1960s and 1970s to achieve equal rights. For some younger women, third-wave feminism is a rebellion against the joylessness of those foremothers whose conviction was that "the way to equality was to reject Barbie and all forms of pink-packaged femininity" (Baumgardner and Richards 136–37). Unlike most veteran feminists, girlie feminists believe that "it is a feminist statement to proudly claim things that are feminine, and the alternative can mean to deny what we are" (135). Girlie culture embraces both sexual pleasure and the childhood girl pleasures of knitting, nail polish, and of course the emblematic color pink (80)—Elle's "signature color."

Following on a turn-of-the-century cultural explosion of media expressions of physical girlpower (think *Powerpuff Girls, Buffy, Lara Croft, Charlie's Angels*), a pop culture fascination with things feminine now runs parallel to third-wave feminism. Merchandising to young girls is dominated by the princess craze and associated "girlie-girl" products, including Mattel's 2001 "World of Girl" line of Barbie princesses, and Disney's princess franchise, which turned around Disney Consumer Products' profits after its introduction in 2000 (Orenstein). "Pink," observes Peggy Orenstein, "is the new gold." The most visible evidence of this trend in Hollywood is a tide of princess tales in 2004, particularly those structured around the Cinderella myth, in which a young woman escapes from a powerless position into both royal prerogative and dreamy ball gowns. The Cinderella story has long provided an outlet for female fantasies of a rise in social class coupled with romance and a new wardrobe, as it did in *Pretty Woman* (1990) and *Maid in Manhattan* (2002), but in these 2004 princess tales the formula is somewhat different. Surveying *The Prince and Me, Shrek 2, Ella Enchanted* and *A Cinderella Story*, along with their 2001 prototype *The Princess Diaries, Time* magazine found that the heroine

> should be pretty, but in a class-president way, not a head-cheerleader way. She should be able to stand up for herself (recall the *Crouching Tiger* moves of *Shrek*'s Princess Fiona). She must be socially conscious —a result, says Meg Cabot, author of the *Princess Diary* books, of Princess Diana's charitable work. And she should above all not want to be a princess—at least until she changes her mind. (Poniewozik 74)

A carefully designed formula is needed, the article suggests, to reconcile the fairy-tale tradition of femininity with the "lessons of feminism": "You can have the girly dream of glass slippers and true love, these films say, as well as the womanly ideal of self-determination and independence—and any contradictions between them are no match for the movies' magic" (Poniewozik 72).

Although such contradictions are not allowed to undermine the heroine's happiness in recent films—whether films about literal princesses or their somewhat more realistic equivalents—I will argue that in these films the contradictions between self-determination and the "girly dream" are frequently explored and tested. Can women have it all? Women have struggled with this dilemma since the second-wave era, but no answer is yet in sight. Younger women may have accepted that family and career are extremely difficult to balance effectively; but they are also trying to make room for recuperating "the privileges that traditional femininity conferred on women despite its costs—doors magically opened, dinner checks picked up, Manolo Blahnicks. Frippery. Fun" (Orenstein). Although women's right to a career seems at this point to be a given in American culture, can women really expect to excel in that career if they jettison "masculine" behaviors in favor of the more frankly feminine appearance and goals sanctioned by girlie feminism? In the visual medium of film, this question is often posed through costume.

## Costume and the debate on femininity

In her 1997 study of the uses of fashion and costume design in cinema, Stella Bruzzi demonstrates that "clothing exists as a discourse not wholly dependent on the structures of narrative and character for signification" (xvi). As such, costume is a key to exploring women's evolving roles in film. Moreover, costume may be especially significant in chick flicks, which are by definition marketed to women. Bruzzi, departing from the line of feminist film theory that has regarded women in film as the objects of the male gaze, posits that the discourse of clothes may be carried on primarily among women. She suggests that "women's fashion—and in a cinematic context emphatic femininity—is an exclusory dialogue between a female image and a female spectatorship" (xix). Choice of costume, then, may be as significant in conveying meaning to the female film viewer as choice of words. Both second- and third-wave feminists, and indeed women in general, are very attuned to the power of dress to make a statement.

"Emphatic femininity" of costume is a striking component of many chick flicks of the twenty-first century. Like all films, these recent chick flicks use costumes to help indicate character, but they also go further. They offer a superabundance of dresses (often pink or sparkly), hairstyles, manicures, designer shoes, clever bags and precious jewels as a celebration of femininity. The films often become, in whole (as in the *Legally Blonde* and *Charlie's Angels* series, and the 2006 hit *The Devil Wears Prada*) or in part (as in most of the Cinderella variants), a dress-up party. Such playfulness is exactly the sort espoused by girlie feminists as a way to take pride in being female.

In the Cinderella variants, a shopping and/or dressing scene always correlates to the fairy-tale heroine's makeover for the ball—even if, as in

*Maid in Manhattan*, the plot has to be seriously contorted to give the heroine an excuse to don Harry Winston diamonds and a fabulous evening gown. In *13 Going on 30* (2004), a young teen transformed overnight into Jennifer Garner rejoices chiefly in discovering a treasure trove of shoes, lacy thongs, and flirty dresses, a display that offers pleasure to the female viewer as well. Even when the heroine rejects the idea of a makeover as inconsistent with her authentic self, as does Anne Hathaway's would-be crusading journalist in *The Devil Wears Prada*, she nonetheless gets to share with the audience the pleasures of a designer wardrobe and, yes, a trip to the ball. More notable still is the prominence of costume in recent films about women who are self-confident and attractive from the outset. For instance, publicity surrounding *Charlie's Angels: Full Throttle* (2003) and *Legally Blonde 2: Red, White and Blonde* (2004) specified the extraordinary number of costume changes in the films—and not only to sell tie-in fashion products, but also to sell the movies themselves.[3] The narrative focus on transformation in recent chick flicks—whether a wholesale transformation into beauty and power (the Cinderella films, *13 Going on 30*) or a "trying-on" of multiple available roles for women (the *Charlie's Angels* films, *The Devil Wears Prada*)—together with the films' visual invitation to revel in the trappings of femininity, shows Hollywood has recognized a cultural tendency among young women to embrace the feminine.

Hollywood's response to that recognition may have been spurred on by the unexpected box office success in 2001 of *Legally Blonde*, in which the heroine sported forty hairstyles and even more outfits. This wicked comedy celebrates both the feminist and the hyperfeminine. The heroine is called Elle, a name suggestive of both femininity and fashion—but the film's extravagant use of the cultural codes pink and blonde tell viewers who don't speak French all they need to know. The ultra-feminine side of Elle, consistent with pre-feminist notions of womanhood, is blatant in the film. Elle applies to Harvard Law School specifically to snare a man, her college boyfriend Warner, who had dumped her by explaining that if he was to become a senator by the age of thirty, "I need to marry a Jackie, not a Marilyn." Elle employs her sexuality to gain admission to Harvard, submitting a video application featuring herself in a bikini. Homecoming queen and sorority president at her California university, Elle confidently enters Ivy League territory in her "signature color," pink. Her extensive designer wardrobe leans toward feathers and spangles, and her long blonde hair is often curled. In Cambridge the only place she comfortably fits in is the feminine world of a local salon, where she bonds with her manicurist. When Elle snares a prestigious internship, her first impulse is to go shopping. Her big legal case is won through her sorority ties to the client, her expertise on Prada, and her girlie knowledge of hair treatments, which helps her trap a witness into admitting to murder.

Although Elle fits so many Fifties stereotypes of femininity and although the relentlessly feminine fashions are *Legally Blonde*'s most visible element, the film also has an agenda consistent with the politics of veteran feminists. Its protagonist is so determined, canny, and diligent that she attains every goal, including success at Harvard Law School and a not-guilty verdict in her big case. She stands up to sexual harassment by her law professor and she is a faithful friend to other women from a range of social classes. These feminist attributes persist in the 2003 sequel, in which Elle (still clad in Jimmy Choo stilettos) storms Washington to change the law so as to save her beloved Chihuahua's mother from animal testing. As Glynis O'Leary points out, in the sequel Elle uses the title Ms and insists on being called a "woman" rather than a "girl" and, when she needs help, organizes a network of women to march on Washington rather than appealing to her Harvard professor boyfriend.

Recognizing the possible contradictions between *Legally Blonde*'s feminism and its obsession with an attractive appearance, feminist commentators disagree on Elle's suitability as a role model. O'Leary, applauding *Blonde 2's* "ideas of grassroots activism, feminist themes of independence, equality, and sisterhood, and subverting patriarchal institutions," argues that the film "becomes a subversive tool for motivating young feminists," who are lured by its humor and then "introduced to some serious progressive ideals." Columnist Ellen Goodman, on the other hand, speaks for many second-wavers as she wonders whether it's possible to tell the difference between the prevailing "new Hollywood message that women can be dolled up and successful" and the "old message that you're successful only if you're a doll." Goodman, placing *Blonde 2* in the context of other popular culture manifestations of third-wave feminist ideals, expresses her ambivalence about Harvard students in the Miss America pageant, about the *Legally Blonde 2* Barbie doll as a "training toy of empowerment," and about producer/star Drew Barrymore's insistence that Charlie's Angels be " 'their own feminine selves' " without acknowledging that the angels are "directed by an invisible male boss" (Goodman A19).

In spite of her reservations about third-wave feminism's embrace of Barbie-ism, Goodman admits to having rather liked the 2001 *Legally Blonde*. Critics and viewers overall agree that the original film is more enjoyable than its sequel.[4] Not only is the sequel less original, but it makes Elle almost a parody of her earlier self. The second film replicates the fish-out-of-water/win-the-big-case structure of the first, imports Elle's familiar girlfriends to Washington with her, parrots small incidents from *Legally Blonde*, and unabashedly celebrates her pink wardrobe and designer shoes. But the sequel loses one of the greatest appeals of the original: Elle's search for her own path. In the first film, the audience was asked to see Elle from outside, sympathizing with her in her early heartbreak, appreciating her charm and spunk, but also laughing at her excesses and naïveté, as when she insists that living across the street from Aaron Spelling is obviously better than being a Vanderbilt. Over the course of the original film, Elle earns the affection of the audience because she is resilient without being blindly determined; rather, she tries on new aspects of herself just as she adapts her wardrobe to her new situations. The audience is asked to consider along with Elle which of her possible options will be most effective or satisfying. The effect is much like that of *Clueless*, the 1995 update of Jane Austen's *Emma*, in which a fifteen-year-old blonde Valley Girl is presented as both ludicrous and lovable as she works her way through self-absorption to adopt more mature and satisfying goals and loves. In contrast to both *Clueless* and *Legally Blonde*, *Blonde 2* starts with the assumption that its heroine is not only charming but always right. Although her difference in appearance may sometimes be played for laughs, in ham-handed imitation of the first film, in the sequel Elle's bright, feminine wardrobe is used chiefly to contrast her idealism to the cynicism of the dark-uniformed Washington insiders.

## Feminine masquerade

In the original *Legally Blonde*, costumes have a more complex role in the film's examination of the intersection of self-expression and social role. Like fashion itself, which attempts to balance a personal style with that year's trends, a young woman's life is often focused on balancing individuality with conformity to appropriate norms. Although the film sometimes engages in the rhetoric of authenticity that seems de rigueur for films about teenagers defining themselves, in fact the question of *Legally Blonde* is not really whether Elle should stay true to herself—after all, her obsession with Prada and pink is less individual expression than adherence to her sorority's norms—but rather which roles her expanding life can accommodate. Can Elle remain a feminine, sexy blonde and simultaneously become a powerful East Coast lawyer? In the age of third-wave feminism and *Sex and the City*, the answer for the film's target audience of young women must be yes. This is a Hollywood comedy, after all. But the film is canny about positioning this optimistic claim against earlier styles of feminism, and in acknowledging the potential dangers of a hyperfeminine self-presentation without devaluing femininity.

*Legally Blonde* shows a keen awareness of the importance of marking out a social role through appearance. When Elle faces the taunt "Malibu Barbie!" on her arrival at Harvard clad in pink leather, she is being given a signal that her appearance, although perfectly adapted to her California sorority house, is inappropriate in a different social setting. A fashion-merchandising major, Elle is highly skilled at adopting costumes to signify various social roles. What would Law School Barbie wear? Soon Elle is donning black-rimmed glasses and layering her pink shirts with earth-

*Image 4.1* Elle (Reese Witherspoon) arrives at Harvard in "Malibu Barbie" attire

toned sweaters that reflect the dominant color scheme of the Harvard students. When she snares a competitive internship, Elle promptly rushes off to shop for more corporate designer suits in blacks or grays, relieved only by a discreet feminine ruffle or tasteful patterned blouse.

Elle is obviously well aware of the importance of masquerade. However, in casting herself in various roles she relies at times too entirely on costuming. In Harvard classes she is belittled, once even ejected, for failing to master the class material. Only after she has swapped her pink feathered pen for a laptop and started to take notes like her classmates does she succeed in the role of law student. Part of her growth in the film is learning the behaviors as well as the costumes appropriate to each social role.

The film too is knowing about masquerade, which it approaches with an irony unknown to Elle herself, who was conceived by the filmmakers as having "the integrity of innocence" (Platt) and was played by Witherspoon as unfailingly perky and nice. The costumes were imagined by director Robert Luketic as a separate "character." The film's postmodern take on feminine fashion is signaled by the immediate reference to Madonna (an icon of the third wave), whom Elle mentions in the first scene. As *Bust* editor Debbie Stoller explains, Madonna, with her canny manipulation of her over-the-top sexual image, mesmerized girls of the 1980s: "Suffocated by the high-school version of the Virgin/Whore complex (dress demurely and you're a prude; dress sexy and you're a slut), girls were happy to have at least one of these options invested with some power" (45). Inspired by Madonna's use of the "trappings of femininity" to make a powerful sexual statement, many girls adopted "a new style of feminine display that involved layers of lingerie and bottles of bleach" (Stoller 45). This sense of the feminine masquerade as a source of power is Madonna's heritage to third-wave feminists, who have developed their own "tongue-in-chic sensibility" (Stoller 46). *Legally Blonde,* a film whose title evokes and ironizes stereotypes, shares this tongue-in-chic attitude by both reveling in its hyperfeminine fashions and winking at their extravagance.

In recent cinema, recognition of the power of feminine display is easiest to see in detective movies like *Charlie's Angels* that involve an "undercover" component, as when the Angels pose as pole-dancers to distract a mark while they recover an encoded ring. Such undercover work is only the extreme expression, however, of naturalized feminine behaviors, a mode of self presentation that Joan Rivière described in 1929 in "Womanliness as a Masquerade." Rivière argued that women who "wish for masculinity," that is, to take their place in a public world then dominated by men, "may put on a mask of womanliness to avert anxiety and the retribution feared from men" (35). Although gender lines in the West are no longer as strongly drawn as they were in 1929, Rivière's insight remains applicable (think about the cultural confusion as to whether, as First Lady, Hillary Rodham Clinton should be overhauling health care or baking cookies).

But especially useful for an understanding of *Legally Blonde* is Rivière's contention that there is no difference between "genuine womanliness and the 'masquerade;'" "whether radical or superficial, they are the same thing" (38). Madonna's or the Angels' use of feminine masquerade as a source of power may be more easily readable because their intentional control of their image is so obvious, but Rivière teaches us that even when a woman does not as consciously plan her effect, she nonetheless adopts womanliness as a role. Elle, who refers to *Cosmo* as "the bible," has been trained into extremes of womanliness that she regards not as deceptive (as a term like *masquerade* might imply) but rather as natural and pleasurable—but her womanliness is powerful either way.

Like girlie feminism, *Legally Blonde* acknowledges and validates the sexual power of feminine masquerade. Elle is unashamed to employ the spectacle of her adorned body to gain her ends. When she designs her admission video for Harvard to feature herself in a spangled bikini, her tactic succeeds. When she determines that she will win Warner back from Vivian, Elle's first move is to display herself "studying" in a bikini top and feathered jacket, knowing that she will rivet the attention of Warner and his fellow football players. When Elle is feeling discouraged about the widespread prejudice against blondes, hunky lawyer Emmett reminds her that being blonde is a "pretty powerful thing" and urges her to "take that power and channel it toward the greater good"—which she promptly does to help her nerdy classmate David get a date.

On the other hand, the film consistently demonstrates that feminine sexuality is not adequate in itself. Although Elle's sexy attire and flirtatious manner pique the interest of the Harvard admissions committee, her 4.0 average and 179 LSAT score are crucial elements of their decision to admit her (as a "diversity" candidate!). Once she gets to Harvard, her professors are impressed only by smart answers, not by Elle's looks. Likewise, it isn't Elle's deployment of bikini or bunny outfit that ultimately wins Warner back, but instead her legal triumph. Even the timing of Professor Callahan's attempt at seducing Elle, which immediately follows her first success in the courtroom, hints that a woman is truly desirable only when her beauty is combined with intelligence and drive.

Moreover, *Legally Blonde* recognizes the potential dangers of flaunting one's femininity. Elle lost the man she loved because Warner assumed that a blonde bombshell could be a suitable partner only for the hot tub, not for a political campaign. Elle, as she complains to Emmett, suffers from feeling that blondes (hampered by the stereotype of being sexy and glamorous but also "dumb" or "ditzy") are discriminated against. But the most compelling dramatization of the dangers of a feminine self-presentation is Callahan's sexual harassment of Elle, which plunges her into self-doubt and almost sends her running back to California. She cries to her friend,

What's the point of staying, Paulette? I mean, all people see when they look at me is blonde hair and big boobs. No one's ever going to take *me* seriously. The people at law school don't, Warner doesn't. I don't even think my own parents take me seriously. I just felt like for the first time that someone expected me to do something more with my life than just become a Victoria's Secret model.

This is Elle's lowest point in the film. And although the film unequivocally condemns Callahan, who had hit on Elle in the context of offering an employment opportunity, it also allows the viewer to wonder whether a man who had come of age in an earlier era might misread signals such as the scented pink résumé Elle had presented to him. Callahan's response to his most dolled-up intern, together with Elle's assessment of the way even her nearest and dearest evaluate her, makes a cogent case that an excessively feminine image can evoke lingering stereotypes that may ultimately limit a woman's opportunities.

*Legally Blonde* joins other recent chick flicks in warning women viewers that extremes of femininity can be socially unacceptable, causing embarrassment and possible misreading. Although fashionable clothing can provide women with pleasurable "fantasies of transport and transformation" (Young 206), these films suggest that women must be watchful about the contexts in which they engage in such types of play. One recurring trope provides a particular caution against naïve use of sexualized roles: the Playboy Bunny, the ultimate image of desirable—and hotly desired—femininity. The Bunny invariably appears in these films in a context of the humiliation of a woman who has failed to completely and accurately read social signals about her role in a public gathering. In *Bridget Jones's Diary* (2001), Bridget's Playboy Bunny costume turns out to be wildly unsuitable for an afternoon garden party after she fails to get the message that the "Tarts and Vicars" theme was cancelled, and her shame is intensified by the presence of her potential lover Mark Darcy. In *Legally Blonde*, spiteful female classmates trick Elle—who might well have suspected treachery from Warner's fiancée—into believing that a law school gathering is a costume party, and laugh heartily when she shows up in full Bunny attire. Although Warner himself is appreciative of Elle's appearance in the skimpy Bunny outfit, it is also at this moment that he tells her that she is not smart enough to do well at Harvard.

Even in the high-school chick flick *Mean Girls* (2004), which reverses the costuming, the Playboy Bunny is linked to the humiliation of the naïve heroine, Cady. Having grown up in another culture, new student Cady doesn't realize that the Halloween party is an opportunity for the girls to dress as "sluts" without consequences. She mistakenly shows up in monster garb, only to lose the boy she likes to queen bee Regina, who uses her Bunny allure to regain her former boyfriend at the party. But the power

*Image 4.2* Elle appears at a law-school party inappropriately dressed

of the Bunny is temporary: by the end of the film Regina will lose the boy and be humiliated herself as a result of the same practices of femininity that led her to don the Playboy outfit. As *Legally Blonde* does for a slightly older group, *Mean Girls* meditates on the uses and limits of femininity for younger teens. Regina and the "Plastics," who dress in pink on Wednesdays, use their command of feminine fashion to achieve a top status in the school, an advantage that temporarily attracts Cady into their ranks. But they are also shown to misuse their power, seducing boys for the sake of competition rather than affection, humiliating classmates who do not mark out their gender so clearly, and discouraging Cady from developing her skills in math. Ultimately Cady returns to her truer friends. *Mean Girls* typifies the Hollywood message to younger girls: don't sacrifice your selfhood to peer pressure; stick with your proven friends; (demure) beauty is good but not at the expense of intelligence; overt sexiness is dangerous to self and others.

But, as *13 Going on 30* recognizes in the magazine-inspired yearnings of its teenage heroine Jenna to be "thirty, flirty, and fabulous," in our society adult women are accorded a larger repertoire of acceptable female roles than are teens. Jenna, Mia, and Cady must all refashion themselves as pretty but demure to achieve a happy ending. A college graduate entering full adulthood, Elle can legitimately select from a wider variety of versions of womanhood, including more frankly sexual femininity. For Elle and Bridget, their Playboy interludes help attract potential lovers as well as embarrassing them in front of other women. Her misjudged role-playing as a Bunny prompts an awakening for the unflappable Elle, who leaves the party and, without pausing to change clothes, storms off to buy a computer so that she can transform herself into a serious student. Elle's encounter at the electronics store with her future boyfriend Emmett, who is moved to appreciate her beauty as well as her brains, suggests that the sexualized femininity encapsulated by the Playboy Bunny can pay dividends in personal relationships. Nonetheless, the overall lesson of these Bunny episodes is that in larger social groups an extremely feminine self-presentation puts women at considerable risk of social failure. To assure maximum success, these films imply, women should moderate their feminine display.

Women should not, however, eliminate feminine display. One version of womanhood that *Legally Blonde* does *not* advise is the sort of feminist who eschews feminine appearance in an effort to be taken seriously in a man's world. *Legally Blonde* pokes gentle fun at almost every featured group (sorority girls, lawyers, gays, Ivy Leaguers), but it especially targets young feminists who model themselves on their second-wave predecessors. Elle's classmate Enid, who holds a Ph.D. in women's studies, represents many of the characteristics of veteran feminism that third-wavers might especially object to. Enid's tirade to Warner, in which she plans a political action against subliminal linguistic male domination by pressuring the college to change *sem*ester to *ov*ester, speaks to the third wave's reluctance to be branded as man-haters as second-wave feminists often have been when contesting patriarchal systems, including language.[5] Enid's nostalgia for her "good times" organizing "Lesbians Against Drunk Driving" seems to critique *any* organized feminist action based on identity politics. Enid even looks like a caricature of a second-wave feminist, as she eschews make-up or contacts, always wears slacks, and is even more fashion-challenged than her pallid female classmates. Yes, she's smart and successful. But she knows nothing about sisterhood, attacking Elle as a sorority type rather than respecting her choice to define herself however she chooses, a value of third-wave feminism.

Although sisterhood was certainly a tenet of 1970s feminism, women of color and third-wave feminists have often critiqued early second-wave praxis as dominated by the concerns of middle-class white women. *Legally Blonde* embraces the third-wave insistence on a more inclusive and multi-valent feminism. When Elle leaves California, she trades her sisterhood in a sorority of glossy and privileged young women, mostly white, for a new sisterhood in the salon where she finds respite from her struggles with the elitist society of Harvard Law School. The female-centered salon world is populated by women of varied colors, ages, and body types, a variety boldly on display as the women take to the floor with Elle to teach her manicurist the "Bend and Snap" method of attracting men. In making this uneducated manicurist, Paulette, into Elle's best friend, the film reinforces both sisterhood and the third wave's demand for a feminism that cuts across class lines. As we see Elle help Paulette regain custody of her dog and, with the assistance of the other salon patrons, win the UPS man, we see sisterhood in action. Finally, the film extends this sisterhood to veteran feminists. When Elle runs to the salon to tell Paulette she is giving up after a male professor propositioned her, it is Professor Stromwell who unexpectedly appears in the salon to convince Elle to keep on fighting. Stromwell is never overtly identified as a second-wave feminist, but her age (actress Holland Taylor was born in 1943) and professorship at Harvard suggest that she was among the pioneers of women in the upper reaches of academia. Her predilection for rather severe suits also seems to align her with the second wave. And her advice to Elle seems almost to embody younger women's perceptions of veteran feminists' rejection of phallocentrism: "If you're going to let one stupid prick ruin your life, you're not the girl I thought you were." Stromwell, who had earlier picked on her pink-clad student and ejected her from class for not having adequately studied precedent, had first been posed as an antagonist to Elle, but in the salon she becomes both sister and savior. Later, in the film's final scene, it is Stromwell who smilingly yields the podium to Elle, a visual statement that second-wave feminism has approvingly handed on the torch to third-wave feminists. Such a whole-hearted reconciliation never extends, however, to Enid, the younger woman who adopts a second-wave brand of feminism whose time has (in the view of many younger women) passed.

*Legally Blonde*, then, rejects for younger women both extremes of feminism and extremes of femininity—one as divisive, and one as inviting stereotypes of womanhood that can prove limiting. Like some other current chick flicks, it seeks a comfort zone in retro sensibility to indulge in especially feminine fashions while critiquing elements of male culture, a critique defused by relegation to the past. A more obvious example of this process is *Down With Love* (2003), a parody of Doris Day romantic comedies, in which Renée Zellweger transforms herself into a beautiful blonde with a bestselling feminist book in order to snare the playboy journalist who had never noticed her when she was his mousy secretary. Since the film is set in 1962, Renée[6] gets to dress up in lots of white gloves and monochromatic dresses in the Jackie Kennedy style, but Renée's masquerade as a "Sex and the Single Girl" type feminist also allows critique of male fear of commitment and of workplace discrimination against powerful women without seeming to attack men of the twenty-first century.

Although *Legally Blonde* is set in the present and draws more selectively from the pre-feminist era, it uses some similar strategies. Script and costuming critique older modes of male attitudes toward women as sex objects and servants. The admissions committee that is bewitched by Elle's bikini consists entirely of suited men, many in tweed and bow ties, looking like "a faculty room circa 1934" (Steyn). Warner derives his limiting categories of womanhood from the elegant and reserved Jackie Kennedy and the sexpot blonde Marilyn Monroe, celebrities of 1960, a time long before he was born. The middle-aged Callahan keeps ordering Vivian rather than Warner to fetch coffee. And then there's the evocation of belittling male desire through the Playboy Bunny, an icon of the Fifties and early Sixties. These attitudes are presented as throwbacks, a far cry from the supportiveness of Elle's soon-to-be boyfriend Emmett, but they give resonance to the film's caution about indulging too deeply in femininity in a world that has not completely rid itself of the old order of male dominion.

Elle's repertoire of feminine costumes combines old and new. Costume designer Sophie de Rakoff Carbonell used up-to-date Vivienne Tam and Moschino in the earlier sections of *Legally Blonde*, but shifted designers and styles as well as colors when Elle moved into her more professional internship mode. Carbonell explains that she referenced movies of the past: "The stuff at Harvard when it's in the winter is much more of an Ali McGraw in 'Love Story' look. And when [Elle]'s interning . . . it's more like a Rosalind Russell '50s [sic] 'His Girl Friday' type of thing" (quoted in Reifsteck). Some viewers, though, read the later Elle, with her Prada cashmere cardigans and Celine pencil skirts, as "more Camelot than California"—that is, more like Jackie (Levy 64). And certainly Jackie was the acknowledged reference for Elle in *Legally Blonde 2*. The pink suit and pillbox hat featured on the film's advertising poster and its tie-in Barbie doll is a direct borrowing from Jackie, and so another return to the era of feminine fashion's ascendancy. The trajectory of the *Legally Blonde* series is to link Elle with a succession of stylish women with increasingly greater power, from the talented student of *Love Story* to the ace reporter of *His Girl Friday* to the trend-setting First Lady (brunettes all), and to move her farther from the Marilyn stereotype without sacrificing her right to be blonde.

## Resolutions and contradictions

Maintaining Elle's right to use the feminine codes pink and blonde was the challenge of the film's ending. After the film's warnings about the dangers of hyperfemininity, how could it restore Elle to her full Valley Girl glory? On the other hand, a film that straddled the line between adult comedy and teen pic could hardly ignore the "be yourself" theme of every teen chick flick; and what about the right to feminine display that third-wavers claim? It was the latter imperatives that prevailed with the creators of *Legally Blonde*. The climactic scene, in which Elle wins her case through a combination of courage and her girlie knowledge of hair care, begins with her triumphant entrance in full pink regalia, visually emphasized by the camera's slow tilt from Elle's spangled pink sandals, to a dress in multiple hues of pink, to a glory of blonde curls. Third-wave Barbie? Actually, what would seem to be a straightforward reclaiming of the right to be girlie is somewhat more complex.

First of all, Elle's triumph is constructed less as a triumph over the opposing side than as a triumph over her sexist male boss, Callahan. When Elle reaches the defense table, she and her blonde sorority-sister client stand tall on either side of the seated Callahan, visually proclaiming their seizure of power from Elle's harasser. When Elle and Emmett then join together to exclude Callahan from the defense team, they are declaring a younger generation's refusal to tolerate the old ways of patriarchy. Secondly, Elle's outfit, which Witherspoon identifies on the DVD commentary as her Dolly Parton look, reinforces Elle's treatment throughout the film as a populist figure whose down-to-earth goodness is favorably contrasted to the elitism of the pruny Harvard students (never mind that she's a rich girl from Bel Air). And might the Parton reference even invoke the well-received feminist fantasy *Nine to Five* (1980), in which Parton joined her female colleagues —among them veteran feminist icon Jane Fonda—in overthrowing their intolerably patriarchal boss? Finally, this closing scene does in fact work to distance Elle slightly from excessive femininity by inserting her ditzy California pals Serena and Margot into the courtroom, where they disrupt the proceedings by squealing about how "cute" the judge and jury are. The contrast between the pals' giddy girliness and Elle's professionalism helps persuade us to take Elle seriously no matter how many shades of pink she is wearing.

Despite the seeming appropriateness of the "be yourself" ending, however, the filmmakers had to add a second ending when test audiences, who felt closer to Elle than the filmmakers had anticipated, demanded a more "credibly successful" ending for Elle and an opportunity for her to take down Warner as well as Callahan (Platt). As a result, the crew had to follow Witherspoon to England, put a blonde wig on her (she had cut her hair for a new film), and shoot a scene of her recapturing and then promptly dumping Warner. They also filmed her giving a commencement speech "two years later," and added titles fulfilling fantasies of sisterhood, romance, and revenge: Vivian had become Elle's best friend; Paulette had won the UPS man and Elle had won Emmett; and Warner was unemployed.

*Legally Blonde* is not the only movie to struggle to find a satisfactory ending. The difficulty for current creators of chick flicks to find a balance between girlie fantasies and real life ideals of self-determination is evident in the oddly mixed iconography of the endings of teen flicks such as *The Princess Diaries* and *Mean Girls*. Cady's costumes show her vacillating between pink (the power of feminine masquerade) and blue (representing more authentic friendship and selfhood), until the ultimate defeat of misused femininity. Regina is discredited, and Cady gets crowned prom queen in her blue-and-gold Mathlete jacket. This mixed image of success, a tiara coupled with casual blue clothes that signify authenticity or intelligence, appears too in the popular *Princess Diaries*, in which Mia accepts her crown as Princess of Genovia while dressed in dripping blue jeans and a royal cape.

In movies featuring adult women, whose choices are more likely to be life-altering than those of teens (for instance, marriage rather than a date), the difficulty of resolving such contradictions is even greater. Thus the doubled endings of *Legally Blonde* and indeed most of the recent chick flicks featuring adult women. *The Prince and Me* (2004), in which a driven American pre-med student falls in love with a handsome exchange student who turns out to be crown prince of Denmark, is a striking example. The marketing campaign of this Cinderella tale promised that "the fairy tale is about to get real," and the script focused not just on temporary obstacles to the romance but also on problems that might persist: for Edvard, the pressure of being unable to choose his profession; for Paige, the loss involved in either of her choices, to become Princess of Denmark or to fulfill her lifelong dream of Johns Hopkins medical school and then Doctors Without Borders. The film, implying that the girlie dream of princesshood is a mixed blessing, offers the feminine fantasies of a roomful of precious jewels and a handsome prince complete with steed, but also emphasizes the uncomfortable clothes and the restrictive limitations on self-expression. But even if the fairy tale castle offered a perfect life, for Paige there is no completely happy alternative: since the Prince cannot abandon his extraordinary duty, Paige can choose only to abandon her lover or abandon her career dream. This extreme situation, this choice in which no compromise is realistically possible and loss is inevitable, severely tests the possibility that women can have it all. The filmmakers had to make a hard choice for Paige, and they did. The original cut of *The Prince and Me* privileged self-determination over fairy-tale dreams. Paige, dressed in blue jeans once again, walks away from both pink ballgowns (never really the yearning of her workaholic heart) and, more painfully, her beloved prince. But, yet again, test audiences demanded a different ending.

In seeking an ending that would satisfy contradictory female yearnings, *Legally Blonde* and *The Prince and Me* resorted to appending the same cultural ritual: graduation. In a commencement scene, the unisex black robes absolve the filmmakers from having to make a statement about femininity through the language of clothes, a crucial level of discourse in these films. Moreover, educational achievement is a value that no one in America, regardless of their notions of proper female roles, is likely to dispute. If Elle had to be made "*credibly* successful" (emphasis added), success in school is a kind of success that Americans assume is completely open to women, and no viewer will doubt that the clever and determined Elle is able to achieve it. In *The Prince and Me*, the promise of continuing academic success represented by Paige's black robe seems to validate her decision to follow her dreams. Moreover, the swell of emotion that surrounds the graduation ritual also helps distract the viewer from the implausibilities of the timely reappearance of Eddie, now King, to insist that he will wait for Paige (five years? ten?) and that the Danes will just have to get used to a "new kind of queen." Reviewers rightly judged this epilogue to lend "a note of absurdity and compromise to its intended message" (LaSalle). But is it surprising that the filmmakers had to back off from portraying Cinderella as choosing a stethoscope over a prince? We don't want to think about making such hard choices—especially in the dream machine of cinema.

There is no option to provide a graduation scene for the older Zellweger character in *Down with Love,* who has left school behind. But the extraordinary level of masquerade in this film, in which Zellweger and her catch "Catch" repeatedly shift personae and philosophies of gender, generates multiple endings that show the lovers uniting, separating, and uniting again, while Renée meanwhile establishes a new career in a female-friendly office, having been convinced by her role-playing that she doesn't want to follow a 1962 model of domestic womanhood. The final ending (unless one counts the song-and-dance routine of the closing credits) achieves a compromise position for Renée and a new willingness from Catch to commit to a "new kind of love." When Catch wishes aloud that Renée could be "someone between the bashful brunette Nancy Brown [her original name] and the cool blonde Barbara Novak [her adopted feminine, feminist persona]," she whips off her white turban to reveal her hair, newly dyed red. This symbolic fusing of competing varieties of womanhood— like the similar red dye-job that reconciles the hit woman and mom aspects of amnesiac Gina Davis at the end of 1996's *The Long Kiss Goodnight* (Dole 98)—provides a promise that women can be everything at once. One wonders how a sequel to either film might look.

The tortuous, even tortured, endings of all these chick flicks make clear that we do not currently have complete cultural consensus on whether women can have it all. In spite of the popularity of attitudes that have been articulated by third-wave feminists, in spite of the recent embrace of femininity in fashion and marketing, there are still some doubts about how fully and how widely femininity is accepted as coexisting comfortably with female power. *Legally Blonde* celebrates the joys of femininity but also hints at certain limits. Nonetheless, as recent chick flicks chart the territory that allows a woman to be what she wants to be and get what she wants to get, the double ambition of third-wave feminism, such films do show a growing acceptance of feminine womanhood. This acceptance is evident not only in the sheer increase in the totems of femininity, but also in the films' very willingness to push the envelope. *Legally Blonde* imagines Elle, after a truly wrenching change of context, not only surviving but improving, reasserting her femininity even as she develops more ambitious goals and finds a better man. *The Prince and Me* goes to even greater extremes to imagine problems that can shut down women's opportunities. To make Paige's choices truly difficult, it must combine an enormous class division, a difference in nationality, an uncommonly ambitious career dream, and a position in one of the world's few remaining monarchies. The extremes to which these films go suggest that most women can now feel that they have many legitimate and non-exclusive choices, and that one of those choices is to be free to be . . . pink.

## Notes

1   Although pink was associated with girls throughout the second half of the twentieth century, it wasn't always. Marjorie Garber points out that before the First World War, boys wore pink while girls wore blue (1–2).

2   Nonetheless, some third-wave feminists position themselves as political activists. For instance, Rory Dicker and Alison Piepmeier's *Catching a Wave* "calls for a third wave of feminism that is politically conscious, grounded in the realities of life in the twenty-first century, and willing to engage in collective action in order to address injustice" (10). It is also interesting to note that since the millennium many activist women's organizations have appropriated the color pink (now firmly associated with breast cancer awareness, for instance) and have sometimes also used the cultural markers of the third wave to attract young women to activism: CODEPINK, a peace and social justice group established by (mostly middle-aged) women in 2002, features on its website (www.codepink4peace.org) not just pictures of marches but lists of movies and merchandise including panties ("No peace, No pussy"), condoms, and a "Peacekeeper Lip Palette."

3   See, for instance, popular press articles such as Critchell's "Clothes Get Top Billing in 'Legally Blonde 2: Red, White and Blonde'" and *People Weekly's* spread on the film's fashions ("Reese's Pieces").

4   Most reviewers compared the sequel unfavorably to its predecessor, and the IMDB.com "user ratings" were 6.5 for *Legally Blonde* but only 4.4 for the sequel. The films grossed roughly the same amount of money in their American theatrical distribution, but the sequel failed to improve its earnings as most sequels of hit films nowadays tend to do. It also netted less as a result of its much higher budget.

5   Even self-defined feminists of the younger generation often differentiate themselves from second-wave feminists, a "product of the past" who "shared the idea that the cornerstone of all women's oppression was a patriarchal system" (Hollows 2, 5). Many younger women have, however simplistically, construed the emphasis on patriarchy to mean that second-wave feminists were man-haters. The reluctance of many young women to label themselves as feminists, even while they assume that women and men should

be treated as equals, is often linked to this perception of 1970s feminists as attacking men. Some third-wave feminists, however, recognize this perception as a distortion: "The anger and passion that feminists express on behalf of women lead many people to label them man-haters. However, most feminist praxis operates not out of hatred of men but out of a deep commitment to women's lives and to redressing the injustices they face" (Dicker and Peipmeier 8).

6  I use the actress's name rather than the character's in my discussion of *Down with Love* because of the difficulty of authenticating the identity of the character, who switches names and roles. During most of the film, viewers along with the other characters believe Zellweger's character to be called Barbara Novak, but her legal name is Nancy Brown. In any case, this metacritical film undercuts the very notion of a fixed identity.

## Works cited

Baumgardner, Jennifer and Amy Richards. *Manifesta: Young Women, Feminism, and the Future*. New York: Farrar, 2000.

Bellafante, Ginia. "Feminism: It's All about Me!" *Time*, 29 June 1998: 54ff.

Bruzzi, Stella. *Undressing Cinema: Clothing and Identity in the Movies*. New York: Routledge, 1997.

Critchell, Samantha. "Clothes Get Top Billing in 'Legally Blonde 2: Red, White & Blonde'." Associated Press, 7 July 2003. 3 June 2004. Lexis-Nexis. <http://web.lexis-nexis.com>.

Dicker, Rory and Alison Piepmeier. *Catching a Wave: Reclaiming Feminism for the 21st Century*. Boston: Northeastern University Press, 2003.

Dole, Carol M. "The Gun and the Badge: Hollywood and the Female Lawman." In *Reel Knockouts: Violent Women in the Movies*. Ed. Martha McCaughey and Neal King. Austin: University of Texas Press, 2001: 78–106.

Garber, Marjorie. *Vested Interests: Cross-Dressing and Cultural Anxiety*. New York: Routledge, 1992.

Goodman, Ellen. "Totally Retro Feminism: Elle Woods, Blond Lawyer, Gets Dumbed Down." *Pittsburgh Post-Gazette*, 23 July 2003: A19.

Hollows, Joanne. *Feminism, Femininity, and Popular Culture*. New York: Manchester University Press, 2000.

LaSalle, Mick. "Pre-med Student, Danish Prince Get Sweet—Smart Remake Tells It From Her Point of View." *San Francisco Chronicle*, 2 Apr. 2004. www.sfgate.com. 17 May 2004.

Levy, Karen. "Legally Blonde." *In Style*, 1 July 2001: 64.

Luketic, Robert. Commentary track. *Legally Blonde* DVD. 2001.

Orenstein, Peggy. "What's Wrong with Cinderella?" *The New York Times Magazine*, 24 Dec. 2006. <www.nytimes.com/2006/12/24/magazine/24princess.t.html?>.

O'Leary, Glynis. "Legally Blonde 2: Dumb, or Just Blonde?" *off our backs: the feminist news journal* 33 (Sept-Oct. 2003): 56ff. <http://web4.infotrac.galegroup.com>.

Platt, Marc. Interview. *Legally Blonde* DVD Special Features. 2001.

Poniewozik, James. "The Princess Paradox." *Time*, 5 April 2004: 72–74.

"Reese's Pieces: Pearls, Dainty Boots, Pink Suits—The Giddiest, Girliest Looks

Onscreen Can Be Found On Reese Witherspoon's Elle." *People Weekly*, 30 June 2003: 150ff.

Reifsteck, Greg. "Pretty in Pink and Rat Pack Chic." *Daily Variety*, 22 Feb. 2002: B8.

Rivière, Joan. "Womanliness as a Masquerade." In *Formations of Fantasy*. Ed. Victor Burgin, James Donald and Cora Kaplan. New York: Methuen, 1986: 35–44.

Steyn, Mark. Review of *Legally Blonde*. *Spectator*, 27 Oct. 2001: 53.

Stoller, Debbie. "Feminists Fatale: BUSTing the Beauty Myth." In *The* BUST *Guide to the New Girl Order*. Ed. Marcella Karp and Debbie Stoller. New York: Penguin, 1999: 42–47.

Young, Iris Marion. "Women Recovering Our Clothes." In *On Fashion*. Ed. Shari Benstock and Suzanne Ferriss. New Brunswick: Rutgers University Press, 1994: 197–210.

# Chapter 5

# A soundtrack for our lives

## Chick-flick music

*Lisa M. Rüll*

Scholarly consideration of popular culture presents special challenges—particularly in those areas that resist easy generic categorization and simultaneously invite the danger of stereotyping. Such challenges certainly arise in any attempt to study chick flicks. If defining the content and audience for chick flicks throws into doubt conventional formulations of genre and potentially reinforces stereotypes of femininity, perhaps we might look to looser ways of approaching the topic. Can we propose instead a spirit and sentiment of chick flicks that can be summed up as success and survival for—and between—soulmates, sisters and girlfriends? And if we do, then what is the place, purpose and meaning of the songs so closely associated with many of these films?

My own first explicit and conscious encounter with the music of chick flicks was certainly tied in with such an experience, a twenty-first-century moment that blurred movie and musical genres as well as any rigidly gendered, familial delineation of roles such as sister. A self-adopted "sibling" (a fellow only child) was anxiously waiting for news of a job and to pass the time we ventured to the local multiplex to view an untypical choice: *Minority Report*. We usually shared ultra-frothy romantic comedies together, but perhaps subconsciously we had chosen a film we could more easily leave if news of her job came through.

As if in compensation for our choice of the sci-fi genre, it seemed acutely appropriate to us that the foyer sound-system should begin to play a series of familiar songs. In sequence we heard "Out of Reach" by Gabrielle; "When You Say Nothing at All" by Ronan Keating; and the power-ballad "Show Me Heaven" by Maria McKee. These were not only easily recognizable tracks; their order confirmed our suspicion that the cinema had begun playing the then recently released CD compilation *The Ultimate Chick Flick Soundtrack*.[1] When the job offer eventually did come through there was only one possible action for us. We eagerly ran to the nearest music store and purchased copies of the compilation album that had provided the soundtrack to our own chick-flick narrative.

It is easy to smile remembering how we had signed our copies to each other with heartfelt commemorations of that day. Yet over time, the compilation, and the series of follow-ups that it spawned, increasingly troubled me. Pleasure in the cumulative "cheesiness" of the lyrics, music and performers—and their associations with that particular day—was gradually overtaken by recognition of the curious, contradictory and ambivalent role these tracks often played in the movies. On one level, the songs could be both enjoyed and (lovingly) derided now they were isolated from the movies they had accompanied. But where the film was familiar to me and the song could be associated with a context, images ultimately flooded in and it became impossible to ignore how the songs simultaneously undermined and reinforced the film narratives—both lyrically and musically.

Consequently, this appropriately personal chick-flick moment initiated a reconsideration of what these films, songs and albums were selling and why the interactions among the three proved so troubling. In this essay, I discuss the place of popular songs in chick flicks, their soundtrack albums and related releases, and themed compilations. Referring to specific films and songs, I also explore how lyrics and music function in filmic narratives and ultimately consider how films, songs and albums are influenced by external commercial considerations. In doing so, I hope to address the complex significance of contemporary popular songs in relation to the spirit and sentiment of chick flicks, and indicate some of the factors affecting why both cultural producers and academics have found it so difficult to pin down either the genre or its associated music.

## From scores to soundtrack songs: music and films

Exploring the relationship between films and their use of popular songs, especially as presented on chick-flick soundtrack albums and compilations, demands an approach that goes beyond most of the existing texts written about both chick flicks and film music. As often occurs in writing about popular culture, blending incisive analysis with consideration of the emotional responses generated—indeed, that such cultural forms are *designed* to generate—is challenging. Fraught with awkward confrontations between language and tone—between interest and disinterest—scholarly writing about popular culture can become burdened by theoretical analyses even as, on the other hand, journalistic discursive material limits the possibilities for nuanced readings. For chick flicks, these conflicts produce a struggle to temper serious analysis of the films' practices and meanings with awareness of their inherently populist appeal. However, writings on film music have faced slightly different challenges, especially regarding the use of popular songs.

Although films have always had music, and indeed have been associated with popular songs since the earliest days of cinema (Smith 27), only in the 1970s did there start to be a significant academic and intellectual interest in film music. While the field continues to be hampered by both music and film being identifiably "discrete areas" with "their own specialist language and terminology" (Reay 1), this problem was particularly acute in those early studies. Authors often approached the topic from an interest in music rather than film and thus concerned themselves almost exclusively with film scoring (e.g., Karlin and Bazelon). This reflected the struggle of music studies to engage with popular music: at least film scoring could draw upon and emphasize its alliances with classical composition, even as its explicit function for establishing mood set it apart from the pure classical repertoire. Driven by musicological approaches, studies of popular twentieth-century music took a considerable time to take off with a slow growth of attention being first paid to those Tin Pan Alley figures who also had an interest in classical influences, such as George Gershwin. Later, the experimental work and practices of jazz were drawn within the fold of musical studies, and writers such as Krin Gabbard have done much to bring popular forms of twentieth-century music to critical attention, even offering substantial studies of the role of jazz in the movies.

Of course, in terms of popular songs, for many years musicals were the main presentation of such music on film. While musicals were studied by both film and music scholars, the broader role of popular music in films was still largely ignored. Most of the musical film projects written about were not created as films, but were films of stage musicals or works for the screen produced by those songwriters who put together stage musicals.[2] Additionally, music-specific analysis for these films was often limited or absent, with specifically musicological studies focusing on the songwriters' overall oeuvre (their film musicals work representing a subset field), and film studies concentrating on stars and performances, or lyrics as a narrative device. Thus, even many studies of musicals denied the full interdisciplinary nature of film music studies, a point noted by Ian Brookes in his review of two anthologies on film music for the online film journal *Scope*. Brookes argued that the limitations of film music studies derive at least in part from the difficulties of analyzing the formal features of texts (music) within a cultural studies idiom that "requires contextualising strategies." Unsurprisingly, then, an engaged analysis of the use of pre-existing pop music songs within film soundtracks remained elusive and film scholars were still coming to terms with musicological methodologies.

Only with the appearance of collections such as Jonathan Romney and Adrian Wootton's *Celluloid Jukebox* (1995) did the use of existing pop chart tracks within film soundtracks begin to attract critical attention. This is surprisingly late considering the long-established tradition of film theme songs, such as those for the James Bond films, becoming pop music chart hits on both sides of the Atlantic. Indeed, Romney and Wooton's work appeared over twenty years after the emergence of influential works such as *Easy Rider* (1969) and *American Graffiti* (1975), which not only *used* pop music as a soundtrack but took that music as a structuring narrative force. However, this turn towards serious writing about pop music in general, and pop music within films in particular, remained shaped by "contextualising strategies" and the influence of cultural studies. Film studies had already begun to move away from solely considering actors and directors, plots and cinematography, towards researching issues related to production and marketing, but in terms of film music, issues of production and musicology remained largely off limits. Instead, contextual analyses of the songs in relation to the on-screen narrative dominated, with analyses that often failed to confront the increasingly complex relationship between the movie and music-making industries or the technical aural functions of musical forms. Even in the most recent texts, efforts to challenge the dominant approach continue to be tentative, although there have been some notable efforts to open up other forms of analysis.[3] As the online discussion featuring leading film/music scholars such as James Buhler and Anahid Kassabian for *The Velvet Light Trap* demonstrated in 2003, virtually everything remains open to exploration in the fields of film sound and music (77). Gradually, but only gradually, both music and film studies are coming to terms with pop music and its role in the construction of the modern film and its soundtrack.

## Compiling the chick-flick soundtrack

If both chick flicks and popular music have been treated as less worthy of serious study within their respective fields, then compilations of the pop songs from such movies must surely qualify as one of the most substantially ignored and critically debased products of contemporary popular culture. (Criticism of the inauthenticity of compilations is rife throughout the popular music press and was at least partially reflected in the decision to separate various artist compilations into a chart of their own in the UK.)[4] But what exactly is being communicated in the soundtrack and specifically the soundtrack *album* of a chick flick? And how are these meanings and messages conveyed, shared or undermined by subsequently placing selected pop tracks from these albums together on compilations defined as chick-flick collections?

Since we have already established the diversity of chick flicks, it is worth clarifying here that I am specifically concerned with contemporary films using a contemporary pop soundtrack. Of course, some chick flicks have made use of Tin Pan Alley songs, the standards created, by and large, in the first half of the twentieth century by songwriters for singers to perform. Ian Garwood contributed one of the most important essays on the use of period recordings, contemporary (period-style) covers of these songs, and their influence on incidental music scoring for *Sleepless in Seattle* (1993). This work has been picked up by other scholars, such as Steve Neale and Frank Krutnick, not only in relation to *Sleepless in Seattle* but also to *When Harry Met Sally* (1989). Such films may be contemporary romances, but their use of Tin Pan Alley tracks was specifically designed to evoke and endorse "the signs of 'old-fashioned romance'" (Neale 295–96) in both a knowing sense—appropriate to the films' own invocations of previous romantic films and narratives—and in an explicitly empathetic sense.[5] As such, contemporary pop songs could never have dominated their soundtracks as this would have countered the ideal of romance established by earlier texts (songs/films). Moreover, the nostalgic significance of the songs potentially grants them significantly higher status in music analysis terms than contemporary pop chart tracks used elsewhere.

Generally, films set in a specific, non-contemporary timeframe, such as historical romances or romantic dramas about the 1950s, 1960s, 1970s and 1980s, also avoid using contemporary pop songs on their soundtracks.[6] *Peggy Sue Got Married* (1986) is a prime example—again, an object of previous scholarly analysis for its use of 1950s nostalgic associations (Babington). *The Wedding Singer* (1998), with its deliberately "straight-faced" adoption of a cheesy 1980s soundtrack, would also fit into that category. Of course, exceptions can always be found, such as the studiously anachronistic *A Knight's Tale* (2001) which invokes modern-day language, behavior and a knowing sense of the future of English literature alongside its rock song soundtrack. The most extravagant example is clearly Baz Luhrmann's *Moulin Rouge!* (2001). Luhrmann circumvents the issue of period-appropriate tracks by presenting his narrative as a musical that flaunts its incongruous use of reworked pop hits. But generally speaking most contemporary chick flicks avoid postmodernist juxtapositions or incongruous uses of songs "from the future."

This leaves us with a range of contemporary movies on the loves and lives of contemporary women, and songs from these types of films certainly dominate compilations such as *The Ultimate Chick Flick Soundtrack*. As texts on chick flicks make clear, a fairy-tale sensibility often pervades such movie narratives and several of the selected songs reflect this old-fashioned sentimentality: "Love Is All Around" (from *Four Weddings and a Funeral*, 1993) typifies this type of track selection.[7]

Yet alongside such classic pop ballads as "Unchained Melody" (from *Ghost*), now associated with an oft-parodied film music moment featuring soaring visual/aural climaxes, chick-flick soundtrack albums and compilations are almost equally dominated by upbeat tracks suitable for dancing. Among these, dance-oriented films inevitably dominate: *Flashdance* (1983), *Footloose* (1984), or the retrospective *Last Days of Disco* (1998). Yet, notably, many of these upbeat tracks come from the end credits or title sequences rather than from the film's internal soundtrack. Rarely do they appear within the film's narrative, in either diegetic (naturally appearing within the film narrative, either as performances or radio/recorded music potentially heard by the characters) or non-diegetic form (superimposed for the audience as narrative accompaniment).

Indeed, despite increased use of popular music in the internal soundtrack, extensive extracts or complete songs are rarely used except where this forms the central premise of the movie, such as in the recent pop music romantic-comedy narrative *Music and Lyrics* (2007) starring Hugh Grant and Drew Barrymore.[8] The commercial motives for including diverse snippets—rather than longer extracts or songs—is obvious, since it boosts the opportunities for additional releases associated with the film. A successful soundtrack album can also generate collections of "more music inspired by the film." Careful attention to the differences and overlaps between works selected for inclusion within a film and those selected for a soundtrack album release (and subsequently to be picked up by chick-flick compilations) can reveal some of the nuances and complex intentions behind musical selections. For example, throughout much of *Serendipity* (2001), the melodically hesitant staccato guitar-line from Nick Drake's depression-haunted track "Black-Eyed Dog" repeatedly accompanies the narrative of delayed fate and missed chances. Yet it is the hopeful and uplifting "Northern Sky" by Drake that appears in the end-credits and on the soundtrack album, and the far less biographically or musically complicated artistry of Annie Lennox ("Waiting in Vain") that is chosen for *Chick Flicks: The Sequel*.

Nevertheless, some chick flicks thrive on using popular songs to register narrative points/counterpoints. Just as we may acknowledge Helen Fielding's *Bridget Jones's Diary* as a typifying example of contemporary chick lit, so its film version and sequel are thrust on UK audiences as archetypal chick flicks *and* chick-flick pop soundtracks.[9] Tracks from the Bridget Jones films constitute the largest contribution to the four compilations released under the *Chick Flick* brand range.[10] So how does this particular soundtrack demonstrate its allegiance to the spirit of the chick flick? How do the tracks and their location both within the narrative and on these albums, reinforce or undercut this spirit and any concomitant typing of gender roles?

### Soul sisters and song narratives: uses of lyrics and music in chick flicks

Several patterns can be identified in the two Bridget Jones films and the albums spawned in their name. First, there is a strong representation of female voices that is rarely seen on non-chick-flick soundtracks. (The relative absence of female pop vocalists in other types of film soundtrack demands a separate article.) These female vocalists include classic soul acts such as Aretha Franklin, who in herself evokes the notion of "soul sister" especially in the self-assured track "Respect," as well as more recent soulful performers such as Gabrielle. Second, a postmodern sensibility pervades many of the sequences in the film, complicating the intertextual meanings of the songs, and their subsequent meanings beyond viewing the films.[11]

Take, for example, the sequence in the first Bridget Jones film that introduces the character of Daniel Cleaver (Hugh Grant). Cleaver appears through a lift door to the opening lines of Aretha Franklin's "Respect": "What you want, baby I got it / What you need, you know I got it." This immediately follows Jones's declaration of the types of men she resolves she will avoid in the New Year—"alcoholics, workaholics, commitment-phobics, peeping Toms, megalomaniacs, emotional fuck-wits or perverts" —with the identifier that the fantasy-worthy Cleaver "embodies all these things." At first glance, the lines appear a heavy-handed exemplar of how Bridget Jones will be unable to keep to her resolutions. Yet on closer inspection, the lines do not just undercut Bridget Jones's ambitions to resist her poor judgment in men, but actually reinforce an ironic identification with the audience and its taste in men. Grant, so often associated with disaster-prone nice guys in romantic comedies, was knowingly cast for his floppy-haired appeal to women. Indeed, director Sharon Maguire notes in her DVD director's commentary how audiences cheered the emergence of Cleaver from the lift even though they were fully aware he was ultimately the villain of the narrative.[12]

Moreover, because the track is so familiar and the audience knows both the lyrics and the sentiments to come, the juxtaposition of "Respect" in the lift scene has a double-edged function. It suggests that Bridget and her audience want to take pride in their identity as Franklin exhorts, but are simultaneously self-aware enough to realize that intention and reality are often at odds with each other. As such, we are waiting for the inevitable appearance of the song's spelled-out title line—"R-E-S-P-E-C-T / Find out what it means to me"—which ultimately bookends Bridget's initial association with Cleaver. Finally taking back some pride following her realization of Cleaver's infidelity, she hands in her notice with some aplomb asserting she would prefer a job "wiping Saddam Hussein's arse" to the option of working with Cleaver again. Cue Aretha. Of course, on the soundtrack album, this track takes a prominent position on the track listing (track two), but the track also reinforces its girlpower sentiments in its appearance on *The Ultimate Chick Flick Soundtrack*. It is positioned as track three on CD2, after Curtis Mayfield's sunny encouragement in "Move on Up" and Donna Summer's enthusiastically ardent "Hot Stuff" as the third in a series of self-assured statements of intent.

As a second example we can look at the song "It's Raining Men," which became a UK number-one single for ex-Spice Girls' singer Geri Halliwell alongside the release of the *Bridget Jones's Diary* film. Halliwell's body, with its ultra-toned suppleness, stirred some public anxieties as potentially anorexic when represented in the track's music video. But, for most of the thirtysomething women of Bridget's generation, the track simultaneously conjured up images of its original successful performers, the Weather Girls. As two substantial black women, the Weather Girls were the visual antithesis of Halliwell's excessively thin body. This dissonance ultimately lends the song a saving grace: a sense of parody. Additionally, because the music-video setting for Halliwell is mostly a gym floor/workout space while Bridget's sole engagement with fitness is a rather unsuccessful and brief period of gym-based cycling, intercutting the video with such clips from the film further undermines the seriousness of each.

Of course, in the film the track accompanies the fight sequence between Darcy (Colin Firth) and Cleaver. As such, it illustrates how the film reinforces the sentiments of the song. It is indeed "raining men" as they crash ineffectively around the street and eventually through a restaurant window. Yet, for knowing audiences—whether familiar with the source novel or not—too much of the film's running length remains for a perfect romantically satisfying ending to be provided by this scene. Bridget cannot, nor with respect to the sentiment of finding the "perfect man" should she ever be, spoilt for choice with men: there has to be just "the one" (even though it may boost the female ego to be fought over). Additionally, with this scene and its musical soundtrack, it is almost impossible not to recall that the Weather Girls were exponents of hi-energy disco music favored by the 1970s gay scene.[13] Consequently, it is also possible to read the flailing struggle and semi-reluctance to fight (to settle things in a "manly" fashion) as highly homoerotic or at least camp. This particular filmic/musical counterpoint or subtext is effectively confirmed when noting that the Bridget Jones's sequel includes an almost identical fight sequence. Choreographed to the falsetto chorus of "I Believe in a Thing Called Love" by the Darkness, a contemporary British band who adopted the highest camp sensibilities and fashion of 1970s Heavy Rock, it is hard to ignore this example of how a soundtrack/film context can offer multiple readings.

On the first *Bridget Jones* CD, "It's Raining Men" appears as track three after Gabrielle's melancholic longing ("Out of Reach") and Franklin's self-assuredly sassy paean to status ("Respect"). In such a setting, the song communicates a much less complex and layered meaning: the infinite possibilities of being single. Yet despite its prominence in the film, the track was not included on the *Chick Flick* collections. As this exclusion indicates, issues of licensing further complicate our engagement with chick-flick music.

## Synergizing chick-flick soundtracks: purposes and meanings in song selection

A series of business links and licenses dictates not only what songs can be used for a film, but also what recordings and subsequent uses of the tracks can be promoted. Ownership of song and performance rights is a key part of media earnings through the licensing of synchronization rights (for a song lyric or tune from a music publishing company) and master rights (for a specific performance from a record company). Thus, when chick flicks make use of cover versions of existing songs this may not only be for the purpose of creating an up-to-date connection between the contemporary artist and the audience, but may also reflect cost or access restrictions to the more familiar original recording. (In the case of the note-for-note rendition Halliwell attempts to make of "It's Raining Men," it is hard to imagine that the original was not the ideal that was in the mind of those constructing the fight sequence.)[14] However, in allying themselves with a new recording, the film company and/or record company may come into conflict with the control the new artist exerts through her or his music releasing company, unless ownership ultimately rests with a single controlling body. Even though media ownership has coalesced in recent years to a handful of businesses with control over both film and music production, there is still sufficient diversity to mean that some works escape over-syndication across compilation CDs.

Nevertheless, the business of "synergy"—the coordination of record releases for the mutual benefit of film and music conglomerates (Denisoff and Plasketes 257–58)—does hold some considerable sway on the industries as a whole.[15] Considering the films and songs that actually are included on the *Chick Flicks* collection reinforces this, as it includes selections of songs more distinctly at odds with the chick-flick sentiment than even ironic intertextual references would allow. Only within the context of the film or trailer do the songs suit the chick flick. Consider the melancholic desperation of Marianne Faithfull's "The Ballad of Lucy Jordan." In *Thelma and Louise*, the song highlights the quiet air of futility entering the women's twilight journey through the wilderness to their ultimate doom. Isolated from the context, the song is a plaintive sigh of quashed hopes. Unsurprisingly, the only place where this song could be accommodated is as the final track on the second of the two CDs. Divorced from any potential uplift it may gain in the film through association with the eventual "death or glory" escape the women make as they "keep going forward," its bleakness is unrelenting. It sends a curious final message for the compilation.[16]

It is not only the songs on *The Ultimate Chick Flick Soundtrack* and the follow-up compilations that challenge the (albeit ill-defined) boundaries of what a chick flick can be, but also the film selections. At times, the selection of tracks seems dictated more by strategic issues of access and efforts of synergy (promoting recent releases or giving new life to relatively obscure recent tracks from other major label releases) than to any notion of chick flicks. For example, few women would define the self-destructive sexual narrative of *91/2 Weeks* as a chick flick. Nor—despite the appeal of Robert Redford for an older generation of chick-flick lovers—would *Indecent Proposal* qualify, though some men might suggest such films could be seen as guy-oriented pseudo-chick flicks. Certainly, the tracks chosen from the latter—"In All the Right Places" by Lisa Stansfield and "No Ordinary Love" by Sade—appeal to the appropriate chick-flick sentiments of romantic desire. But it is hard to envisage how "Slave to Love" by Bryan Ferry from *91/2 Weeks* fits the definition. In a similar vein, other films that appear to be designed to provide men with acceptable incarnations of the chick flick, such as the romantic-gross-out-comedy hybrid *Along Came Polly* (2003), also donate tracks to the *Chick Flick* collections. In this case, the suitably retro feel of "Let Your Love Flow" by the Bellamy Brothers fits perfectly with the cross-generational construction of the 3-CD set *Chick Flick Diaries*. Isolated from the films themselves, such tracks blend the right amount of kitsch, sentiment or camp appeal to slot into the *Chick Flick* albums.

## Living in the moment of a chick-flick soundtrack

In consuming chick flicks and their associated music products—singing along with the film, buying the soundtrack CD, accumulating compilations of these (loosely) connected tracks—audiences highlight the difficulties in pinning down singular definitions and meanings even as the companies producing these products seek to commercially manage and construct such definitions. Such tensions, combined with academia's belated and still developing analysis of the role of popular music in film, explain why both cultural producers and academics have found it so difficult to analyze either the genre or its associated music. But, of course, to really understand the chick-flick albums, you have to be in the moment, preferably with some fellow chick-flick aficionados, ready for a night in (or out). This is the tone that these compilations are seeking, a tone that cannot quite be fulfilled by other compilations that are driven more by straightforward sing-a-longs (*Hairbrush Divas*) or weep-a-longs (*All-Time Classic Tearjerkers*). That the original *Chick Flicks* collection proved successful enough to warrant three sequels suggests that the marketing teams of film soundtrack producers and the broader media conglomerates have correctly gauged our appetite for such material. Nevertheless, audiences are perhaps aware of meanings and associations between tracks and films that alter their relationship to these products in ways not entirely understood by either filmmakers or music producers. As such, songs selected for film sound-tracks will always retain elusive power and meanings not quite controllable by their masters.

## Notes

1  This collection, along with the subsequent compilations *Chick Flicks: The Sequel, Ultimate Chick Flick Love Songs* (both 2003), and *Chick Flick Diaries* (2004), were all released in the UK through Warner Strategic Marketing (WSM). Although some of these are available on import in the USA, similarly named products have been released elsewhere in the world. However, collections such as *DJ Smash Hit Chick Flicks Movie Themes* focus much more explicitly on film theme songs or tracks accompanying the credits sequences.

2  Examples such as the films of Elvis Presley and other (popular music) star-vehicle musicals complicate such definitions. Rick Altman has noted the debates around categorizing Presley's musical films as musicals (7). Given that these films were so popular with female audiences, and often—as in Altman—casually derided both in film and music studies, one might provocatively consider the extent to which they encapsulate the narratives and music associated with chick flicks.

3  While Justin Wyatt's volume on "high concept" films discusses cross-platform marketing strategies for music and film, the role of multi-media conglomerates is best addressed in Jeff Smith's *The Sounds of Commerce: Marketing Popular Film Music*. However, Smith concentrates mostly on film scoring, albeit from a standpoint of the influence of popular songs and their musical structures. Essays in Pamela Wojcik and Arthur Knight's anthology *Soundtrack Available* (2001) and in Steve Lannan and Matthew Caley's recent collection *Pop Fiction: The Song in Film* (2005) represent a more substantial move towards discussing the particular role of pop music in movies.

4  The Official UK Charts split off compilations into a separate Top 20 in January 1988, and this included the majority of various artist pop music soundtrack albums for films (Roberts 8). The US charts, as is reflected in the ever-increasing number of categories at the annual Grammy awards, have a longer tradition of separating out genres and products from mainstream listings.

5  Similar arguments regarding the signification of romantic nostalgia can apply to the film *Moonstruck* (1987) with its mix of 1950s Italianate swing tracks by Dean Martin and the ultimate in doomed operatic romance, *La Bohème*.

6  Theme songs or songs specifically designed to be themes for a lead acting performer, perhaps even to be sung by one of the leads, have always been permitted inclusion within period-set films. *Dirty Dancing* (1987), with its 1950s/early 1960s soundtrack, was able to accommodate examples of both of these: lead Patrick Swayze sang "She's Like the Wind" and the theme song "(I've Had) The Time of My Life" was both a major chart hit and an eventual Oscar winner.

7  Still there is increasingly a postmodern sense of awareness about signified meanings associated with such songs and films. Witness writer/director Richard Curtis confronting head on the syrupy emotional associations of this iconic track and indeed Curtis's own over-association with British romantic comedy: the song is self-referentially reworked as a diegetic Christmas single, "Xmas Is All Around," for Bill Nighy's has-been rock sex-god character in Curtis's December 2003 film, *Love Actually*.

8  As enjoyable as Grant's performance is in *Music and Lyrics*, one senses that there is a limited appetite for a second album dominated by his vocal pastiches of 1980s pop or the recent revival of that genre.

9  This marks a key difference between the UK and US markets where the Bridget Jones films are much less noted. The US compilation *Chick Flix* (2003) did not include any tracks from the Jones films, but did accommodate "Kiss Me" by Sixpence None the Richer. This airy pop track has been used on at least two different chick-flick soundtracks (*She's All That* [1999] and *How to Lose a Guy in 10 Days* [2003]).

10  Of the 170 tracks across the four releases, ten are from the Bridget Jones films. (This does inevitably include some repetitions.) Tracks included from the first film are "Out of Reach" by Gabrielle and "All By Myself" by Jamie O'Neal, both also featured on the *Love Songs* and *Diaries* collections; "Respect" by Aretha Franklin; "Someone Like You" by Dina Carroll from the closing credits (rather than the Van Morrison version that plays in both the middle and end sequences of the film); "I'm Every Woman" by Chaka Khan; and "Don't Get Me Wrong" by the Pretenders. *Chick Flick Diaries* (2004) almost simultaneously coincided with the cinematic release of *Bridget Jones: The Edge of Reason*: alongside some duplicates from the earlier CD compilations, this 3-CD set featured seven further tracks from the second film.

11  See Brackett for discussion of the kinds of multiple meanings and associations created by a compilation film soundtrack.

12  Grant's shift to caddish sexual appeal also dominates in *Two Weeks Notice* (2002), whose soundtrack unsurprisingly includes the hyper-sexual thrusting breaks on the down-beat of James Brown's funk classic "Papa's Got a Brand New Bag."

13  My thanks to my partner, Neil Roberts, for reminding me of this.

14  However, alternative songs are sometimes used for different countries' cinematic releases, and this may or may not be reflected in the soundtrack albums' track listings.

15  Pauline Reay's book *Music in Film: Soundtracks and Synergy* is one of the more recent contributions on this topic, but scarcely touches on anything within the chick-flick genre.

16  The UK CD release *New Woman: Hits From the Chick Flicks* (Virgin TV), sponsored by a woman's magazine, included the Faithfull track, but located it in the middle of disc 2, between Des'ree's "I'm Kissing You" (from *William Shakespeare's Romeo + Juliet*) and Ferry's "Slave to Love" (from *9½ Weeks*).

## Works cited

Altman, Rick. "A Semantic/Syntactic Approach to Film Genre." *Cinema Journal* 24.3 (1984): 6–18.

Babington, Bruce. "Time Trips and Other Tropes: *Peggy Sue Got Married* and the Metaphysics of Romantic Comedy." In *Terms of Endearment*. Ed. William Evans and Celestino Deleyto. Edinburgh: Edinburgh University Press, 1998: 93–110.

Bazelon, Irwin. *Knowing the Score: Notes on Film Music.* New York: Van Nostrand Reinhold, 1975.

Brackett, David. "Banjos, Bio-Pics and Compilation Scores: The Movies Go Country." *American Music* 19.3 (2001): 247–90.

Brookes, Ian. Review of *Film Music: Critical Approaches*, ed. K.J. Donnelly, and *Music and Cinema*, ed. James Buhler *et al. Scope*, 28 Jan 2005. <http://www.nottingham.ac.uk/film/journal/bookrev/books-february-04.htm>.

Buhler, James, Caryl Flynn, and David Neumeyer (eds). *Music and Cinema*. Hanover, NH: Wesleyan University Press, 2000.

Buhler, James, Anahid Kassabian, David Neumeyer, Robynn Jeananne Stilwell, and Kyle Barnett. "Panel Discussion on Film Sound/Film Music." *The Velvet Light Trap* 51 (2003): 73–91. Project Muse. 6 Jan. 2005. <http://muse.jhu.edu/journals/the_velvet_light_trap/v051/51.1buhler.html>.

Denisoff, R. Serge, and George Plasketes. "Synergy in 1980s Film and Music: Formula for Success or Industry Mythology?" *Film History* 4.3 (1990): 257–76.

Donnelly, K. J. (ed.). *Film Music: Critical Approaches*. Edinburgh: Edinburgh University Press, 2001.

Evans, William, and Celestino Deleyto (eds). *Terms of Endearment: Hollywood Romantic Comedy of the 1980s and 1990s*. Edinburgh: Edinburgh University Press, 1998.

Frith, Simon, Andrew Goodwin, and Lawrence Grossberg (eds). *Sound and Vision: The Music Video Reader*. London: Routledge, 1993.

Gabbard, Krin. *Jammin' at the Margins: Jazz and the American Cinema*. Chicago: Chicago University Press, 1996.

Garwood, Ian. "'Must You Remember This?': Orchestrating the 'Standard' Pop Song in *Sleepless in Seattle*." *Screen* 41 (2000): 282–98.

Karlin, Fred. *Listening to Movies: The Film Lover's Guide to Film Music*. New York: Schirmer-Simon & Schuster Macmillan, 1994.

Krutnick, Frank. "Love Lies: Romantic Fabrication in Contemporary Romantic Comedy." In *Terms of Endearment*. Ed. William Evans and Celestino Deleyto. Edinburgh: Edinburgh University Press, 1998: 15–36.

Lannan, Steve, and Matthew Caley (eds). *Pop Fiction: The Song in Film*. Bristol: Intellect, 2005.

Neale, Steve. "The Big Romance or Something Wild? Romantic Comedy Today." *Screen* 33 (1992): 284–99.

Reay, Pauline. *Music in Film: Soundtracks and Synergy*. London: Wallflower, 2004.

Roberts, David (ed.). *The Guinness Book of British Hit Singles and Albums*. 17th ed. London: Guinness World Records, 2004.

Romney, Jonathan and Adrian Wooton (eds). *Celluloid Jukebox: Popular Music and the Movies since the Fifties*. London: BFI, 1995.

Smith, Jeff. *The Sounds of Commerce: Marketing Popular Film Music*. New York: Columbia University Press, 1998.

Wojcik, Pamela Robertson and Arthur Knight (eds). *Soundtrack Available: Essays on Film and Popular Music*. Durham: Duke University Press, 2001.

Wyatt, Justin. *High Concept: Movies and Marketing in Hollywood*. Austin: University of Texas Press, 1994.

# Chapter 6

# The southern-fried chick flick

## Postfeminism goes to the movies

*Deborah Barker*

The emergence of the southern chick flick comes on the heels of what Susan Faludi saw as a conservative reaction against the gains that women made during the women's movement of the 1960s and 1970s. In her 1991 book, *Backlash: The Undeclared War Against American Women*, Faludi argues that Hollywood producers, influenced by the backlash trend in the media, created a series of movies that pitted the angry career woman against the domestic maternal "good woman."[1] These 1980s films, such as *Fatal Attraction*—which Faludi sees as the ultimate anti-feminist, anti-career woman movie—portray women as rivals (and often deadly rivals); the women rarely seek solace or help from other women, only from men. Arguably the chick flick goes against the trend Faludi documents in the 1980s backlash movies that depict little or no female bonding.[2] Yet the name alone—*chick flick*—flies in the face of the feminist movement's objection to the demeaning gender appellation *chick*. The films are further denigrated as *tearjerkers*, another dismissive title used to belittle the earlier category of "woman's films" from the 1930s and 1940s. Is the chick flick then a product of the backlash or a feminist reaction against it?

My answer is that the chick flick is responding simultaneously to feminist principles and to the backlash mentality, and that the southern setting facilitates the sleight of hand necessary to negotiate this contradictory impulse. Although the chick flick is not typically defined as a regional genre—and certainly not all chick flicks are set in the South—in this essay rather than simply dismissing the genre as trite or formulaic, I will examine the cultural significance of the southern chick flick and its relationship to postfeminism. In doing so, I am not suggesting that the southern chick flick is fundamentally different from other chick flicks, but neither do I think that the southern setting is arbitrary or incidental. The southern locale helped to establish the genre as a whole, and especially its emphasis on the lives of white women, because 1) while the cinematic South has often been the setting for dealing with issues of racial discrimination and the struggle of the Civil Rights Movement, it has not been associated with the women's movement of the 1960s and 1970s, and 2) the cinematic South simultaneously links the southern chick flick to the tradition of—and nostalgia for—the white southern lady (the antithesis of the villainous, feminist career woman of the 1980s films) as well as to strong female characters such as Scarlett O'Hara, an extremely assertive, if not necessarily feminist character.[3] The southern setting, therefore, serves as a place to explore issues of female empowerment without invoking the political problems or solutions associated with feminism and womanism and/or as a place where traditional feminine values still reign. (Whether this is a cause of celebration or criticism in the various films is not necessarily a clear-cut issue.) In the southern chick flick, typically the personal is the personal, not the political.

Significantly many of the films are set not only in the South but also in the past, further distancing the audience not only from the 1970s women's movement but also from the Civil Rights Movement and justifying the emphasis on white women as the subjects of film, while African-American characters play supporting roles. The southern past in the chick flick evokes nostalgia for both the female solidarity celebrated in the feminist era and nostalgia for the pre-feminist era in which Gloria Steinem's "click" has not yet been heard and when women's dissatisfaction was still "the problem that has no name." In other words, the white southern chick flick is the perfect postfeminist film genre. It emerges in the gap between feminism and postfeminism, between second wave and third wave; at the same time it acts as a bridge to cross the gap. As such, the chick flick invokes the conflicts and contradictions of postfeminism.

While various popular definitions of the chick flick have been put forth, I would like to reconsider the basic elements associated with the genre and to define it more narrowly as a film that emphasizes female empowerment through female bonding.[4] The emphasis on female bonding distinguishes the early chick flick from its predecessor, the woman's film of the 1930s and 1940s. As Molly Haskell argues, in the woman's film the heroine "is at the center of the universe," and the other women play supporting roles, serving as foils to highlight her capacity for self-sacrifice, bravery, jealousy, or despair (155). Chick flicks, especially southern chick flicks, emphasize either groups or pairs of women who share center stage. But female bonding also distinguishes the genre from the more general category of the romance or date movie. While a chick flick can include romance, it is not the central focus of the film. For this reason I do consider *Thelma and Louise* (1991) a chick flick, whereas the romantic comedies, or date movies, such as *When Harry Met Sally* (1989), *As Good as It Gets* (1997), *What Women Want* (2000), and *Sweet Home Alabama* (2002) are a separate genre. To paraphrase the title of a recent chick flick, boys are on the side. A chick flick does not have to be produced, written, or directed by women—though many of them are—but it does have to feature women and their concerns as the focus of the film.

If we look at the salient features of the genre as it emerged—female empowerment through female bonding—without automatically accepting the pejorative connotations of the label, several southern films fit these criteria: *Terms of Endearment* (1983), *The Color Purple* (1985), *Crimes of the Heart* (1986), *Steel Magnolias* (1989), *Fried Green Tomatoes* (1991), *Daughters of the Dust* (1991), *Rambling Rose* (1991), *Thelma and Louise* (1991), *Passion Fish* (1992), *Ruby in Paradise* (1993), *Bastard Out of Carolina* (1996), *Hope Floats* (1998), *Where the Heart Is* (2000), *Divine Secrets of the Ya-Ya Sisterhood* (2002), and *Cold Mountain* (2003), to name a few. Significantly, however, southern movies that consider the lives of African-American women (*The Color Purple* and *Daughters of the Dust*), or the relations of black and white women (*Passion Fish*) have not been labeled chick flicks, even though *The Color Purple* is often negatively characterized as melodramatic and as women-centered, two characteristics often associated with the chick flick. To understand the emphasis on white women and on the predominance of southern settings in the early chick flicks, it is necessary to look at the cultural climate that produced the chick flick and the concurrent development of postfeminism.

## Postfeminism

The debates surrounding postfeminism have often taken the form of a generational divide between second- and third-wave feminism.[5] In her interviews with second-wave feminists and their daughters, Judith Stacey found a strong desire among daughters of feminists not to share in their mothers' anger and not to see their lives in political terms, even though the daughters sought and felt entitled to equality in the workplace and the home. The daughters' reactions to their mothers' feminism is not atypical of other time periods. In looking at feminist writing over the past one hundred years, Alice Rossi suggests that there have been three distinct peaks in political activities: the 1850s, 1900–1920, and the late 1960s. Although Rossi sees no reason to assume that the daughters of activists held radically different values from those of their mothers, she does argue for the existence of a "generational dialectic in the spheres of life in which those values are acted out. It may be that the public heroines of one generation are the private heroines of the next" (616). The southern chick flick seems perfectly suited to the "quiet second generation" that "struggle[s] for status," but that also explores the limitations of feminism.[6]

In looking at the various forms of postfeminism, not all reflect a generational divide. For example, one approach that Toril Moi refers to as the "disenchanted feminists" sees feminists as a "bunch of fanatics" and holds feminism as responsible for women's maladies (1738). Feminism, especially in the academy, is seen as too powerful, too monolithic, too theoretical, and too repressive. Within this group are the women who lived through the women's movement but who felt shunned, excluded, or left behind by it, most notably Christina Hoff Sommers and Camille Paglia. As postfeminists they receive the (media) attention they felt they were not given by the feminist movement.

But the postfeminist discourse that is most associated with this generational divide is not necessarily antifeminist. To many postfeminists, feminism is seen as old-fashioned and out of date, precisely because it has been successful in establishing economic opportunities and sexual equality, so that gender discrimination is no longer the problem it once was. In this postfeminist world, second-wave feminists are seen as holding on to an unproductive victim mentality (Roiphe, Wolf). Postfeminists espousing such views have been severely criticized by second-wave feminists and are often put in the role of ungrateful daughters. Another variation can be seen in the postfeminist emphasis on girlpower, which maintains that women should have choices, including the choice to be feminine and sexy. Second-wave feminists, therefore, are seen as repressive and judgmental, as killjoys who see sexism everywhere.

From a second-wave perspective, however, what these various post-feminisms have in common is "the simultaneous incorporation, revision, and depoliticalization of many of the central goals of second-wave feminism" (Stacey 8). Postfeminism's adaptation of feminism focuses on individual economic and sexual freedom, often ignoring collective political action and systemic gender inequality. Feminism is thus reduced to individual choice, which ironically blames women and the choices they make for the existence of gender inequality. Furthermore, such "choice" feminism tends to focus on women who have the greatest economic opportunities. While women of color were challenging the narrow conception of feminism and making it more responsive to issues of race, class, and nationality, postfeminism declares feminism defunct and freezes it for all time as a movement that focused only on the economic liberation of white middle-class women.[7]

Third-wave feminism and postfeminism share some characteristics; however, there are important differences between their respective reactions to second-wave feminism.[8] Third-wave feminism is more politically active and continues and expands the second-wave agenda, especially in terms of issues of race, class, sexuality, and global issues, as outlined in Jennifer Baumgardner and Amy Richards' *Manifesta: Young Women, Feminism and the Future*. These third-wave feminists criticize second-wavers for focusing too narrowly on white, heterosexual, privileged, middle-class women (ironically the same charge that second-wavers level at postfeminism). The films in question often collapse the more individually oriented, apolitical postfeminism with the more socially, politically, and globally minded third wave, thus managing to push boundaries without actually breaking through them.

The generational divide between feminists and postfeminists is seen within the chick flick in the form of the mothers and daughters who confront each other as sexually mature women. The daughters are often on the verge of marriage or motherhood themselves and have to choose which elements of southern womanhood/motherhood to keep and which to reject, while the mothers have to come to terms with the decisions they have made as mothers and wives and how these decisions have affected their daughters. The appeal of the mother–daughter pair is that it simultaneously speaks to very different audiences and age groups. The *Shorter Oxford English Dictionary* has recently added *chick flick* to its lexicon and defined it as a film "perceived or marketed as appealing to young women"; however, I would not limit the chick flick by age. On the contrary, the female audience for the chick flick is made up of both women who lived through the women's movement and their daughters. The chick flick is therefore able to capitalize on the generational divide and appeal to both feminists and postfeminists, both mothers and daughters.

## The southern chick flick

To explain the salient features of the southern chick flick and how it incorporates feminist issues within the nonpolitical backdrop of postfeminism, I will focus on *Steel Magnolias*. The title itself suggests a way to describe women's strength within the context of traditional southern womanhood. Although the mother–daughter pair in the film, M'Lynn and Shelby Eatenton, argue whether Shelby should continue to work after she marries, whether her future husband will help with the children and housework, and whether she should start a family, these issues are completely removed from a feminist context and displaced onto a discourse of disease, in keeping with the backlash tendency to use metaphors of disease and death to characterize the end of feminism. In another context these questions could be considered "feminist," but in *Steel Magnolias* Shelby's acute diabetes, not her political beliefs or individual ambitions or lack of them, frames the mother–daughter conflict. Furthermore, these discussions about Shelby's future are set in traditionally feminine spaces (the beauty parlor and the kitchen), and during traditional family and community events—a wedding, an Easter egg hunt, Christmas festival/party, Halloween/wedding shower, and a funeral—over which women traditionally preside.[9]

M'Lynn is not overtly feminist, yet she is a woman "who has it all." Unlike the masculinized and lonely career women of the 1980s movies, M'Lynn has a career, a husband, and children, but she has something else that many of the filmic 1980s women do not have—close female friends. Even though the narrative of *Steel Magnolias* is based on Shelby's wedding, pregnancy, and death, the focus of this early chick flick is clearly on the mother's generation. Shelby has nine bridesmaids at her wedding, but we never see her interact with her own friends, only those of her mother. As such, the relationship among M'Lynn and her friends takes center stage in the movie.

Upstaged by all the big hair, ubiquitous holiday decorations, and colorful southern aphorisms, women's economic independence in *Steel Magnolias* is treated as a given. In an earlier movie, *Terms of Endearment*, neither the mother Aurora nor daughter Emma works outside the home, and the working women depicted in the movie are condescending New Yorkers who treat Emma's lack of employment with the same embarrassment and lack of grace as they treat the news of her cancer. However, in *Steel Magnolias* all of the women work, run their own businesses, or have independent incomes and are "richer than God," as Ouiser puts it. Truvy's marriage is under stress because her husband Spud, a contractor, is temporarily out of work, but there is no suggestion that Truvy's successful beauty parlor is to blame. On the contrary, the beauty parlor signifies her husband's inadequacy both romantically and economically. When Truvy asks Shelby if she and Jackson did anything romantic before the wedding, it is not just idle gossip she is looking for. She wistfully declares, "The last romantic thing my husband did for me was back in 1972. He enclosed this carport so that I could support him." Ironically, the "happy ending" of the film includes a scene in which Spud presents Truvy with yet another beauty shop—another way for her to support him—although it is not clear where he got the money to pay for it.

What in a more overtly feminist venue would be seen as male-bashing, in the traditional world of *Steel Magnolias* is presented as charmingly humorous. Husbands in this film are either absent, as are Ouiser's two husbands, "the most worthless men in the universe," dead (Clairee's husband), selfish (Jackson wants a son even though it may kill his wife), sulking (Spud spends most of his time in bed), or a nuisance (M'Lynn's husband Drum sets the neighborhood in an uproar shooting birds out of the trees before the wedding). The tension between M'Lynn and Drum is kept low-key, but Shelby feels she must defend her father and admonishes her mother not to be "so hard on Daddy." We rarely see the husband and wife together, a point that Shelby brings home when she tells her mother that she is pregnant. Shelby comments that she wanted to tell her parents when they were together, "but you two are never together." The same undercurrents of tension between Shelby and Jackson are subtly revealed when Shelby, justifying her decision to go ahead with the life-threatening pregnancy, describes Jackson's desire for a son, adding that she thinks having a baby "will help things a lot."

While all the women in *Steel Magnolias* are fairly conventional, initially the daughter displays the most traditionally feminine attributes. M'Lynn makes fun of Shelby's excessively pink wedding, commenting that the chapel looks like it has been "hosed down with Pepto-Bismol." Wrapped in a protective feminine pink bunting (like the church), which would prevent any viewer from seeing her as feminist, Shelby is nonetheless instrumental in prodding her mother's friends to take new chances. She tells Clairee that life isn't over because her husband is dead and encourages her to buy the local radio station, even though Clairee says she has no interest in business. Shelby even fixes up the curmudgeonly Ouiser with an old boyfriend. Shelby's encouragement proves successful and both women break out of their shells.

Shelby's own ambitions, however, are downplayed in the film. Asked if she will quit working (as a pediatric nurse) after she marries, Shelby responds with an emphatic "Never!" Significantly she does not use feminist rhetoric to explain her desire to work; she asserts that she just loves those babies, crinkling her nose as she says "babies." In this same scene we learn that her doctor has told her that she should not have children because of her medical condition. Shelby's desire to work seems, therefore, to be a sublimation of her more traditional desire to have children of her own. Yet, even after the birth of her own child and after a kidney transplant has further compromised her health, she is still working as a nurse and trying to "do it all." The only time we see Shelby in her own world and not that of her mother is just before her collapse, when, after finishing her shift at the hospital, she is going home to get dinner ready and then to go trick-or-treating. Shelby's efforts to live up to her mother's example literally kill her. As Annelle says, "her poor little body was just worn out. It wouldn't let her do all the things she wanted to, so she went on to a place where she could be a guardian angel." The not so subtle postfeminist message of *Steel Magnolias* seems to be that the model of the superwoman is too much for the daughters of the next generation. Only in heaven can they "do it all." Rose Glickman, in talking with daughters of feminists found that some did not embrace the term *feminist*, not because they did not believe in the principles, but because they did not feel they had earned the title, that they had not done as much as their mothers (14). In *Steel Magnolias* the daughter does not have the steel, or in this case the insulin, to duplicate her mother's life.

Another facet of *Steel Magnolias* connecting it to postfeminism is the exclusion of African-Americans, what Tara McPherson refers to as the "almost unrelenting whiteness of the film," its desire for "a safe—and segregated—space" that reflects "national anxieties and agendas around multiculturalism" (164). Although the film is set in the contemporary south, the film's opening scenes create a sense of nostalgia for the segregated past. We see a series of stationary, low-angle, long shots of Annelle as she walks slowly towards the camera. From this distance it is difficult at first to gauge the exact time period, especially as Annelle walks past tree-covered lanes, the ubiquitous old pick-up trucks, and even an old-fashioned white milk

*Image 6.1* Washing windows for Shelby's wedding

truck. The all-white groups of children riding by on their bicycles or walking across the center of the town square in their Little League outfits still do not pinpoint the historical moment. The sentimental harmonica-laced music, reminiscent of the opening music in *To Kill a Mockingbird,* likewise suggests an earlier time. The first African-American character we see in the film is a woman in a maid's outfit washing windows at the Eatenton home in preparation for Shelby's wedding. This tableau almost seems to be a bad joke about getting good help. In 1970s TV land even the Jeffersons' maid refused to wash windows or wear a uniform. As we move indoors we see more African-American women in maids' outfits working in the kitchen and cleaning the chandeliers. And at the wedding itself there are only four African-Americans, and one of them, again in a maid's outfit, is serving food. The erasure of race appears to "express the white South's (and the nation's) inability to conceptualize what racial contact might even look like" (McPherson 166). The film collapses the past into the present, creating a 1950s small southern town, minus any signs of racial unrest or protest. Not until the end of the movie in the hospital, one of the most public of the spaces in the film, do we see African-American women working as equals with white women.[10]

McPherson maintains that the characterization of "Shelby and M'Lynn draw[s] on the mythologies of the plantation mistress," thereby "sneaking the southern woman back on the pedestal, still caught within the confines of the big house" (164). The mother–daughter pair emerge "as a sort of latter-day Ellen and Scarlett" from *Gone with the Wind.* Although

McPherson's overall argument about *Steel Magnolias* is persuasive, I do not agree with her characterization of M'Lynn and Shelby as Ellen and Scarlett. Important differences distinguish the two pairs of mothers and daughters that correspond to the differences between the woman's film and the postfeminist chick flick. The concept of the "lady" is associated with class as well as race and, while the Eatentons live comfortably, they are clearly middle class. M'Lynn runs her home with the efficiency of Ellen O'Hara and both serve the community, but significantly M'Lynn's work is not a matter of charity—she works at the mental health clinic. It would be more appropriate to say that M'Lynn represents the middle-class lady of the New South. Although we do see uniformed black maids at the wedding, we do not see them at any other time in the Eatenton home. M'Lynn, unlike Mrs O'Hara, seems to raise her own children and to run her own home, without the almost ubiquitous presence of an African-American maid/nanny that characterizes so many other southern films. One of the main reasons that Ellen is able to remain a serene and gentle mother, never raising her voice to Scarlett, is that she does not know the first thing about her. It is Mammy who understands Scarlett and who struggles with her to make her live up to the rules of being a proper young lady. M'Lynn combines the roles of Ellen and Mammy; she attempts to remain calm and serene, like Ellen, but she is also willing to fight her own battles with her daughter. In a movie that seems otherwise oblivious to racial issues, *Steel Magnolias* revises the white southern mother/lady, giving her more of a hands-on position in her own household. She is not sheltered by her family or treated as if she is made of glass. In the first scenes of the Eatenton family, we see the children teasing and talking back to their mother. When M'Lynn tells Shelby that she did not raise her daughter to talk back to her, Shelby rejoins, "Yes, you did, Mamma."

Rather than simply reinscribing the elements of *Gone with the Wind* in a contemporary setting, as McPherson suggests, *Steel Magnolias*, along with other southern chick flicks, revises many of the basic features of its predecessor.[11] As I've already argued, *Steel Magnolias* reconnects the white mother and daughter, warts and all, without the black mammy as the intermediary who plays the heavy—literally and figuratively. But it also rewrites the mother–daughter dynamic in relation to death. In *Gone with the Wind* it is the mother who dies, forcing Scarlett to take on the role of both her mother and her father (who is mentally enfeebled with the strain of Ellen's death). Scarlett represents the woman of the New South who does not have the luxury to maintain the role of the lady; Scarlett must be made of sterner stuff to survive. In *Steel Magnolias*, M'Lynn is the survivor, who must raise the next generation. But M'Lynn, like Scarlett, must also bury her own daughter. In *Gone with the Wind*, Rhett's grief over his daughter's death takes center stage; we never see Scarlett grieve. *Steel Magnolias* (like *Terms of Endearment*) puts the mother's grief front and center. M'Lynn is allowed to lose her composure, to get angry and to yell. Indeed, M'Lynn's gravesite outburst is the climax of the film and cements the bond not between M'Lynn and her own family (and certainly not her husband), but between M'Lynn and her female friends, the real stars of the movie.

Steel Magnolias' success ushered in a series of southern chick flicks. Two of the most commercially successful were *Fried Green Tomatoes* and *Thelma and Louise*, which both came out in 1991. Although *Thelma and Louise* fits my definition of a chick flick, and indeed has been referred to as such, it does stand out from the other southern chick flicks as being too obviously about feminism. Callie Khouri, who wrote the screenplay, resists the label *feminist*, saying, "The issues surrounding the film are feminist. But the film itself is not" (quoted in Read 103). Khouri may have been attempting to use the postfeminist sleight of hand that worked so well in *Steel Magnolias,* but many viewers and critics were not buying it.[12] Although the movie begins as a typical chick flick, using comedy to poke fun at the male characters, particularly through Thelma's naïve viewpoint, it turns more serious after Thelma is attacked. Peter Travers, in a *Rolling Stone* review, comments that the movie "begins like an episode of *I Love Lucy* and ends with the impact of *Easy Rider.*"

The movie is considered feminist "male-bashing" not simply because Louise shoots the man who attempts to rape Thelma or because she kills him after she has prevented the rape in response to his insulting and unrepentant comments. The pair are not condemned for this action, for Thelma's vulnerability and Louise's fear create a certain amount of sympathy for the heroines. Their real crime is blowing up the flammable cargo of the trucker just because he insults them. He calls them "bitches from hell," a moniker that, I believe, many audience members find appropriate. Female critics in both *Time* and *Newsweek* focus on this scene, commenting on it as a fantasy of female power and revenge, which carries power in the real world. *Newsweek*'s Laura Shapiro reports, "Last week four women who had seen the film were walking down a Chicago street when a truck driver shouted an obscenity at them. Instantly, all four seized imaginary pistols and aimed them at his head. 'Thelma and Louise hit Chicago,' yelled one" (Willis 101–02). For women to show fear is much more acceptable than for them to show unmitigated anger at being insulted or objectified. The truck scene, even more than the earlier rape scene, links them to "unacceptable" feminist anger, but more transgressive than their anger is their laughter and derision after they blow up the truck.

In many ways *Fried Green Tomatoes*, Fanny Flagg's film adaptation of her novel *Fried Green Tomatoes at the Whistle Stop Cafe,* is even more controversial and seems to represent the political sensibilities of third-wave feminism by productively confronting inequality as it applies to class, race, and sexual orientation. Yet it has not been labeled *feminist* in the same way as *Thelma and Louise*. *Fried Green Tomatoes* is the southern chick flick exception that proves the rule. It is one of the few "feel good" movies to include both cannibalism and the Klan, and achieves this effect by using the depoliticizing techniques of postfeminism. Not only is a white man killed, as in *Thelma and Louise*, he is killed in cold blood for attempting to retrieve his own son. Furthermore, he is butchered, barbecued, and served up to the white sheriff who is trying to find the murderer. What should be seen as a heinous act becomes an occasion for humor, exploited by the producers in marketing the film. The punch line, "the secret's in the sauce," plays on the fact that the secret of Frank's death and the evidence of his murder—his body—is literally in the barbecue that the sheriff eats. *Fried Green Tomatoes* not only vilifies the white male body, it cannibalizes it.

While the film acknowledges cannibalism—certainly the most taboo of subjects—the relationship between Ruth and Idgie is downplayed. Although almost everyone associated with the film, including and especially the author Fannie Flagg, deflected the possibility of a lesbian relationship, the film clearly allows for such a reading (which the novel makes more apparent). Why then was so much more controversy created over Thelma and Louise and their farewell kiss than by two women living together as in *Fried Green Tomatoes*?[13] The secret is not only in the sauce; it is also in the past. *Fried Green Tomatoes* does not just hint at the past, as does the opening of *Steel Magnolias,* it literally incorporates it into the movie in a series of flashbacks to the 1930s, through the storytelling of Ninny Threadgoode, an elderly woman living in a nursing home in Alabama, who tells her friend Evelyn the stories of Ruth and Idgie.

In the depoliticized past of both the book and the film, a pregnant woman (Ruth) can leave her abusive husband (Frank) for another woman (Idgie) with whom she lives, works, and raises a child without being labeled feminist or lesbian.[14] Avoiding such labels is crucial for a postfeminist chick flick: as both Rose Glickman and Paula Kamen found in their interviews with young women in the early 1990s, many women who held feminist beliefs shied away from defining themselves as feminists for fear of being labeled lesbians (Glickman 1–17; Kamen 23–27). In her attempt to avoid the term *lesbian*, Fannie Flagg demonstrates how both the South and the past help to deflect the issue of homosexuality in the film. When asked about the possibility of a lesbian relationship between Ruth and Idgie, Flagg does not deny the possibility, but maintains that in the context of the past, because it is unacknowledged, it is tacitly accepted: "Well, I'm not sure. Those were innocent times in that part of the world, and . . . I'm not sure people knew the word 'lesbian.' Maybe they didn't have a name for the girls, and maybe it didn't matter" (LaBadie B1).

The nostalgia for a lost world of (nonfeminist) female empowerment and bonding is, as the title of the film suggests, most evocatively signified through the many sensuous depictions of food. In the past, both public and private spaces—the homes and the café—are spacious and filled with friends and families and an abundance of fresh, homegrown, homemade food, over which the camera lingers in a series of sensuous close-ups. Homegrown food and home cooking not only represent the nostalgia for the simplicity and bounty of an earlier era, they also represent a lusty sensuality that is used to depict the homoeroticism between Ruth and Idgie. Just as the secret of Frank's cannibalization is hidden in the sauce, the secret of lesbian sexuality is coded in the depictions of "down-home cooking" in which Ruth (feminine, domestic, and religious) tries to teach Idgie (butch, wild, and irreligious) to prepare fried green tomatoes.[15]

I'd like to focus on the details of this scene because they reveal how the film uses not only the past, but the filmic techniques of Production-Code-era Hollywood to present a coded lesbian love scene. The sequence opens with a sizzling pan of fried green tomatoes and then jump-cuts to a series of sumptuous close-ups of ripe tomatoes, chocolate frosting, eggs, and blackberries. The close-ups of food in this scene connect back to the earlier close-ups of food at the wedding of Idgie's sister. In the background music of the cooking scene we hear the husky voice of Marion Williams singing "Cool Down Yonder," establishing the sexual tension of heating up (sizzling) and the promised release of that tension in the cooling down. The title of the hymn presents a sexual double-entendre that capitalizes on the Production Code era's use of blues, and especially African-American female blues singers, to suggest illicit or primitive sexuality. At the same time, the hymn sanctifies the scene by tying it to rural southern spirituality.[16]

From the close-ups of food, the camera moves to a tight two-shot of Idgie hand-feeding Ruth an overcooked fried green tomato. In the classic heterosexual Hollywood romance, hand-feeding a member of the opposite sex is a standard prelude to sex. This device also links it to the wedding scene in which the bride and groom feed each other cake. As Ruth laughingly admits that Idgie's cooking is terrible, the camera cuts to a medium shot of the two women, and Idgie, offended, turns her back on Ruth saying, "Oh well, don't be shy. Tell me how you feel," to which Ruth replies, "I will." The intimacy of the earlier shot is resumed when Idgie puts her arm around Ruth only to throw a glass of water in her face, telling her in a seductive voice that she could use a "little cooling off." In the classic heterosexual film, throwing water in a man's face is the ultimate insult and indicates the woman's lack of interest, but in a lesbian love scene, getting "wet" is not necessarily synonymous with a "cooling off" of passions. Ruth then throws water on Idgie and the scene escalates into an all-out food fight in which the women smear the beautifully rendered food on one another and end up rolling together on the floor.

The narrative structure of *Fried Green Tomatoes* is based on secrets that are "both announced and suggested," "openly revealed, and variously concealed" (Berglund 130). Ruth and Idgie bond through a series of shared transgressive secrets that are connected to food, starting when Idgie brings Ruth along to ride the rails and distribute food to the needy out of the railroad cars and including Idgie's revelation that she can charm bees, a secret she shares only with Ruth. The most "obvious" secret, which is both revealed and concealed in the food fight, is that Ruth and Idgie are lovers. The intimacy between the two women is revealed in Ruth's willingness to drop her lady-like politeness and tell Idgie the truth, even if it is insulting. Although the scene is comic, the dialogue between the women in the context of a love scene displays their intimacy. Ruth's "I will" mirrors the "I do" of the wedding scene.

The forbidden nature of the scene is further suggested by Sheriff Grady's negative reaction. The scene cuts from the women smearing food on each other to a shot of cherry pie and then tilts up to show Grady's look of consternation. As Sheriff, Grady represents patriarchal authority's disapproval of "lesbian" love, but as Idgie's unsuccessful suitor he also represents the excluded heterosexual male. Idgie's mocking, "Go ahead," in reply to Grady's threat to arrest the women for disorderly conduct links the food fight to the cannibalization of Frank and to Idgie's eventual arrest for Frank's murder. Ruth participates in flaunting the law by smearing Grady with a spatula full of chocolate icing. Her act, rather than bringing Grady into the food fight, into a ménage à trois, reaffirms his distance and disapproval. Like the scene in *Thelma and Louise* when the women laugh after blowing up the truck, Ruth and Idgie laugh in Grady's face and continue their fight.

*Image 6.2* Idgie's (Mary Stuart Masterson) bad influence on Ruth (Mary-Louise Parker)

The erotic food fight is the culmination of Ruth and Idgie's transgressive behavior in relation to race and class as well as gender orientation. Before this scene we witness the opening of the café and the women's "inappropriate" kindness to the poor and down and out: Ruth brings soup to a sick African-American family and refuses any payment; both women show kindness to Smokey Joe, even though he is an alcoholic and a hobo; and they also serve African-Americans—not inside with the white customers, but outside. The latter act is enough to get them in trouble with the Klan, yet Idgie is defiant in the face of Grady's warning.

The movie deals with race more directly and positively than the average chick flick. Ultimately, despite Idgie's suspicion that Grady is himself a Klan member, it is Grady who protects Big George from the Georgia Klan and even the minister lies to protect him from the charge of murder. Yet, the film omits narratives of African-American characters present in the novel, which are told through the local African-American newspaper, *Slagtown News Flotsam & Jetsam*. For example, the story of Artis Peavey, Big George's son, provides a more detailed look at African-American life in Birmingham, to which Artis is drawn. In the film, Artis's experiences in Birmingham are omitted and the African-American characters conform more closely to the stereotype of the "loyal servant." They are not fully developed and function merely as signifiers of Ruth and Idgie's progressive attitudes about race (Holmlund 40–41; Vickers 26). Not until the end of the film do we learn that Sipsey (not Idgie) killed Frank with her frying pan, after he knocked her to the floor. Although this would seem to be an assertive and transgressive act, it is easily contained within the conventions of the loyal servant. Even in *Birth of a Nation*, the mammy character used violence to protect her white master. After whacking Frank with the frying pan, Sipsey explains that no one is going to take Miss Ruth's baby. She does not show the same determination to save her own son, Big George, when he is accused of murdering Frank and she remains silent throughout the trial.

In the sterile suburban present of the movie, food comes prepackaged from the Piggly Wiggly, and "home" is the institutional "old folks home" where Ninny lives, and the suburban track house where Evelyn Couch lives. Although sex is talked about more openly than in the past, the women are nevertheless divorced from their bodies and their sexuality.[17] Evelyn's attempt to find empowerment through feminism is laughable at best, and totally ineffectual. The movie lumps together the feminist and traditional routes to self-improvement, lampooning both. To save her marriage, Evelyn first attends a seminar reminiscent of the 1970s *Total Woman* by Marabel Morgan in which the leader (played by Flagg herself) teaches the women how to put the "magic" back into their marriage. When Evelyn imagines opening the door for her husband wearing only cellophane, even in her fantasy her husband just thinks she is crazy. The next week she is supposed to "reclaim [her] power as a woman, to realize the source of [her] strength and [her] separateness" by looking at her vagina. Unfortunately she can't get her girdle off to get in touch with her power. Female bonding through feminism and/or self-improvement courses is depicted as a poor substitute for the earthy, "innocent" lesbian sexuality of the past.

Only through the power of the prefeminist past is *Fried Green Tomatoes* able to rewrite the earlier women's film, *Gone with the Wind*. Rhett's romanticized rape of Scarlett (when he carries her up the stairs as the scene fades to black) and Scarlett's subsequent "accidental" fall down the same stairs (when Rhett learns she is pregnant) are conflated and refigured on the stairs of Frank's run-down, Depression-era version of Tara. Absent in *Fried Green Tomatoes* are all the visual elements that allowed the 1939 audience to ignore Rhett's threat to smash Scarlett's head like a walnut, her disgusted rejection of Rhett's advance, and her attempts to fight back. The plush red staircase, the handsome leading man, the fade to black, and most importantly, Scarlett's morning-after scene of singing and giggling in bed, deflect the sexual violence of the night before. In contrast, *Fried Green Tomatoes* presents a very unglamorous view of wife abuse. When Idgie comes to Georgia to rescue Ruth, Frank roughly throws his pregnant wife over his shoulder and takes her upstairs declaring his power over her, including the power to beat her. Frank, unlike Rhett, is outnumbered, because Idgie does not come alone. Big George's knife convinces Frank to let Ruth go, but not before he unceremoniously pushed her down the stairs.

The influence of the prefeminist past also empowers Evelyn finally to stand up for herself. Evelyn calls on Idgie's alter ego, Towanda, the Amazon

*Image 6.3* Frank (Nick Searcy) claiming his wife

warrior, the name that Idgie calls out when she rescues Ruth from Frank. In her newly emboldened state, Evelyn threatens to "take out all the punks" and "machine gun [the] genitals of all the wife beaters," but her threats remain imaginary and comical, such as putting little bombs in *Playboy* and *Penthouse* and banning all fashion models under 130 pounds. Unlike Thelma and Louise's spectacular truck blow-up or Idgie's decision to barbecue Frank, Evelyn's only real act of aggression is directed at other women. Although the incident that sent Evelyn crying to Ninny was brought on by a young man who shoves her and then calls her a "fat cow" and an "old bitch," she takes her revenge out on two young women who have taken her space at the grocery story and flaunted their youth, by saying "Face it, we're younger and faster." Evelyn, as "Towanda," proceeds to ram their car repeatedly, but her parting quip "Face it, girls, I'm older and have more insurance," while humorous, also indicates that Evelyn, even in her most outrageous act, is not a threat to men or women; indeed, she is already thinking in terms of paying for the damages.

*Divine Secrets of the Ya-Ya Sisterhood* proves that thirteen years after *Steel Magnolias* the basic elements of the southern chick flick are virtually unchanged. It clearly follows in the footsteps of its predecessors in its southern setting, uses of nostalgia, focus on the lives of the female character, emphasis on female empowerment through female bonding, and marginalization of the male characters. Like *Fried Green Tomatoes*, *Divine Secrets of the Ya-Ya Sisterhood* literally incorporates the past into the present through a series of flashbacks of the mother's life, triggered by the daughter's examination of the Ya-Ya scrapbook. As in *Steel Magnolias*, the ostensible focus of the film is the daughter's (Siddalee Walker) impending wedding, but again it is the mother Vivi and her friends, the Ya-Yas, who are the real focus.

Although the movie version of *Divine Secrets* was released in 2002, it is set in the early 1990s, having been based on Rebecca Wells's two novels: *Little Altars Everywhere*, set in 1991, and *Divine Secrets of the Ya-Ya Sisterhood*, set in 1993. The film therefore takes us back to the period of the backlash and the emergence of the southern chick flick, but although almost ten years separate the setting of the film and its release, aside from the size of the cordless phones, there is almost no way to tell that the movie is set in the 1990s. The postfeminism it depicts is virtually indistinguishable from that of the next millennium.

There is, however, a marked difference between Wells's 1991 *Little Altars Everywhere* and the 1993 *Divine Secrets of the Ya-Ya Sisterhood*, which explains why *Divine Secrets*, rather than *Little Altars*, was made into a successful chick flick. *Little Altars Everywhere* moves into the dangerous 1960s, dealing directly with the politics of the Vietnam War, as well as with issues of race and homosexuality. The novel is structured as a series of alternating first-person accounts in which the husbands, sons, and African-American workers, who typically are left out of the chick flick (Shep, Shep Jr., Baylor, Willetta, and Chaney, respectively) tell their own accounts of life in Pecan Grove from their often critical perspectives. Willetta, the African-American housekeeper, is particularly critical of Vivi, presenting her as a spoiled, mean-spirited white woman who does not take proper care of children. Shep Jr.'s chapter describes not only the physical abuse that is the subject of *Divine Secrets*, but an even darker suggestion of sexual abuse at the hands of his drunken mother (229–39). In *Little Altars*, only two chapters are devoted to Vivi's version of reality, while in *Divine Secrets of the Ya-Ya Sisterhood* the critical voices are marginalized and the third-person narrative focuses on Sidda, Vivi, and the Ya-Yas.

Absent from the film are the politics of feminism, race, and sexual orientation. Callie Khouri, who wrote *Thelma and Louise* (1991), directed *Divine Secrets* and she has learned the postfeminist lesson of how to use the southern setting to create a kinder and gentler chick flick. Because of the movie's emphasis on Vivi's past (1930s to early 1960s), it is divorced from the 1970s feminist films chronicling the problem that had no name. Yet the story behind Vivi's 1963 breakdown could have come straight out of *The Feminine Mystique*, which was published that same year (Travis 151). Vivi's thwarted ambition, her sense of being overwhelmed by motherhood, and her absentee husband are the sources of her discontent. Furthermore, Vivi's attempt to be a traditional woman, with the help of religion and prescription drugs (her priest sends her to the doctor who prescribes the drugs), sends her over the edge and causes her to "drop her basket," a euphemism for the night she takes her children out into the rain and beats them, after which she is committed to a mental institution for six months. Like *Steel Magnolias*, *Divine Secrets* eschews feminism in favor of a disease model of addiction that "represses both history and feminism," by proposing only individual and not systemic solutions (Travis 151). The movie taps into women's feelings of isolation, but by presenting women's solidarity in the pre-feminist past, it avoids depicting feminist solidarity. The Ya-Yas' rebellions are mostly induced by alcohol and not politics.

The mother's past ends abruptly with her 1963 breakdown and we flash forward to 1993. If Vivi's thwarted ambition represents the problem that has no name, Siddalee's illustrious career as a New York playwright embodies the feminist ideal. Unlike in the 1980s backlash film, neither Sidda's career nor her ambition prevents her marriage; she is not struggling to choose between work and family for she has a loving and supportive fiancé, Conner McGill. Instead, she is afraid she will abuse her children as her mother, Vivi, abused her. While Scarlett fears that she cannot live up to the role of the lady set by her upper-class, white mother, Sidda fears that she might. She compares her own mother, however, to Scarlett and not Miss Ellen: "I'm sick to death of this whole center-of-the-universe-holier-than-thou-nothing-is-ever-good-enough-oh-how-I've-suffered-

nobody-understands-me-somebody-fix-me-a-drink-and-hand-me-a
Nembutal-worn-out-Scarlett-O'Hara-thing."

*Divine Secrets* self-consciously and directly invokes the cultural past,
the cinematic South, and the woman's film when the Ya-Yas attend the
premiere of *Gone with the Wind*. This event reveals the nostalgic desire
for the prefeminist past in which girls and women can "innocently"
indulge in politically incorrect pleasures of popular culture, regardless of
its racist or sexist content, at the same time that it allows the Ya-Yas to
emerge as good liberals even during segregation.

Both the film and the novel, however, seem uncomfortable allowing the
Ya-Yas thoroughly to enjoy the segregated premiere. Willetta accompanies
the Ya-Yas as their maid and chaperon, much like Mammy going with
Scarlett to Atlanta, but Vivi is chastised for her unthinking racism when
she assumes that Willetta is having as much fun as she is.[18] Willetta's
reaction to wearing a maid's uniform and waiting on the girls is "I have
died and gone to hell." Ultimately, however, Vivi and the Ya-Yas defend
Willetta when Teensy's snobbish cousin calls Willetta a "nigger." The Ya-
Yas hurl their own insults and their breakfasts upon Junior, an act for
which they are banished from the Coca-Cola palace, just as the movie
suggests Margaret Mitchell was banned from the Junior League for her
infamous Apache dance. In the film's present time racism is presented as
a non-issue: when Sidda, a privileged white woman, is released from her
lakeside confinement by the Ya-Yas, she sees Chaney, Willetta's husband.
He says "Free at last," to which she replies, "thank God All Mighty"—
certainly one of the most apolitical and inappropriate references to Martin
Luther King Jr.'s most famous speech.

As in *Fried Green Tomatoes*, in *Divine Secrets of the Ya-Ya Sisterhood*
homoerotic desire is contained in the past and is redefined under the guise
of friendship. In *Little Altars,* in which lesbian desire is directly discussed,
Sidda falls in love with her female dance teacher, whom she discovers is
having an affair with her favorite aunt (23–41). After walking in on her
aunt and her dance teacher together in bed, Sidda rushes out and kisses
one of her girlfriends and then threatens to "ruin [her] whole life" if
she tells anyone (40). Any reference to this episode disappears completely
from *Divine Secrets of the Ya-Ya Sisterhood*, as does any discussion of
lesbianism, but in the novel, the homoerotic element of the Ya-Yas' past
is depicted as the solution to the working woman's isolated and overly
structured life.[19] Through the Ya-Ya memorabilia Sidda is able to
participate in her mother's world:

> She longed for porch friendships, for the sticky, hot sensation of
> familiar female legs thrown over hers in companionship. She pined
> for the *girlness* of it all, the unplanned, improvisational laziness. She
> wanted to soak the words 'time management' out of her lexicon.

> She wanted to hand over, to yield, to let herself float down into the
> uncharted beautiful fertile musky swamp of life, where creativity and
> eroticism and deep intelligence dwell. (81)

The homosexual desire in *Little Altars Everywhere* is redirected into the homosocial and homoerotic world of the past in which female friendship ("girlness") is only a "simple, innocent, sensual act with a woman" (40). Homosexuality in the present is kept at bay with assurance of Sidda's desire for Connor (including steamy love scenes in the novel), and her reluctance to marry is explained solely on the basis of her fear of being a bad mother. Sidda's desire for female friends, as presented in the novel, and her complaint that women today are not as close is a sentiment also voiced by the daughters of feminists in Glickman's study. These daughters, however, attribute their mothers' friendships to their commitment to feminism, not to unproblematic "girlness." As one daughter said, "These days everything is fragmented and scattered, people are so stressed about work or home life. I just get the feeling that there isn't the same kind of community there was twenty years ago" (118).

The movie ends with the reconciliation of the mother and daughter, the promise of Sidda's wedding taking place in her hometown, and with Sidda's initiation into the Ya-Ya Sisterhood, after learning the secrets of her mother's life.[20] Presumably if Sidda only *knew* all of her mother's secrets she would also know how to keep them. The happy ending depicts mother and daughter coming together on the porch swing in a scene that is the ultimate validation of the abused child. Vivi presents Sidda with her ring and acknowledges her shortcomings as a mother (though without any specifics), maintaining that she doesn't expect to be forgiven by her children or her God. The ring, however, is an ambivalent legacy to hand down from mother to daughter. Its history is tied to maternal jealousy and abandonment. In a humiliating scene, Vivi's mother tries to take the ring away, implying that it was a sign of an incestuous relationship between Vivi and her father. Vivi later hocks the same ring to escape from her children when she can no longer stand her responsibilities. The movie allows the daughter to revise yet participate in her mother's traditions, but not without a cost. Sidda trades her own painful memories of childhood as presented in *Little Altars Everywhere* for those of her mother in *Divine Secrets of the Ya-Ya Sisterhood*, thereby both revealing and preserving the family secrets.[21]

Both mother and daughter get to live, love, and marry, though only the daughter gets to have a successful career, and only the straight white women get to tell their stories. For the southern chick flick, however, this is a progressive move. Most films in this genre depict either the death of the daughter (*Terms of Endearment, Steel Magnolias*) or the death of the mother (*Crimes of the Heart, Hope Floats,* and *Fried Green Tomatoes*),

*Image 6.4* Sidda's (Sandra Bullock) initiation

or the death of both (in the quasi mother–daughter pair of *Thelma and Louise*), a trend which seems to suggest that women can only be sexually and personally fulfilled in the absence of their daughters or mothers, that the mother–daughter relationship itself is confining and repressive. *Divine Secrets of the Ya-Ya Sisterhood* deals more directly with serious mother–daughter conflicts than any of the other movies mentioned; yet the resolution of these conflicts does not involve the death of either the mother or daughter. The initiation into the secret world of women achieves the reconciliation between mother and daughter, but the question remains: What is sacrificed to create this reconciliation? Or, perhaps, what has to remain secret to allow this reconciliation and to celebrate girlpower?

Ironically, while most producers and directors of southern chick flicks have become adept at downplaying issues of race and sexual orientation and have avoided the labels *feminist* and *lesbian*—labels they fear will limit their audience—they now fear the label *chick flick*. Bonnie Bruckheimer, who co-produced both *Beaches* and *Divine Secrets of the Ya-Ya Sisterhood*, once admitted to being "chick-flick producer of the year" for her role in *Beaches* and accepted "whatever flak" she had taken over the years because of the response she received from women who told her "how much they loved the movie" (Koltnow). However, when *Divine Secrets of the Ya-Ya Sisterhood* was first released, she was quick to distance herself from the label, regardless of how many women might love the movie: "I cringe when people call this a chick flick. It is an unfair label for this movie. I think a lot of men can relate to it." Bruckheimer's denial does not actually speak to any of the salient elements of a chick flick as I've defined them in this essay. Her definition of a chick flick has narrowed to "a movie a man does not relate to." She also makes it clear that her real reason for objecting to the term has nothing to do with whether the film really is a chick flick; it has to do with the box office: "We know the engine that drives the movie business. It is the first weekend's box office. The problem with being labeled a chick flick is that women don't run to the movies that first weekend. Women have to get baby sitters and they have to convince their husbands and boyfriends to go. That takes time. Only young boys run to the theatre the first day."[22] Bruckheimer's comments reveal the limitations of postfeminism: in a society that still undervalues women's concerns and emotions, it does not matter how traditionally, apolitically, or noncontroversially the women are represented; if the film focuses on women it is by definition not of interest to men. After downplaying the presence of "objectionable" women—feminist and lesbian—the only thing left to take out of the chick flick is the *chick*.

Tyler Perry's series of Madea plays and movies, in which he plays an assertive, gun-toting, cigarette-smoking African-American woman, has indeed eliminated the *chick*. Wearing a wig and a fat suit, Perry, as Madea, goes where the southern chick flick has feared to tread.[23] Taking many elements of the standard white chick flick—including the southern setting and an emphasis on female bonding and empowerment—and combining it with a strong dose of Christianity, Perry has generated the kind of weekend box office take that rivals that of the popular chick flick. His first feature film, *Diary of a Mad Black Woman* (2005), self-consciously invokes plot elements and references to earlier feminist films and to more recent chick flicks. Most obviously, it takes its title from the 1970s feminist film *Diary of a Mad Housewife* (1970). The 1970s version satirizes the domineering, narcissistic husband. Perry's 2005 version contains literal male-bashing. The mad housewife, Madea's niece Helen, gets revenge on her arrogant lawyer husband, by beating, starving, and almost drowning him, while he sits helplessly in his wheelchair. The film also references *Thelma and Louise, The Color Purple,* and *Waiting to Exhale,* the first African-American chick flick, which was heavily criticized for its male-bashing and materialism. Although *Diary,* like *Waiting to Exhale,* visually revels in beautiful clothes and expensive houses, ultimately, the message of *Diary* is not that all men are dogs, but that success and wealth corrupt. Helen must forgive her husband and denounce all claims to his money in order to be at peace and to marry her new blue-collar boyfriend.

Perry's presentation of Madea could be seen as an insulting caricature of strong black women, but he has been endorsed by Oprah Winfrey, the most vocal and successful supporter of choice feminism, whom Perry acknowledges as his inspiration.[24] As the title of Perry's first film indicates, he has been able to do what second-wave feminism, postfeminism, and the southern chick flick have not: he has put black women's concerns center stage and has attracted a Christian, working- and middle-class African-American audience of both men and women. In his second film, *Madea's Family Reunion* (2006), Perry actually features African-American feminists. He shares the creative process with Maya Angelou, who steals the scene and speaks for herself (and to Madea's filmic family) on the porch of a former slave cabin.

If the chick flick is a barometer of Hollywood's attempt to balance feminism and postfeminism, it would seem that the forecast is gloomy. Looking at the trends in the genre as a whole, two patterns emerge: the absence of women or the absence of feminism. Focusing on the second trend, many of the most recent films referred to as chick flicks (that actually feature women) have more in common with the 1980s backlash movie than with the earlier southern chick flick. In films such as *Bridget Jones's Diary* (2001), *Sweet Home Alabama* (2002), *How to Lose a Guy in 10 Days* (2003), *Bridget Jones: The Edge of Reason* (2004), *13 Going on 30*, (2004), *Raising Helen* (2004), *The Devil Wears Prada* (2006), and *The Holiday* (2006), work is the impediment to successful romance because the inappropriate man is a co-worker/boss, and/or because the demands of work preclude a social life. But, more important, work threatens to turn women into the vicious caricature of the 1980s evil career woman.[25] Typically, the heroine must give up her successful job, reject her female mentor, and choose the simple life in order to find love. Certainly these films are responding to the real problem that both men and women face today in trying to balance a career and a family (whatever form that takes), but the chick flick's balance between feminism and postfeminism seems to be tipping in favor of the latter. The above films, like the woman's film of the 1940s, focus on the lives of individual women. The heroines sometimes have a sidekick girlfriend, but she remains a peripheral character. This new trend results not simply in the vilification of work or the career woman, but the absence of the crucial element of the southern chick flick: female empowerment through female bonding. The "new" solution to the heroine's alienation and isolation is based on an old story: she just needs to find a man.

## Notes

I would like to thank Suzanne Ferriss, Mallory Young, Ivo Kamps, and Jamie Harker for reading various versions of this essay and for their insights and suggestions.

1 Faludi contends that 1970s movies, which featured women's fight for independence and/or their dissatisfaction with traditional marriage (*Diary of a Mad Housewife, A Woman Under the Influence, An Unmarried Woman, Alice Doesn't Live Here Anymore, Up the Sandbox, Private Benjamin, Norma Rae, My Brilliant Career, Julia,* and *The Turning Point*), gave way to the 1980s movies in which career women were either highlighted as heartless, neurotic villains or were depicted as disenchanted with the work world and looking for love and motherhood (*Fatal Attraction, Surrender, Crossing Delancey, Broadcast News, Baby Boom, Overboard, The War of the Roses, She-Devil,* and *I Love You to Death*).

2 In her discussion of 1980s films, Faludi lists *Terms of Endearment* in the category of films in which "housewives guard their families from predatory single women." She does not mention the 1989 *Steel Magnolias* film at all, and, because her book was published the same year as the 1991 chick flicks *Thelma and Louise* and *Fried Green Tomatoes,* she was not able to comment on the emerging genre of the chick flick.

3 Like many of today's postfeminists and third-wave feminists, Margaret Mitchell was the daughter of a feminist. Mitchell recalls being the darling of her mother's circle of suffragettes and marching in parades (Pyron 40–52).

4 A *USA Today* article claims the chick flick is "heavy on emotion and relationships," "escapist, brain-vacation entertainment" with a "bevy of can-do independent female leads" ("A Trio"); E!Online's "Top 10 Chick Flicks," claims that the genre's emphasis on "traditional values" rules out movies like *Thelma and Louise,* whose heroines are too tough; while recent shows such as Women Entertainment's *Three Men and a Chick Flick* have expanded the genre to include almost any movie a man might not like. In her review of *Divine Secrets of the Ya-Ya Sisterhood,* which she characterizes as a "chick flick pattie," Alex Kuczynski maintains that the genre of the chick flick is based on a set of clearly defined rules. The typical chick flick includes "platitudes about life and love," which are delivered "with the delicacy of a meat cleaver," and features divorced and alcoholic characters with "names that bludgeon you with their stark regional authenticity," like "M'Lynn and Clairee in *Steel Magnolias*; Idgie, Ninny and Sipsey in *Fried Green Tomatoes*; Flapp in *Terms of Endearment.*" Sarcastic dismissals are characteristic of many reviews of films labeled *chick flick,* but what I find significant is the inclusion of regional names as part of the "rules" of the genre. In fact, the names and the setting of the films—*Steel Magnolias, Fried Green Tomatoes,* and *Terms of Endearment* —are not simply regional, they are specifically southern.

5 Although the generational model is often criticized, it is nonetheless a persistent trope for discussing the changes in feminist criticism and theory. For example many of the articles in recent roundtables on the current status of feminism in both *Signs,* "Beyond the Gaze: Recent Approaches to Film Feminisms" (Autumn 2004) and *PMLA* "Feminist Criticism Today" (October 2006) employ these terms.

6 While historians have charted the rise and fall of the women's movement, Rossi looks at the "off-peak" years of the 1870s–1880s and again in the 1930s–1950s as times when women's participation in higher education and in the job market showed strong increases, suggesting that "the quiet second generation, unnoted by historians, may consolidate gains and provide the foundation on which the third generation takes off again into public and historical notice. After a generation of testing feminists' ideas in work and in the family, the limitations of those ideas may be realized, and the third generation returns again to challenge and action" (619).

7 As Astrid Henry points out, African-American women in the nineteenth century "began to theorize the intersectionality of identity" ("Feminist Deaths and Feminism Today" 1718).

8 Not all critics distinguish between nonpolitical postfeminists and political third-wave feminism. In *The F-Word: Feminism in Jeopardy* (2004), Kristin Rowe-Finkbeiner characterizes third-wave feminists as belonging to the same generation and as reacting to second-wave feminism, but she sees them as having no set goals and no formal political agenda, even though she also cites the work of the Third Wave Foundation, which specifically promotes social activism (90). Rowe-Finkbeiner includes the lipstick feminists in the third wave, noting that it is the "edgy, pop-culture" aspects of the third wave that get the most media attention with their "lipstick and push-up bras, stitch'n' bitches (power-knitting circles), short dresses and attitudes, and feminist porn" (90). Unlike the emphasis on white women of the postfeminists, Rowe-Finkbeiner does acknowledge the sexual and racial diversity of third-wavers (90). For a more detailed history of the emergence of third-wave feminism and post-feminism see Astrid Henry's *Not My Mother's Sister*, 23–36.

9 This technique is repeated in other nonsouthern chick flicks, such as *Legally Blonde* I and II. Both films are set in major urban areas, but they nonetheless preserve intimate feminine spaces: the first uses the feminine space of the sorority, and the second, like *Steel Magnolias*, focuses on the beauty parlor.

10 In the director's commentary, which accompanies the DVD version, Herbert Ross explained that they used the actual nurses who worked in the hospital, rather than actresses.

11 Although the term *chick flick* was of course not used in 1939, *Gone with the Wind* has many of the elements of what was known then as the "woman's film." One chick-flick fan has even called *Gone with the Wind* the ultimate chick flick in her all-time best chick flick web list (see <http://www.amazon.com/exec/obidos/tg/listmania/list-browse/-/1600WW7SXQUHN/002-3657929–8230407>).

12 For an excellent reading of the feminist and the postfeminist potential of *Thelma and Louise*, see Projansky 121–53. Although *Thelma and Louise* can be read as postfeminist, it does not use postfeminist strategies, as do the other southern chick flicks, in a way that masks feminist issues and thereby avoids controversy.

13 I teach a course on the South in film at the University of Mississippi and am constantly surprised that my students, both male and female, embrace *Fried Green Tomatoes*. Not only are students not offended by the murder and cannibalization of Frank, but, when I ask them which film best depicts their own image of the South, many point to this film and argue that it really captures small-town life in the South, though none of my students lived through the Depression.

14 Only one of the women, however, can live. Ruth, the lady to Idgie's tomboy/Amazon warrior, is too good for this world and succumbs to cancer, leaving Idgie to raise Buddy Jr. The movie was both praised and blamed for its understated depiction of a lesbian couple. The director, Jon Avnet, received an award from GLAAD (Gay and Lesbian Alliance Against Defamation) for his positive portrayal of lesbians, while David Ehrenstein cited it as one of the many instances of "delesbianization" in Hollywood movies (Holmlund 47).

15 Ostensibly, Ruth has been called in by Idgie's mother to serve as a "good" influence on her wayward daughter. Teaching Idgie to cook should be a sign of Ruth's domesticating influence, but, as this scene shows, Idgie has an equally strong non-domestic influence on Ruth.

16  Peter Stanfield focuses specifically on the use of St. Louis Blues as a marker of transgressive sexuality in connection with a white actress "as a means to articulate racial instability in the characterization of women who represented problems in terms of their sexuality, their morality, and their (lower) class status" (84).

17  In the film's suburban present, race is presented as a non-issue. The book depicts a much more segregated South in the present: Mrs Threadgoode lives in an all-white nursing home and her friend Mrs Otis is white. In the movie we eventually learn that Mrs Otis is Sipsey's daughter, indicating that Ninny's best friend is African-American and that the ties that existed in the past have remained strong in the post-Civil Rights South.

18  In the film Willetta is a composite of Ginger and Willetta in the novel.

19  Even in the movie version the Ya-Yas display little interest, sexual or otherwise, in their husbands, and the happiest times of their lives are depicted as their summers at the lake when all the men are gone.

20  The initiation not only gives Sidda a "community" of women friends, it also gives her an alternative pseudo-ethnic origin, without giving up the privileges of whiteness. The Ya-Yas invoke the priestesses who came before them "from Indian holy ground, from the jungle of the ancients, the prairies of the Norwegians and the shores of Gitchy Gumi."

21  Rebecca Wells's latest version of the Ya-Ya story, Ya-Yas in Bloom, follows the trajectory away from family secrets. In this version the secrets revealed are about women outside the Ya-Ya circle, who secretly envy the Ya-Yas and their happiness.

22  Bruckheimer did have good reason to be concerned; in 2002 she faced competition from such action blockbusters as Spiderman, Harry Potter and the Chamber of Secrets, Star Wars: Episode II—Attack of the Clones, and Lord of the Rings: The Two Towers. However, another chick flick, My Big Fat Greek Wedding, despite a slow start, ended up coming in fifth in box office totals for 2002 films. After Divine Secrets did well at the box office, and before the release of the DVD, Bruckheimer modified her position on the chick flick, stating "if used to describe a movie by women, about women, for women—then it doesn't bother me" (Cella 67).

23  Surprisingly for a film that features a man in drag, the film does not address the presence of homosexuality or transgenders in the African-American community. In Madea cross-dressing remains a visual joke, but it is left out of the film's content.

24  The potential for this type of film to devolve into insulting caricature is realized in Eddie Murphy's performance in Norbit (2007), a film whose one visual "joke" seems to be that fat women are disgusting.

25  I would like to thank Suzanne Leonard for her insights on the relation between work and romance in recent chick flicks, as presented in her recent conference paper, "She Works Too Hard: Postfeminism's 'Exploited' Workers." (The exceptions to this trend are the Legally Blonde films.)

## Works cited

Baumgardner, Jennifer and Amy Richards. Manifesta: Young Women, Feminism, and the Future. New York: Farrar, 2000.

Berglund, Jeff. "'The Secret's in the Sauce': Dismembering Normativity in Fried Green Tomatoes." Camera Obscura 14.42 (September, 1999): 125–59.

Cella, Catherine. "Khouri is Ga-Ga over Ya-Ya." *Billboard* 114, 44 (2 November 2002): 67.

"Chick Flick." *Shorter Oxford English Dictionary*. 5th ed. 2002.

Ehrenstein, David. "'Fried Green Tomatoes' Caps a Banner Year for Delesbianization." *Advocate* (February 11, 1992): 67.

Faludi, Susan. *Backlash: The Undeclared War against Women*. New York: Crown, 1991.

"Feminist Criticism Today." *PMLA* 121.5 (October 2006): 1678–741.

Flagg, Fannie. *Fried Green Tomatoes at the Whistle Stop Cafe*. New York: Fawcett Columbine, 1987.

Findlen, Barbara (ed.). *Listen Up: Voices from the Next Generation*. Seattle: Seal, 1995.

Glickman, Rose L. *Daughters of Feminists*. New York: St. Martin's, 1993.

Harde, Roxanne and Erin Harde. "Voices and Visions: A Mother and Daughter Discuss Coming to Feminism and Being Feminist." In *Catching a Wave: Reclaiming Feminism for the 21st Century*. Ed. Rory Dicker and Alison Piepmeier. Boston: Northeastern University Press, 2003: 116–37.

Haskell, Molly. *From Reverence to Rape: The Treatment of Women in the Movies*. 2nd ed. Chicago: University of Chicago Press, 1987.

Henry, Astrid. *Not My Mother's Sister: Generational Conflict and Third-Wave Feminism*. Bloomington: Indiana University Press, 2004.

——"Feminist Deaths and Feminism Today." *PMLA* 121.5 (October 2006): 1717–21.

Holmlund, Chris. "Cruisin' for a Bruisin': Hollywood's Deadly (Lesbian) Dolls." *Cinema Journal* 34.1 (Fall 1994): 31–51.

*In Full Bloom: Remembering Steel Magnolias*. Dir. Michael Gillis. Columbia Tristar Home Video. 2000.

Kabir, Shameem. *Daughters of Desire: Lesbian Representations in Film*. London: Cassell, 1998.

Kamen, Paula. *Feminist Fatale: Voices from the "Twentysomething" Generation Explore the Future of the "Women's Movement."* New York: Fine, 1991.

Koltnow, Barry. "The Label That Scares Hollywood." *Orange County Register* 28 May 2002.

Kuczynski, Alex. *Weekend Edition Sunday*. National Public Radio. 16 June 2002. Transcript.

LaBadie, Donald. "Friend's Life in a Shoebox Inspired Flagg." *Memphis Tennessee Commercial Appeal*, 10 January 1992: B1.

Leonard, Suzanne. "She Works Too Hard: Postfeminism's 'Exploited' Workers." Post-Feminist "Chick" Narratives. Society for Cinema and Media Studies Conference. Hilton, Chicago. 10 March 2007.

McPherson, Tara. *Reconstructing Dixie: Race, Gender, and Nostalgia in the Imagined South*. Durham, NC: Duke University Press, 2003.

Moi, Toril. "'I'm Not a Feminist, But . . .': How Feminism Became the F-Word." *PMLA* 121.5 (October 2006): 1735–41.

Potts, Kimberly. "Top Ten Chick Flicks." *E! Online* 16 May 2005. <http://www.eonline.com/Features/Topten/Chickflicks/10.html>.

Projansky, Sarah. *Watching Rape: Film and Television in Postfeminist Culture*. New York: New York University Press, 2001.

Pyron, Darden Asbury. *Southern Daughter: The Life of Margaret Mitchell.* Oxford: Oxford University Press, 1991.

Read, Jacinda. *The New Avengers: Feminism, Femininity, and the Rape-Revenge Cycle.* Manchester: Manchester University Press, 2000.

Rogers, Mary F. *Barbie Culture.* London: Sage, 1999.

Roiphe, Katie. *The Morning After: Sex, Fear, and Feminism on Campus.* Boston: Little, Brown, 1993.

Rossi, Alice (ed.). *The Feminist Papers: From Adams to de Beauvoir.* Boston: Northeastern University Press, 1988.

"Roundtable: Film Feminisms." *Signs* 30.1 (Autumn 2004): 1209–92.

Rowe-Finkbeiner, Kristin. *The F-Word: Feminism in Jeopardy: Women, Politics, and the Future.* Emeryville, CA: Seal, 2004.

Schrobsdorff, Susanna. " 'Brokeback Mountain': A Hit with Red State Women." *ArtsExtra. MSNBC.com.* 2006. *Newsweek.* 20 January 2006 <http://www.msnbc.msn.com/id/10930877/site/newsweek/> .

Stacey, Judith. "Sexism by a Subtler Name? Postindustrial Conditions and Postfeminist Consciousness in the Silicon Valley." *Socialist Review* 17 (1987): 7–28.

Stanfield, Peter. "An Excursion into the Lower Depths: Hollywood, Urban Primitivism, and *St. Louis Blues*, 1929–1937." *Cinema Journal* 41.2 (2002): 84–108.

Travers, Peter. *Rolling Stone*, 16 April 1991. 5 Feb. 2001 <http://rollingstone.com/reviews/movie/5948343/review/5948344/thelma_louise>.

Travis, Trysh. "Divine Secrets of the Cultural Studies Sisterhood: Women Reading Rebecca Wells." *American Literary History* 15.1 (Spring 2003): 134–59.

"A Trio: 'Apocalipstick' is Hilarious, 'Better' is Fanciful and 'Sangria' is Heart-wrenching." *USA Today* 20 February 2003, Life Section: 4D.

Vickers, Lu. *"Fried Green Tomatoes: Excuse Me, Did We See the Same Movie?" Jump Cut* 39 (1994): 26–39.

Wells, Rebecca. *Divine Secrets of the Ya-Ya Sisterhood.* New York: HarperPerennial-HarperCollins, 1996.

——*Little Altars Everywhere.* New York: HarperTorch-HarperCollins, 1996.

——*Ya-Yas in Bloom.* New York: HarperCollins, 2005.

Willis, Susan. *High Contrast: Race and Gender in Contemporary Hollywood Film.* Durham, NC: Duke University Press, 1997.

Wolf, Naomi. *Fire with Fire: The New Female Power and How It Will Change the 21st Century.* New York: Random House, 1993.

# Chapter 7

# Something's gotta give

## Hollywood, female sexuality, and the "older bird" chick flick

*Margaret Tally*

In a February 23, 2004 article in *The Guardian*, cultural critic Cherry Potter identified a new film genre for women, the "older bird" chick flick. Commenting on these films, Potter compared this term to another recent coinage, "chick lit":

> Sorry, that ["older bird"] doesn't have quite the same ring as "chick-lit." But what else are we to call the recent trend for comedy dramas about the sexual awakening of middle-aged women, particularly those who discover that some men actually find them beautiful without their clothes on? The question is why these comedies are appearing now.
>
> (Potter 16)

Diane Keaton, who starred in one of the recent "older bird" chick flicks, *Something's Gotta Give* (2003), thinks these films may be appearing now, in part, because they explicitly speak to the questions of relationships and sexuality in middle age. Despite these relatively positive assessments that Hollywood has finally begun to create films with older female audiences in mind, annual production is still dominated by films with more conventionally "male" themes of the hero or anti-hero on some kind of quest, either alone or with a buddy figure. Women, where they are portrayed, are usually young women who play a supporting role; middle-aged women are relegated to even more subsidiary roles.

The dearth of good roles for women may be due, in turn, to the fact that men still predominantly hold positions of power in Hollywood and believe that young men are the most attractive demographic to pursue. In this view, the conventional wisdom has been that while men won't go to see films with a central female character, their girlfriends or wives will accompany them to male-oriented movies. Younger men themselves are occupying more decision-making positions in Hollywood than ever before. As film writer Mimi Swartz wryly notes, "You know, if you're a 28–32-year-old Hollywood studio executive, it probably is a stretch to think that anybody wants to see a bunch of 56-year-old women naked in a movie."

Studio executives defend their decisions by charging that female audiences can't "open" a picture, that is, that films targeting women can't draw large crowds on the opening day, which is viewed by the film business as crucial to whether a film will ultimately be profitable or not. As Amy Pascal, Chairwoman of Columbia Pictures, has commented, "Women don't open pictures, older, younger, in-between. No, they don't" ("Profile").

While conventional wisdom holds that female audiences don't open films, some recent films have directly challenged this long-held supposition by demonstrating that, while they may not be able to attract large crowds on their opening day, they nevertheless have "legs"—the ability to attract a good number of viewers over a longer period of time. These films include *The Banger Sisters* (2002), *Under the Tuscan Sun* (2003), *Something's Gotta Give* (2003), and *Calendar Girls* (2003). All of these films, in addition to providing a central female character, celebrate older women's sexual reawakening. One reason these positive films about middle-aged female sexuality are finally being made is that a few voices in Hollywood, mostly female themselves, have successfully argued that an older female demographic is a viable niche audience (Peterson).

While these films offer a welcome departure from the preponderance of films with male themes, other recent films portraying middle-aged women end up playing into the worst stereotypes of middle-aged female sexuality as somehow deviant and inimical to the interests of the family. In these films, which range from the controversial film *Thirteen* (2003) to the more standard woman's "weepie," *Anywhere But Here* (1999), to even the tween comedy *Freaky Friday* (2003), the older female's sexuality is portrayed as toxic to the other family members, threatening to upend the fragile relationships within the family.

Although the more upbeat "older bird" films such as *Something's Gotta Give* would appear to present a more positive view of older women expressing their sexuality, both kinds of film share one central theme: that an "older" woman who is sexually alive and aware and has her own needs must nevertheless be contained within the family. Thus, it is fair to say that the more upbeat "older bird" films, while seemingly affirmative, also express a sense of ambivalence about older women's sexuality.

## When mom is too hot: *Thirteen, Anywhere But Here, Freaky Friday*

In the more negative films I have identified, one persistent theme is that a sexually active middle-aged woman impedes her daughter from becoming fully developed, both sexually and emotionally. In these films, the mother's desire to be sexually attractive to men becomes an intense focus of the teenage daughter's own sexual conflicts associated with coming of age.

In the film *Thirteen*, for example, a young woman named Tracy (Evan Rachel Wood) is shown living with her divorced mom, Melanie (Holly Hunter). Although her mother is portrayed as loving and caring, we soon discover that the mother is hanging on by a thread, attending AA meetings, and letting a boyfriend who had used drugs and abused her back into her life. Tracy is furious with her mother for allowing him to insert himself into their lives again, and finds herself adrift as she returns to middle school in the fall. There, she comes under the influence of Evie, the prototypical "bad girl," who gets Tracy involved in a netherworld of substance abuse, shoplifting, and other self-destructive activities. Tracy's mother is portrayed as trying to keep her relationship with her boyfriend afloat in the face of an increasingly belligerent and uncontrollable "thirteen"-year-old.

In the film, the mother's need to have the boyfriend in her life wreaks havoc on the daughter's fragile sense of emotional stability. Other cues that the mother is too needy to the detriment of her daughter's well-being include the fact that the "bad" girl Evie is able to successfully flatter and thereby manipulate Tracy's mother into ignoring their escapades by telling her how sexy and young she looks. The mother is invited to be "one of the girls," as evidenced by her own sexy, young wardrobe, make-up, and hair, while also being a maternal figure, cooking them food, and driving them to the mall.

The larger point in this cautionary drama is that the mother has supposedly precipitated her daughter's downward slide by asserting her own sexual needs, that is, by having the problematic boyfriend move back in. The only way the crisis is ultimately resolved is when another, previously absent mother figure, Evie's alcoholic guardian, confronts them with Tracy's drug use. This other, unstable mother triggers Melanie's own need to save her daughter and protect her from Evie.

The ending of the film implies that the mother–daughter bond is the only thing that will save the child from her descent into hell. The mother's own sexuality, her own neediness, is intentionally buried in this portrait, as she instead asserts the primal maternal bond to save her child. The implication is that motherhood requires an intense and primary focus on the child, with little room left over for the articulation of the mother's sexual desires or other needs.

The theme of a mother's sexuality contributing to the daughter's conflicts in adolescence is brought into even greater relief in the slightly older film *Anywhere But Here* (1999). In this film, based on Mona Simpson's 1987 novel, the dynamic again is that of a mother, whose inability to act conventionally maternal leads to an unstable situation for the daughter. Susan Sarandon, who plays the character Adele August, is a frustrated, slightly unbalanced woman who lives with her daughter Ann (Natalie Portman) in a small town. Wanting her daughter to escape her own fate, she packs up everything and moves them to Beverly Hills, where they live precariously on her salary as a teacher. In the film, the daughter is portrayed as the sane one, sober, conservative, and bitter that her whole world was taken away to pursue her mother's dreams.

The mother, on the other hand, is portrayed as a kind of manic, sexually inappropriate woman who is so fixated on living through her daughter that when a real opportunity for her daughter comes along to attend an excellent college in the East, the mother does everything she can to stop her daughter from leaving. The mother's sense of unreality is continually highlighted throughout the film. That disconnection with reality is tied to her sexually inappropriate behavior, as she is shown to "act out" by wearing outrageous and sexy outfits, as well as flirting and otherwise acting too young for her age. The daughter, on the other hand, is portrayed as sexually repressed, except when she finally relents and allows a would-be suitor to help her lose her virginity. Her sexual coldness throughout the film, however, seems to stem from her mother's overt sexuality.

While *Thirteen* and *Anywhere But Here* seem to be very different kinds of film, the first an "edgy" cautionary tale, the second a more standard melodrama in the tradition of a "woman's weepie," both films nevertheless reveal a deeper cultural assumption about middle-aged mothers and their daughters. In both films, the middle-aged women are shown to be acting inappropriately for their age. Furthermore, the ability to "mother" is undermined by the needy sexuality of the older women, and a kind of role reversal takes place between the conservative younger daughter and the middle-aged mother.

This role reversal is explicitly presented in yet another recent film, *Freaky Friday* (2003). This film, which stars Jamie Lee Curtis as a psychiatrist raising her fifteen-year-old daughter Anna (Lindsay Lohan) is at first glance worlds apart from both *Thirteen* and *Anywhere But Here*. In this film, the mother Tess is a widow who is trying to combine her high-pressure job with raising two children and planning marriage to a new man. The daughter Anna is conflicted about her mother's decision to get remarried so soon after her father dies, and some of her rebelliousness—along with the tension in her relationship with her mother—stems from her mother's impending remarriage.

In a comic turn involving a fortune-cookie curse at a Chinese restaurant, Anna and Tess switch bodies. The daughter is horrified to have her middle-aged mother's body, exclaiming, "I look like the crypt keeper!" The mother, on the other hand, while initially horrified, begins to appreciate her new-found attributes as she feels her own buttocks and is pleasantly surprised to see how firm they are now that she inhabits a fifteen-year-old's body.

In terms of the mother's sexuality, the film is able to offer its older female audiences multiple pleasures as the middle-aged mother is portrayed as looking sexy and younger, causing young men to fall for her. Unlike *Thirteen* and *Anywhere But Here*, *Freaky Friday* allows the mother to "act out" as a fifteen-year-old for the bulk of the film, without the dire consequences implicit in the other two films.

At the same time, however, *Freaky Friday* does not allow the mother to remain in this "immature" stage of flaunting her sexuality, but rather has her relinquish both the younger body and the handsome younger man, as the curse is finally reversed. While she is still allowed a sexual identity, that is, with her new husband, this sexuality is placed in the service of reconstituting a nuclear family. Her sexuality is tamed, as she re-enters her "old" body and life, and allows the daughter to reclaim her younger body and get the handsome young man who had initially fallen for the mother.

What all these films share, despite their differences, is the portrayal of mothers who must restrain their sexual natures in order to parent their adolescent daughters. Whereas the two earlier films offer the cultural stereotype of the "sexy Momma" as deviant and narcissistic in relation to her own daughter's needs and emerging sexuality, *Freaky Friday* allows middle-aged women to celebrate their sexuality for the better part of the film, only to safely recontain it by the end.

## Momma's got a brand new bag: *The Banger Sisters*, *Under the Tuscan Sun*, *Calendar Girls*, and *Something's Gotta Give*

Like *Freaky Friday*, *The Banger Sisters* focuses on a previously uptight mother who is loosened up as she gets to re-experience her sexual desire in the wake of something or someone entering her carefully constructed, yet stifling life. While in *Freaky Friday* the plot device is the introduction of a body-switch initiated by a fortune cookie, in *The Banger Sisters*, the plot device consists of the re-entry of an old friend who allows the main character to get back in touch with her younger, more sexually liberated self.

The plot of *The Banger Sisters* revolves around the relationship between two middle-aged women, Lavinia (Susan Sarandon) and her old friend Suzette (Goldie Hawn). Once groupies to rock stars, they are both now over fifty. While Lavinia has become a straight-laced, over-achieving "soccer mom," Suzette has, on the contrary, remained true to her wild past, and thirty years later, is still acting and dressing as she did in her twenties. When Suzette loses her job as a bartender in LA and needs money, she decides to look up her old comrade-in-arms Vinnie, now Lavinia. One of the conceits of the film is that Lavinia has made such a radical transformation into an uptight, respectable Mom that her whole family has no clue about her earlier wild days as a groupie.

The initial impetus for Lavinia's desire to return to her more youthful "Vinnie" self occurs in a jarring scene at the dinner table, where her daughters make fun of her after hearing about her sexually adventurous past. This ridicule, combined with her friend's ability to remind her of her freer self, propels Lavinia to jettison her lifestyle and go out with her friend to an all-night club. Lavinia cuts off her hair, puts on skin-tight clothes, goes out dancing and stays out all night. When she returns with Suzette to her suburban house, they go to the basement, discover some ancient pot, and smoke it as they giggle over old snapshots of the penises of their past sexual conquests. It may be that the truly radical dimension of the film is not when the Sarandon character is allowed to step out and express herself as a sexual being again, as much as the taken-for-granted sexuality of the fifty-something Hawn character. Hawn's sexuality is all the more radical because the more conventional Hollywood trope would be to show a middle-aged female character who had never married or had children as somehow deeply regretting her life choices. Although Hawn's character is shown as fully capable of being a maternal figure to Sarandon's daughter, as when the daughter gets sick from taking drugs on her prom night and Suzette helps her through it, the film does not lapse into a story of regret and recrimination for Suzette's lack of a nuclear family.

The film does take the more conventional road, however, towards its end, where Lavinia reclaims her mothering role to help the family when her younger daughter experiences a crisis. The final scene portrays the family banded together, with the mother at the center, all staring happily at Suzette, who is walking off into the sunset like a sexualized Mary Poppins. The entire family has, in other words, presumably been transformed for the better by Suzette's openness, and there is the sense that Lavinia will take more opportunities to explore her newfound old self. Yet, by placing her squarely back as the center of the family, the film reinscribes her burgeoning sexuality within the nuclear family.

*Under the Tuscan Sun* (2003) features a middle-aged woman who is not a mother, yet who also finds herself re-discovering her sexuality in middle age. The film stars Diane Lane, an actress who has played a similar role in several other films, including *A Walk on the Moon* (1999) and *Unfaithful* (2002). In *Under the Tuscan Sun*, Lane plays Frances, a married San Francisco author who, on discovering her husband's infidelity, leaves her marriage and, jettisoning everything along with it, sinks into a deep depression. Her gay best friend (Sandra Oh) tries to lift her out of her depression by giving her a ticket for an upcoming gay bus tour to Tuscany, Italy.

On the tour Frances is freed from any marital constraints and allowed to be anonymous since she is in a bus full of primarily gay men where, as her friend tells her, "nobody will hit on [her]." She finds herself getting off the tour bus and, in an impulsive move, making an offer to purchase a beautiful old villa in Tuscany. The film follows Frances, who, with the help of her real-estate agent, hires illegal workers from Poland to help her renovate the long neglected house.

These characters, along with a neighbor's adolescent daughter, form the basis of what Frances will come to view as her quasi-family. This sense of family only intensifies when her gay friend arrives on her doorstep, pregnant and abandoned by her female lover. Frances takes her in, and with the Polish workers, teenage neighbor and real-estate agent, she creates a new, blended family. As if this new family were not enough to help her heal, into the picture walks a handsome younger man who sweeps her off her feet. As we can see in several other recent films, including *Lovely and Amazing*, *Freaky Friday*, *Something's Gotta Give*, *Laurel Canyon*, and *Tadpole*, as well as television shows directed to women such as *Sex and the City*, the figure of the "cougar," or older woman who dates younger men, is becoming one way of displaying middle-aged women's newfound sexuality. In *Under the Tuscan Sun*, this May–December union signifies that Frances has rediscovered her buried sexuality. This sense of sexual empowerment is amplified in a scene where, after making love with the younger man, Lane is shown bouncing up and down on her bed, clutching her loins and pumping her fists in the air, shouting "Yes, Yes! I've still got it!"

While the conceit of the film is that the beautiful and relatively young (39) Lane is supposed to be a woman of a certain age who has been dumped, the film nevertheless delivers on its promise of an escapist fantasy for middle-aged women. For, while there are a few romantic setbacks, including the fact that the nice, sexy real-estate agent is too noble to cheat on his wife and the young Italian man ends up having another girlfriend, in the end Frances gets to have another younger man in her life, as well as an alternative family. In fact, the last scene of the film shows Frances presiding over her newly renovated villa, with an assortment of friends and quasi-family, including her new lover and her gay friend's baby, all basking in the light of the "Tuscan Sun."

In this way, the film parallels such films as *Freaky Friday* as well as, arguably, *The Banger Sisters*, in allowing the female character to rediscover her presumably lost sexuality, while at the same time re-containing it within a kind of extended family. In this film, however, there is more space given to the woman to, in a sense, have her cake and eat it too, in that she is allowed to keep a younger man and have a family and a home. The film allows for the idea that one can, in middle age, recreate oneself and find a family, even if it wasn't created conventionally. And, by allowing her to have a younger man in her life, *Under the Tuscan Sun* offers a vision of a female who is not punished for her sexual desires, but actually rewarded with a man and a new family.

In yet another film of the "older bird" genre, *Calendar Girls* (2003), the female, middle-aged characters are also allowed to rediscover their sexuality, through the display of their bodies. In this film, best friends Chris (Helen Mirren) and Annie (Julie Walters) become a catalyst for a larger social transformation in their town among the older women, as they too become reawakened to their own physical beauty in mid-life. The plot, based on a true story, concerns a group of women in rural Yorkshire, England. When Annie's husband dies of cancer, her friend Chris decides they should raise money for a new couch in the sitting room of the cancer ward where he died. Chris devises a plan to raise the money by asking members of their Women's Club to pose in the nude for their annual calendar.

Drawing on a comment comparing the women of Yorkshire to its flowers made by Annie's husband before he died—"The last stage is always the most glorious"—the film quaintly affirms this stage of life for women. Some tensions arise, not because the older women agree to be photographed nude, but because of what the newfound notoriety does to their families, their communities, and themselves. Chris, for example, begins to neglect her husband and son as she finds herself enamored of all the attention and adulation. With the help of her friend Annie, however, who points out to her what all that fame has done to her relationship with her son, Chris returns to her family from her publicity tour in America, chastened and humbled. In this film, then, the mother's sexuality threatens to unravel the family both because of what it does to the mother, who becomes swept away with all the newfound attention, as well as because of its impact on the community as a whole, which is put under the spotlight of intense media attention. The older women's sexuality, more generally, transgresses the "older" values of family and community for the "newer" values of sexual freedom, mass marketing, and Americanization, as the mothers are swept off to the United States to appear on television talk shows.

*Image 7.1* The "Calendar Girls" (Helen Mirren, Julie Walters, *et al.*) are temporarily seduced by the bright lights of LA

While a threat to the family has been introduced, the end of the film portrays the family strengthened as a result of this trial. As in *Under the Tuscan Sun*, the characters, with the exception of Chris, are not punished for discovering their sexuality, and are allowed to experience themselves as physically attractive and, at the same time, ultimately firmly embedded within their families.

## Love and death in the Hamptons

Like *Calendar Girls* and *Under the Tuscan Sun*, *Something's Gotta Give* also presumably celebrates a middle-aged woman's sexual awakening. The story is about a fiftysomething woman named Erica (Diane Keaton), who is a successful, divorced mother of a grown daughter named Marin (Amanda Peet). The daughter is dating a much older man, Harry Sanborne (Jack Nicholson). Horrified that her daughter is dating a man her own age, Erica nevertheless allows them both to stay in her house in the Hamptons with her. When Harry suffers a heart attack during foreplay with the daughter, he is rushed to the hospital and treated by a young doctor named Julian (Keanu Reeves). Julian takes an instant interest in Erica, who is both flattered and flustered at the attentions of a younger man. In this May–December flirting, as well as in a subsequent dating scene, Erica is portrayed as thinking Julian must be somewhat delusional, as if it were inconceivable that a man so young would find her remotely attractive:

JULIAN MERCER:  You really are a very sexy woman.
ERICA BARRY:  No, really, swear to God, I'm NOT.

When Harry is released from the hospital, Erica's house is the logical place for him to stay. To her horror, Erica is asked to be his nurse, since her daughter has to go back to Manhattan to return to her job. Erica at first rejects the notion that she must play nursemaid to a man who only the night before had referred to her as a "woman your age." In a scene used in the trailer for the film, one night Harry stumbles into Erica's bedroom by accident, where she has undressed to shower. She begins screaming, as does he, with the joke supposedly being that he has never seen a woman Erica's age in the nude, or as he puts it, "I've never seen a woman that age naked before."

For the remainder of the film, the story reveals the blossoming relationship between Harry and Erica, and much of the dialogue that ensues revolves around Harry's and Erica's evolving sexual and romantic interest in one another. Before they begin a sexual relationship, however, Erica must lose her frigid exterior, as suggested in the following exchange:

HARRY:  I just have one question: What's with the turtlenecks? I mean it's the middle of summer.

*Image 7.2* Erica (Diana Keaton) finds an age-appropriate mate in Harry (Jack Nicholson)

ERICA:  Well I guess I'm just a turtleneck kind of gal.
HARRY:  You never get hot?
ERICA:  No.
HARRY:  Never?
ERICA:  Not lately.

Erica's initial frigidity is slowly melted, both because she falls in love with Harry and because she becomes the recipient of sexual attention from the young doctor, Julian. For example, at one point after she and Julian kiss, she remarks, "Good. That's very good." While enjoying the attention of the young Julian, Erica is still portrayed as being ambivalent about his sexual interest in her, both because of her attraction to Harry and, presumably, because she still can't believe a young man would find her attractive.

Despite the attentions of the younger Julian, the film soon reveals that she has fallen in love with Harry, and they finally consummate their relationship. Erica remarks on what it is like to make love again, after being celibate for such a long time:

ERICA:  I DO like sex!
HARRY:  You certainly do.

Although she has fallen in love, Harry finds it much more difficult to let himself go and make the same kind of emotional commitment. Whereas Erica's sexual self-discovery, then, occurs as a result of letting herself open up to and fall in love with Harry, a central tension of the film lies in how Harry will be able to reciprocate, given his own emotional armor.

Despite his seeming intransigence (or perhaps because another ending didn't play well with test audiences), by the end of the film Harry does realize that he wants to be with Erica. And, in the last scene, viewers are supplied with the requisite happy ending, complete with Harry and Erica taking Marin and her new, age-appropriate husband and baby out to dinner at a fancy New York restaurant. Her choice of Harry over the younger Julian demonstrates that her character is allowed to go only so far in experimenting with her sexuality before she must "come home" and return to a more conventional pairing with a similarly aged male.

Looked at from another angle, we can ask whether such films, in portraying middle-aged women's sexuality with relative approval and openness, might be said to be sustaining the stereotype that equates women with their (hetero)sexuality. There's a fine line, in other words, between portraying women as sexually free and reducing them to essentially sexual beings. However, in a culture which has effectively reduced middle-aged women to a kind of invisibility with respect to their sexuality, these newer films at least reopen the question of whether accomplished, professional, middle-aged women can be portrayed as having sexual lives as well, or whether they must renounce their sexuality because they are no longer young.

In sum, what distinguishes these films from their precursors is that the characters are not punished for expressing their sexuality. In fact, their sexual experimentation is viewed as a kind of necessary corrective to the overly constrained lives they have created for themselves as type-A career women or soccer moms. What these relatively more affirmative visions of female middle-aged sexuality offer is that, although the re-introduction of their sexuality might shake things up for the other people in their lives, it is still ultimately a positive and enriching experience for the female characters themselves.

## Conclusion: "What do women want?"

In writing about the history of how middle-aged women are portrayed in Hollywood films more generally, Karen Stoddard has noted that they are usually viewed as either mothers or spinsters, and their sexuality is constrained by cultural assumptions and prohibitions surrounding their role in the family. Film writer Mimi Swartz, commenting on the "coming-of-middle-age" sagas in the earlier film period of the 1950s, points out that when middle-aged women are portrayed, they are shown as either going crazy or disappearing, citing such films as *Sunset Boulevard* (1950) and *All About Eve* (1950) as paradigms of the aging female losing her social powers and sinking into depression and madness. Swartz finds that older female characters of the 1960s do not fare much better, represented as sexually starved and humiliated in films such as *The Graduate* (1967). By the 1990s, Swartz finds what she terms a "calcification" of these themes. Against this backdrop, the recent "older bird" films appear to challenge stereotypes of middle-aged women as sexless and over the hill.

For the female characters in these new "older bird" films, then, their newfound sexuality is experienced as a kind of recovery of a lost self, and a way to be in the world that is not defined solely by their role as a parent, wife, or worker. In fact, the sexual reawakening often serves as a life-affirming event, one that will help them eventually be stronger and better family members, community members, and adults.

The films' ambivalence towards women's sexuality lies in their almost compulsive need to show that these women come back into the family fold. None of the women, in the end, are shown reveling in their solitude or living alone willingly. In *Calendar Girls*, for example, it is only the widow who remains alone. And even in *The Banger Sisters*, the unrepentant and single Suzette is portrayed as possibly getting together with a man she meets during the course of the film.

Unlike leading male characters "of a certain age," furthermore, the women in these films are shown "discovering" their sexuality at mid-life, with the assumption being that a "normal" middle-aged woman has somehow jettisoned her sexual identity along the way. These "older bird" films do not address why it is assumed that middle-aged women have "lost" their sexuality in the first place. This kind of assumption is never present in films featuring *male* middle-aged characters. Indeed, when it comes to actors such as Harrison Ford or Mel Gibson or Clint Eastwood, viewers are expected to assume that the older male character has remained virile and sexually attractive throughout his life. In this way, then, even the most progressive portrayals of middle-aged women's sexuality in the recent "older bird" films are still reproducing old stereotypes.

Ultimately, while the endings to all these films reveal Hollywood's ongoing ambivalence toward older women's sexuality separated from their place within the family, these films do nevertheless represent a welcome departure from earlier representations of older women's sexuality as deviant and toxic. Whether these kinds of films which allow middle-aged women to be sexually expressive will continue to be made, however, is less clear. Perhaps only when more women who are Hollywood executives themselves become women "of a certain age," will they begin to make decisions that allow more "older bird" films to be created.

## Works cited

Brand, Madeleine. "Two New Films Celebrate the Sexuality of Older Women." *Day to Day*. National Public Radio. 9 January 2004.

Peterson, Thane. "Aging Women: Movies' Golden Oldies." *Businessweek Online*, December 16, 2003. <http://www.businessweek.com:/print/bwdaily/dnflash/dec2003/nf20031216_7457_db028.h>.

Potter, Cherry. "Sex and the Older Woman: Both Film and TV Have Discovered That Women Over 50 Don't Lose Their Allure When They Lose Their Clothes." *The Guardian*, Feb. 23, 2004: 16.

"Profile: Recent Hollywood Phenomenon of Movies Giving Older Women More Sexual Roles." *All Things Considered*. National Public Radio. 18 December 2003. Transcript. <http://search.epnet.com/direct.asp?an=6XN200312282008&db=tth>.

Stoddard, Karen M. *Saints and Shrews: Women and Aging in American Popular Film*. Westport, CT: Greenwood, 1983.

Swartz, Mimi. "Sunset Strip: Hollywood Casts an Unexpectedly Realistic Eye on Aging Womanhood." *Slate* 5 January 2004. <http://slate.msn.com/toolbar.aspx?action=print&id=2093444>.

# Chapter 8

# Simple pleasures

## Lesbian community and *Go Fish*

*Lisa Henderson*

The summer of 1994 saw the release of the independent feature film *Go Fish*, a charming, episodic, and much awaited lesbian romantic comedy. Written and produced by Rose Troche and Guinevere Turner (Turner also stars), directed by Troche, and executive produced by Christine Vachon and Tom Kalin, *Go Fish* was picked up for distribution by the Samuel Goldwyn Company following several seasons on the festival circuit as a work in progress. After years of sitting through films whose lesbian leads ended up dead, straight, or suffering, or of creatively reclaiming (from opportunists like Michael Douglas and Paul Verhoeven) the bad-girl possibilities of characters such as Sharon Stone's in *Basic Instinct* (1992), lesbian audiences found deliverance in *Go Fish*, in its soothing rhythms, its fond typifications of a foibled and venturesome group of lesbians, and its quirky laugh lines. As on so many other occasions on and off the record of lesbian history and culture, survival meets humor in *Go Fish* and both are the better for it. It is against this ground—of the felt survival value of whimsy, self-irony, and representations of group culture—that I read *Go Fish*'s narrative and stylistic gestures. How do they animate utopic thoughts of community and a life within it? This query invokes larger questions about popular representation, about the work of images in constructing and reconstructing social subjects, and is perhaps best addressed by looking into the reception and circulation of cultural forms among both loosely connected and tightly knit groups. Although precisely how subjectivity takes shape in the time and space beyond the text is a complicated question, people do come together in their engagement with popular materials. They assemble in movie theaters and concert arenas, show up at readings and demonstrations by authors and artists, and gather in public spaces (such as bars and dorms) to watch and discuss their favorite television programs. Such gatherings make concrete both the presumption and possibility of common repertoires, of cultural practices that link people across a maze of different and competing social positions. But are these groups really communities? Not necessarily. Indeed, in the practical language of social theory and cultural criticism, such links constitute "taste formations." However, they also signify communal potential and even produce (at least fleetingly) the symbolic bonds they appear only to represent. In their stories and characters, their deployment of subcultural tropes and sensibilities, and their enactment of the lived possibility of connectedness, popular texts and performances offer a point of entry into what Benedict Anderson has famously called *imagined communities*.

I argue that, in moving back and forth between its lesbian characters' and audiences' senses of longing, humor, and self-recognition, *Go Fish* produces a communal ethos. Impatient with bullet and mirror metaphors for understanding media effect (in which we are either shot through with undue influence or simply reflected by a transparent form), I imagine instead a reciprocal dialogue between films and audiences, a mutual constitution made all the more intimate (and thus more powerful) in and around works by, for, and about nondominant collectives. On the one hand, it is well-charted territory in cultural studies of representation that people accustomed to hostile infidelities between popular depictions of their social groups and their own senses of self are mobilized by jolts of recognition, those occasions when a text makes familiar (salient, plausible) references to a reality little known outside the group itself. On the other hand, the mapping of this territory changes as the repertoire of texts and references expands. English-speaking lesbian movie fans no longer have only villains, victims, and the films *Personal Best* (1982) and *Desert Hearts* (1985) to look to for the simple pleasure of keeping company with lesbian characters. Scores of new films and videos are screened each year at urban and regional festivals; a small handful of lesbian- and gay-targeted magazines feature regular film and video reviews; and a diverse, energetic film and video movement, tentatively promoted as the "new queer cinema," has been underway since the early 1990s, with *Go Fish* executive producers Vachon and Kalin among its high-profile members.[1] Amid this symbolic profusion, the kick of recognition has changed enough to require both a new account of how lesbian audiences are hailed—or not—by "lesbian" texts and a new understanding of the narrative figures and interpretive frames invoked as lesbian filmmakers and audiences produce, embrace, or refuse a text as their—our—"own."

A handful of inventive (and persuasive) scholars of film, television, and other popular forms have investigated these questions, seeking to understand how both current and historical texts produced for and within mainstream culture still manage to be, in myriad senses, "queer." Patricia White, for example, has read Robert Wise's 1963 horror classic *The Haunting* for its construction of a deviant female subjectivity that can be understood as lesbian in its implications. Observing the film's dramatic reliance on an unresolved and borderline perverse relationship between two women characters, White traces "the haunting of Hill House as it shifts between homo-sexuality and homophobia" ("Female Spectator" 153). *The Haunting* is "not a film about lesbians," observes White; "it is (pretends to be) about something else. I would consider 'something else' to be a useful working definition of lesbianism in classical cinema" ("Female Spectator" 154). In another essay, on the "queer career of Agnes Moorehead," White undertakes considerable historical and interpretive labor to connect Moorehead's many performances, the terms of her reception in the mainstream press, and the gossip surrounding her career and constructs a kind of lesbian hagiography within classical Hollywood cinema. This kind of recuperative reading also figures in Judith Mayne's work on Dorothy Arzner, one of the very few successful women directors in the classical period. Mayne responds to feminist film scholarship on Arzner that makes explicit the question of whether and how female authorship might interrupt male subjectivity in cinema but leaves implicit the many filmic and extrafilmic opportunities available for reading Arzner as a specifically lesbian author. Desire is at the core of Mayne's analysis—both the desire among women characters in Arzner's films (the "textual Arzner") and the desire projected by the director herself (the "very visible Arzner"), in public and in print, through such gestures as dress, language, and bodily style and engagement. Invoking psychoanalysis, subtext, and hitherto suppressed biographical detail, Mayne and White reveal a lesbian/nonlesbian tension at the heart of dominant forms of cultural expression that challenges the heterocentric grain of both Hollywood cinema's and feminist film theory's (over)emphasis on a masculine spectator.

In contrast, the declaratively lesbian universe in *Go Fish* demands a different kind of reading, one that is more explicitly social than psychic, self-consciously linking particular filmic gestures to other texts and to extrafilmic participation in cultural discourses and social relationships. Read at the juncture of texts and social life, *Go Fish* produces a fictional community at once diverse and harmonious, self-actualizing and tentative, witty and vulnerable, sexual and sexually judgmental. In the tradition of Jan Oxenberg's *Comedy in Six Unnatural Acts* (1975), the *Go Fish* ensemble is a mixed array of comic type and countertype that presumes (rather than promotes) lesbian identity and identification.[2] The film is neither a coming-out story nor an excruciating drama of recognition and loss (although these themes are present) but a buoyant, urbane depiction of a few weeks in the lives of a dozen or so avowed young dykes gathered together in an early 1990s lesbian scene. Within a cinematic tradition populated by few lesbian characters and amid a potentially liberatory but easily divided and vulnerable lesbian sexual culture, *Go Fish* offers a modest lesbian utopia. In doing so, it accomplishes what Richard Dyer argues is also characteristic of mainstream entertainment films: it manages the contradictions between viewers' experience of how things are and how they might want them to be ("Entertainment and Utopia" 229).

## The problems and pleasures of positive images

In Dyer's analysis, films' mediation between reality and utopia signals the pleasurable if fundamentally conservative tendency of commercial entertainment forms: their incorporation of real-world struggle, dissatisfaction, and longing into narratives and images of energy and abundance. Such a description is premature, however, for films intended for audiences who have long been deprived of (or spared) fantasies of fulfillment. Lesbian audiences, for example, hardly suffer from a historical surplus of romantic and communal images featuring openly lesbian characters and settings. As such images do emerge, their cultural and political value—and their audiences' social and emotional investments—are keyed to a long history of symbolic marginalization. This is neither surprising nor problematic, but it may produce too great a faith in the power of "positive images." The question of positive lesbian images was raised early on by Edith Becker, Michelle Citron, Julia Lesage, and B. Ruby Rich in their co-authored essay "Lesbians and Film," a summary of the sorry state of lesbian portrayals in popular cinema, of the productive moves then underway by openly lesbian filmmakers, and of the place of lesbian pornography and erotica in the formation of a public and autonomous lesbian identity. The authors were prescient in their early critique of the "positive images" framework, and in re-reading their essay recently, I thought about all that has come to pass since 1981. Film scholars and critics have raised questions about what is "positive"—or not—about positive images, noted that "positive" is a context-specific quality (positive to whom? when? under what circumstances?), and argued that a positive-images approach to cultural criticism bespeaks a naïve commitment to absolute value and essential identity. I am hesitant, however, to dismiss the significance and utility of positive images, although, like Becker and her co-authors, I am concerned with the dense particularities of when and why an image becomes positive. "Positive" no longer means portraying members of historically marginalized groups in mainstream or high-status positions or simply rewriting the rules about who can and cannot be represented as a member of the social and symbolic club. "Positive images" are better understood, I think, as transformations of common sense through the progressive appropriation of popular forms. This redefinition signals a shift from the static logic of "good" role models (doctors, lawyers, elected officials) to a more dynamic articulation of symbolic value, in which goodness is liberated from conventions of status to become contingent on narrative context and identification and in which the social terms of goodness are themselves opened to question.

*Go Fish*, I argue, makes a number of such progressive appropriations through the mechanisms and operations of humor. In cinema, and at other moments in cultural practice, humor both reveals and produces intersubjectivity, a cultural mortar or strain of recognition and alliance among even the most tenuously related persons. As illustrations of the lesbian case apart from the film, consider two tales from the sapphic imaginary.

*One.* A couple of years ago I had the good fortune of an English holiday. After ten days of cream tea and romance, I returned to Philadelphia via the Continental Airlines hub in Newark, New Jersey. Arriving exhausted at the gate for the second leg of my return trip, I plunked down my book bag to wait out the layover. My attention was riveted, moments later, by an announcement over the public address system: "Kay-Dee-Lang, Kay-Dee-Lang, please meet your party at Gate 23." Always the vigilant cultural critic, impervious to the effect of popular celebrity, I fell apart. I was sitting at Gate 21, and 22 was across the concourse. Twenty-three couldn't be far. Face flushed, heart racing, I turned discreetly to my left. The electronic signboard at Gate 23 said San Francisco. Plausible. Didn't I read once that k. d. lang divides her time between Vancouver and the Bay Area? Still bound by an overidentification with critique, I sauntered toward Gate 23, pretending to stretch, to wander, to pass the time, but really just to catch an undetected, heart's-a-flutter glance at Miz Lang.

Well, there were no celebrities at Gate 23, but there was also no shortage of lesbians such as myself, wandering back and forth past the ticket counter like tropical fish meandering around a small tank. Despite our conspicuously similar t-shirts, haircuts, blazers, shoes, lambdas, and pink triangles, we struggled not to stare too hopefully down the concourse. Traveling-class women stricken by coolness, we treated each other like strangers, but I was smiling to myself, thinking about the wry announcer who had flushed out the dykes flying Continental that night. Were we a lesbian community? Hardly, but shared style and affect were working overtime at Gate 23.

*Two.* In their oral history of a working-class lesbian community, Elizabeth Lapovsky Kennedy and Madeline Davis chart the recollections of dozens of middle-aged and elderly women about the perils and grace of stepping out as butch and fem in the 1940s and 1950s in Buffalo, New York. It was an urban community under siege, well before Stonewall, where the women got by on modest resources and an abundance of grit and humor. Matty, one of the contributors to Kennedy and Davis's study, tells her own origin tale with a subversive nod to essentialist doctrine: "People ask me . . . when I tell them I've been gay all my life . . . 'How did you get to be gay all your life?' And I tell them the story. I say, 'Well you see, when I was born the doctor was so busy with my mother, it was a hard birth for her. . . . It was the nurse that slapped my ass to bring that first breath of life into me. And I liked the touch of that feminine hand so much that I've been gay ever since'" (348). Gay all her life, indeed, but it was the nurse's hand that did it, not fetal biology; Matty's recipe for making a lesbian calls for a sexual newborn sensitive to a gendered touch, and a slap to the ass, not the more maternal gestures of patting or cradling. I laughed out loud at Matty's story, loving her bristle and her sassy confidence about lesbian life, however marked it must have been by sadness and duress. I imagine the same qualities abundant in the communities of Kennedy and Davis's account—the mythic heroism of ordinary people, a psychological richness and energy produced against the grain of social indifference and brutality. To the cachet of lesbian in-jokes (ardor for k. d., for example), Matty's humor adds the survival value of refusal, wherein female desire replaces pathology as an explanation of lesbian origin.

*Go Fish* offers similar pleasures—of cachet and survival, of humor with a lesbian cast—and many lesbian viewers have received the film as being solidly by, for, and about a "lesbian nation." Nonlesbians, of course, are welcome to watch, and have done so in numbers enough to provoke crossover dreams—and anxieties—among lesbian moviegoers and critics (d'Erasmo), but lesbian audiences revel in the film's telling details of everyday life and sexual etiquette, not because others in the theater will not get the jokes (though many will not) but because those who will are likely to be lesbians.[3] Two male friends, for instance, one gay and one straight, recounted their confusion during festival screenings of *Go Fish*, when lesbian spectators fell into the aisles laughing as two characters prepared to consummate their romance by clipping each other's fingernails. For the men, it was an unconventional bit of business, charming, but not uproarious—a reaction suggesting that neither was attuned, at that spectatorial moment, to the public evocation of sexual hand play, male or female, gay or straight. But for lesbian viewers the foreplay was explicit, a gesture whose humor crystallized in the goofy slippage between sex and hygiene and the whimsical editing of a first-date montage. We do, after all, wear some of our sexual equipment naked, in public, at the ends of our sleeves, and engage such manual pickup techniques as comparing the diagonal width of our own hand with that of a prospective partner, speculating, under the coy bat of an eyelash, whether or not she'll fit. And, patiently or gruffly, we have lived through seductions interrupted midarousal by a girl getting up to trim her nails. In sexual practice, it may be an ill-timed annoyance ("Couldn't you have done that earlier?") but, projected as fantasy for public consumption, the gesture is metonymic, sparking a repertoire of lesbian signification with fragments as material and experiential as fingernails and midsex manicures. There is, of course, subcultural momentum in reading against the grain—where *Laverne and Shirley* and *Cagney and Lacy* become lesbian narratives; where a televised duet by Anne Murray and k. d. lang is just another Canadian love story; or where, in Barbara Smith's words, Toni Morrison's *Sula* "works as a lesbian novel" (3).[4] But under the press of symbolic annihilation, or even commercial chic, it remains true that there is delight and momentum in a grain of one's own, particularly when a narrative world appears to be sufficiently about one's self (the self one imagines and projects) that typifications seem fond, rather than lazy or cruel, and irony feels humane, rather than judgmental or self-hating.

It is rarely the case, however, that audiences make sense of humor from only one "inside" position (a position, that is, historically on the outside of mainstream commercial culture). Narratives offer multiple points of connection, and thus quite different audience segments are likely to make simultaneous claims to be insiders in the reception of humor. Some in the audience will find themselves cognitively in the dark, unmoved, while those around them laugh knowingly. But among those laughing there will be varied, perhaps incompatible motives, a jumble of funny bones tickled or made tender by different cultural materials, sometimes in the same scene. (Archie Bunker's appeal to both cultural liberals and conservatives was a case in point.) Thus the promise of inside recognition in humor may be partly illusory, or at least promiscuous. We may think the text is just for us (an especially enticing prospect among queers, for whom invisibility and enforced secrecy are reclaimed as knowledge), but others may think so too, others whom we imagine, at that moment, to be pointedly different from ourselves in at least one critical respect. The "we," finally, is rarely as univocal as our chorus of laughter implies. It is a fictional unity (though, for that, no less real), a suspension of uneven, crisscrossing multiplicities of cultural positions, inside and out.[5]

Thus my reading of community in and across Go Fish is framed by the pleasures and contradictions of humor. Along with other funny texts and other occasions of wit and irony among lesbians and lesbian characters (such as Matty's birthing story, microphone high jinks at the Newark Airport, Aerlyn Weissman and Lynne Fernie's film Forbidden Love [1992], Cheryl Dunye's video narratives, and Alison Bechdel's comic strip Dykes to Watch Out For, of which Go Fish is arguably the live-action version), the film relocates survival and ethos in epic and everyday acts of cultural production and refiguration. But as it does, it also raises hard questions about the limits of symbolic attachment in the struggle for social change.

## Genre

The role of humor in appropriating popular forms bears on a reading of Go Fish as an instance (and anti-instance) of that Hollywood staple genre, romantic comedy. In Go Fish, the generic conventions, transformations, and refusals typical of romantic comedy secure lesbian identity as unproblematic, while also challenging the heteronormative presumption of Hollywood romance (Wexman).

Set in Chicago, Go Fish opens in a women's studies classroom presided over by Kia. A college instructor in her early thirties, Kia is the oldest, sagest, and least impulsive of the film's five lesbian leads. She is also the lover of Evy, one of the five. Shortly after the classroom scene, we meet

Max (a.k.a. Camille) West, Kia's former student, her current apartment mate, and a self-described "lonely lesbo, lookin' for love." Through Kia, Max meets Ely, who shares an apartment with the coolly promiscuous Daria. Ely is chronically uneasy, a sensibility Daria attributes to her lapsed relationship with Kate, her long-distance lover (and another former student of Kia's), who never appears on screen. Kate "lives in Seattle" and Ely, we learn, has seen her only three times in two years. On several social occasions, Kia, Evy, and Daria make impatient but sisterly efforts to bring Max and Ely together. At first unimpressed by Ely's appearance and her nervous countenance, Max, a hip young thing in knee-length cut-offs, backward baseball cap, and Doc Martens, eventually comes around to Ely's attractions, and Ely summons the nerve for a romantic affair with Max. Amid the others' scheming, their documentary-style commentary, and a handful of everyday incidents, the two finally spend the night together, and the film ends with Max's joyful, no-nonsense appeal to the audience: "Don't let yourself forget," she tells us in voice-over, "the girl is out there."

The narrative hallmarks of romantic comedy are all there: conflicted desire, romantic awkwardness, internal and external barriers blocking the path to true love, and a marked contrast in persona and sensibility—first between Max and Ely, and later between them and the other characters —that makes the couple appear especially compatible in their quirky difference and thus destined for togetherness (Neale and Krutnik 132–73). But conventional romantic comedy ultimately produces heterosexual engagement (a qualification that has been routinely articulated in academic film criticism only within the last ten or so years), which makes *Go Fish* a romantic comedy with a twist. It appropriates narrative and stylistic gestures for women lovers, offering the audience both the comforting familiarity of genre (we know how these things turn out) and a new narrative context for lesbian characters, whose source of conflict is romance itself and not (hallelujah) lesbianism. Max, Ely, Kia, Evy, and Daria are sometimes stricken by youthful identity crises, family strife, and sexual uncertainty but not by shame or by essential doubt about their social and cultural legitimacy as lesbians.

Ely, for example, signals her delicate emotional guardedness in early interactions with Max, explaining (over a cup of herbal tea selected from the legions of boxes cluttering the foreground moments before) that indeed she has a girlfriend, who, uh, lives in Seattle, whom she hasn't seen in months, but, uh, with whom she has a "nonmonogamous" relationship. On the one hand, the description mixes all manner of lesbian self-irony: nonmonogamy as an earnest (if slightly tortured) challenge to conventional sexual propriety, the protective appeal to another woman somewhere on the planet (guarding against both commitment and the image of loneliness), and the ubiquitous "long-distance relationship," itself a modern condition aligned by sheer contemporanaeity with chic lesbian romance, a "Nineties" sort of thing. But while Ely's story marks her as a little tentative ("she thinks she's in a nonmonogamous relationship but really she's just lying on the sofa," jabs the film's publicity material), it does not mark lesbianism itself as neurotic or incomplete. There are other, contrasting practices among a range of lesbian characters, and Ely herself is transformed about halfway through the film toward boldness and romance by a butched-up kitchen haircut by Spike, another member (though not a lead) of the film's lesbian community. In this deceptively simple and marked-as-lesbian ritual, gone are Ely's hippie looks, replaced by a sharp mixture of shaved and straight and a healthy measure of lesbian attitude. What primes Ely, then, for love and humor in this romantic comedy is not lesbian disavowal (unlike, say, the denouement in *Personal Best*) but precisely the contrary: the intensification of a conspicuously lesbian style. Some of the endearing tentativeness remains, however, as Max encounters Ely in a local women's bookstore-café, barely recognizing her and then commenting that the cut looks good, that it looks butch. "Too butch?" Ely nervously asks. "Oh no, that's not what I meant," says Max, "yeah, the butch/fem thing, so oppressive." Their exchange marks sexual-political positions in lesbian communities (butch/fem vs. anti-gender role), along with Max's and Ely's momentary ambivalence. But the passing critique is visually contradicted by the butch/fem contrast between petite, curvy, and long-haired Max and tall, lean, short-haired Ely. This is especially true in the climactic love scene, as Max evolves from impish sprite to fem princess, her long hair released from the baseball cap and freshly wet from a predate shower, her body loosely draped in a silky robe. Max and Ely's palpable attraction, along with that between Kia and Evy and between Daria and her many lovers, humorously recuperates the sexual and romantic value of butch/fem difference. The romantic effort, moreover, is communal: Ely's and Max's friends gently nudge them toward connection, Spike cuts Ely's hair free of charge, and Daria proposes a potluck dinner party to give Max and Ely a chance to get together. Daria later presents Ely with a homemade cardboard heart after her first all-night date with Max. Unlike the usual familial objections in lesbian romance films (including *Desert Hearts*), the girls of the *Go Fish* community grease the wheels, happy to see Max and Ely lucky in love.[6] Although the audience may be denied the emotional excitement of romantic sabotage (will the lovers beat the opposition?) (Stacey), lesbian viewers can relax, knowing that Max and Ely will get there eventually, and enjoy a comedy of lesbian manners along the way. While Jackie Stacey argues in her insightful reading of *Desert Hearts* that the requirement of lesbian affirmation may override romantic tension and thus flatten a film's emotional effect, I would say that in *Go Fish* the genre pleasures of comedy enhance the emotional payoff alongside, not despite, the appealing predictability of Max and Ely's romantic success. In other words, the pleasure of the film is not diminished—and perhaps enhanced—by the audience's knowledge that Max and Ely will get together eventually.

*Go Fish*'s lesbian re-articulation of romantic comedy is thus "positive" because it invests romantic capital—long used to affirm characters as worthy—in unions that are elsewhere symbolically and socially excluded. In doing so, though, it also exposes the limits of convention, drawing some of its humor from a self-conscious commentary on the history of a film form long devoted to naturalizing heterosexuality. Late in the film, for example, when Ely leaves Max's apartment after their first night together, she gently pulls a blanket from frame-left to frame-right over Max's naked, sleeping body (as the camera pans with her in modeled and languorous close-up) and then lets herself out. A brief montage sequence shows Ely in the early morning sun with a grin on her face, a step-lightly gait, and a clenching of her elbows to signify "yes!" Diegetic sound fades under a Latin melody, returning only briefly to punctuate the scene with streetwise commentary—"congratulations, Ely!"—from passersby, playing on the youthful fantasy (and apprehension) that strangers can tell when someone has just had sex. It is the film's queer homage to *Singin' in the Rain* (1952) and *An American in Paris* (1951), along with dozens of other heterosexual falling-in-love musical sequences. Deployed so self-consciously, the montage "highlight[s] the 'otherness' of dominant culture" (Stacey 112). Midway between convention and parody, the style of the scene conveys the giddiness of lesbian romance, but it also exposes the absurd lengths to which Hollywood cinema has taken normative heterosexuality.

The effect of the montage sequence is similar to that of a campy series of nondiegetic inserts throughout *Go Fish* that simultaneously invoke feminist consciousness-raising groups, Greek choruses, and the over-the-top formation shots of swimmers or dancers in the musical production numbers of classic Hollywood. In these sequences, Kia, Evy, Daria, and Daria's lover of the moment lie on their backs in aerial close-up, in a row or in a circle with the tops of their heads pointing toward each other. For about a minute, and leaving behind spatial continuity with most of the film, the women discourse on sex and romance and their expressive idioms, debating, for example, whether (and why) "honey pot," "beaver," "love mound," or "cunt" is the preferable nickname for female genitalia. In form and dialogue, the sequences are hilarious, reminiscent of the sweet conspiracies of teenage girl-talk, of lesbian processing, and of hot and clumsy lesbian pornography (love mound?).

Other formal gestures signal the film's simultaneous evocation of and departure from contemporary genre convention, beginning with the selection of black-and-white stock. In combination with nondiegetic transitions, cropped compositions, instances of direct address to the camera, poetic voice-over, and nonreferential uses of sound, the monochromatic image addresses more than the budget constraints of an independent first feature. *Go Fish* presents itself as a romantic comedy *and* as an art film, at once inside and outside the genre mainstream. Such a strategy indicates a search for art-house as well as more general theatrical distribution and an appeal to a mixed audience of lesbians and others likely to be drawn to romantic narrative, to a text that speaks to questions and critiques of representation, or, in some instances, to both. These choices also can be understood in terms of the aesthetic desires of art school-trained film-makers (e.g., Troche and Kalin), but they are familiar strategies, perhaps necessary ones, for "crossover" success in the sharply targeted distribution of independent feature films.

What *Go Fish* preserves from traditional romantic comedy, however, is the happy ending. I do not accept that producers who represent their own nondominant identities, experiences, and communities ought to be bound by best-light, "positive-image" portrayals and restricted to good, moral characters and happy resolutions by mainstream standards. In political and representational practice, this is a form of assimilation that suppresses and thus stigmatizes (in this case as negatively queer) the struggling, fatigued, miserable, fearful, conflicted, contemptuous, irreverent, or just plain lackluster existence that everyone leads at least some of the time.[7] But, as I suggested earlier, it is precisely against the long history of such pathologized misery in dominant cinema that a happy lesbian ending, where girl gets girl, gains its momentum and generates effervescence.[8] Admittedly, in its conformity to the myth of romantic love, the ending can also be read as ideologically compromising, since it depicts a sociocultural position (lesbianism) defined in part by a refusal of dominant gender, sexual, and romantic standards. It remains true, though, that many lesbians in the audience, sexual radicals among them, will recognize aspects of their own practice in the serial monogamies of *Go Fish*. And alongside Ely and Max's more conventional relationship, Daria troubles the film's romantic compliance. As a happily, openly, unapologetically, and (the dialogue implies) safely promiscuous character, she extends the film's image of sexual possibility among women.

## A sense of place

Some comments about *Go Fish* from the lesbian diaspora (all dialogue guaranteed overheard):

> It's so Northampton (Massachusetts).
> It's so Philadelphia (Pennsylvania).
> It's so Brighton (Sussex, England).

What is it about a film vaguely set in Chicago that elicits attributions of locale from so many different places? My answer is that it is the image of city life that *Go Fish* presents, and the claiming (or reclamation) of lesbian space signaled by its forms of narration.

In *The Practice of Everyday Life*, Michel de Certeau aligns language and space, arguing that both languages and cities are characterized by recognizable systems. In the case of language, the system is grammar, and in the case of cities, a technocratically and architecturally rule-governed plan. But languages are always more than their grammars, and cities more than their plans. Language is uttered by speakers who are not grammarians, cities are traversed and inhabited by people disengaged from the technocracy of urban life, and both populations also create rhetorics against and resistance to the impositions of systems (Certeau 100).

In *Go Fish*, storytelling is harnessed to spatial trajectories in images of city life.[9] On the one hand, cities are familiar environments in the history of Hollywood cinema, although New York, not Chicago, is the paradigmatic location. City life is also a frequent setting in romantic comedy, and again New York is the most consistently mythologized example, a place where anything is possible for protagonists who are desirable but romantically incomplete. Images of city life in *Go Fish*, however, extend beyond the conventions of romantic comedy for lesbian and gay viewers, especially those personally or narratively party to the history of urban queer migration (D'Emilio; Chauncey), and here the resistant character of spatiality emerges.

As Charles Musser points out, a wealth of film historiography on the United States of the early-to-mid-twentieth century has explored the cinematic common ground of immigrant and city life (39–43). Both for those newly arrived in the United States and for US-born rural dwellers, American cities became culturally cacophonous venues, where newcomers were reconstituted as Others by a perilous nativism but also where they could try out new identities and practices. The port cities of New York and San Francisco became famous settings for lesbian and gay community formation in the United States, although, as innovative work in oral history, anthropology, and cultural geography shows, many other North American cities can tell similar stories.[10] As is true for other nondominant groups (constituted by race, class, ethnicity, nationality, religion, language, political commitment), cities are historically important places for queers, who found refuge in urban numbers and diversity and who, still, often have to go from country to city to encounter others like themselves. Alongside anomie and danger (and, in the United States, legislative and popular contempt), cities offer protection in the chance to be (relatively) spared surveillance of one's sexual nonconformism, to enjoy, potentially, the luxury of unselfconsciousness.

Indeed, the safety of *Go Fish*'s urban milieu, I would argue, is a big part of its communal sensibility and its humor, which both blossom in the film's protected and protective city enclaves. It is not unconflicted space,

but it is largely untroubled by some of the harsher realities of lesbian life
—queerbashing, misogyny, and, for some, racist contempt. To be sure,
nondominant communities also take root in rural and town locales
(northern New Mexico and Northampton, Massachusetts, for instance),
but cinematically, city life sets the stage for the dense imbrication of
intergroup and intragroup struggle and survival, as several recent
independent features illustrate (e.g., *Just Another Girl on the IRT* [1993],
*Mi Vida Loca* [1994], *Kids* [1995]).

*Go Fish*'s narrative is further spatialized and specialized by a repertoire
of stereotypically lesbian urban haunts. We first encounter Kia in her
women's studies classroom, raising questions to sometimes impatient
students about the history of lesbian (in)visibility. The names of openly—
or hopefully—lesbian public figures appear on the chalkboard, a list long
made famous (and mobile) by the chants and placards of Pride marches.
From the college scene, *Go Fish* winds episodically through the small,
shared walk-up apartments of its middle- and working-class characters,
through cafés and diners, women's bookstores and potluck get-togethers,
and finally to the rocky lakefront where Ely and Max smooch their way
through a lovers' stroll. In reality, these sorts of spaces are public and
private, both inside and outside the lesbian universe, but, attached to the
journeys and trajectories of the *Go Fish* women, the spaces—the troubling
as well as the comforting—are refigured as lesbian territory. The film's
depiction of generic lesbian enclaves (with familiar distributions of
commercial and noncommercial space), along with its placement of lesbian
characters in generic urban spaces, produces a nonspecific though recognizable synecdoche for "urban lesbian culture." It makes sense, then, that
*Go Fish* can offer nary an image or sound of Sussex yet remain "so
Brighton" for lesbian fans from that southern English city.

Some characters, more conspicuously than others, find themselves
crossing among many worlds, and this commute too is spatially represented.
Evy, for example, a bilingual Latina who switches fluently between English
and Spanish on the telephone, finds herself in a fight about lesbianism with
her ex-husband and her mother in her mother's home. Furious and upset,
Evy leaves, traveling on foot and by city bus to Kia and Max's apartment.
It is a thoughtful and uncertain journey, presented as a montage with an
unsubtitled Spanish voice-over of a conversation between a young girl
and an adult. Coinciding with the cross-town trip, the voice-over seems
to be an interior reflection on Evy's past and her present, one that marks
(in one way for those who understand Spanish, differently for those who
do not) the spatial distances she routinely travels and the cultural
environments and conflicts they map. As in this example, spaces in *Go
Fish* become readable as "lesbian" through a narrative articulation or
linking of spaces and movement to lesbian characters and through an
infusion of affect that also connects them to characters' most deeply felt

experiences (of pleasure and pain) as lesbians. Such connections heighten the emotional realism of place and the spatial realism of feeling, eliciting a poignant tension between the real world of the lesbian audience and the imaginary world of the film.

The image of a lesbian community with spaces of its own does indeed register "positively" in relation to the tiresome, pervasive portrayal of queers in straight settings in mainstream movies. Jonathan Demme's *Philadelphia* (1993), for example, which was hailed as an open-minded breakthrough in popular narratives of the AIDS crisis, tells the story of Andrew Beckett, an ambitious and promising young gay attorney fired from a top law firm in Philadelphia under the unspoken suspicion that he has AIDS. After nine other firms decline to represent Beckett in an employment discrimination suit, his case is finally accepted (if none too readily) by a consciously homophobic independent attorney. Throughout *Philadelphia*, Beckett is placed in conspicuously heteronormative (though often homosocial) spaces, including the law firm, its senior partners' preferred steam baths, the office of the independent attorney, a hospital emergency room (and later a ward), a courtroom, and the home of his parents and family. He is shown receiving regular intravenous medication in an apparently "gay" clinic (populated by many young men, some with Kaposi's lesions visible on their faces), but we never see—indeed cannot see if we are to accept the film's premise—any community-based legal centers. Where, in Beckett's search for representation, are the legal service organizations for people with AIDS, long established by gay communities of all colors in urgent and heroic response to the ongoing AIDS crisis? Not in *Philadelphia*, though certainly in Philadelphia. It takes, then, some self-abnegating suspension of disbelief on the part of gay folks, people with AIDS, and AIDS activists for *Philadelphia*'s story to work. Or it takes an audience well outside those groups. That, of course, was precisely the point: to produce a high-budget, popular-appeal film about a (privileged, white) man with AIDS but principally for a straight and HIV-negative audience. People with AIDS, of course, are invited to watch along.

*Go Fish*, a no-budget production by *Philadelphia* standards, does things differently, claiming its spaces, characters, and structures of feeling as deeply and socially "lesbian." Ironically, however, this articulation of group and place extends the film's address to both lesbian and nonlesbian audiences. For lesbian viewers, it preserves the humor of romantic comedy, making it possible for them to laugh, not bristle, at the characters' foibles and rocky romantic progress. However, that same framing largely sets aside the enduring struggles of all queers (though of some more than others) in a heterosexist and homophobic universe. Within the protected enclaves of this "lesbian community," heterosexual viewers are spared visible signs of heterosexist complicity. They can read the film as a charming tour through usually closed territory, where the comic pleasures of romance and friendship are largely uninterrupted by pointed political critiques or by the raised fists of queer activism, gestures that might implicate even those straight folks interested enough to attend a lesbian independent feature. Perhaps this is partly why *Go Fish* attracted a mainstream audience; framed as travelogue to and through the exotic, its genre and setting may offer more crossover potential than its lesbian in-jokes prohibit.

Finally, *Go Fish*'s textured and evocative visual and musical transitions also contribute to the film's lesbian identity. The images include a wooden top spinning in extreme close-up on a checkerboard, connoting the contingent nature of lesbian identity, always in motion in a landscape of social possibility; three thin columns of white paint dripping on to a dark, flat surface (as though poured or spilled from just above the frame); candle flames flickering in slow-motion close-up; hands plunging into water to the amplified and elongated sound of a synthesized cymbal crash; instrumental phrases clipped from Latin melodies; a grainy, sunlit, slow-motion and low-angled image of a black child flying through the air on a skateboard; and cream hitting coffee in clear glass. The images are tactile, ephemeral, and intimate, paying fond attention to the sentience of everyday life and homage to a tradition of feminist filmmaking that locates experience (particularly women's experience, if not always so fondly) in domestic environments and the unspectacular (Kuhn 150). The images are sensual, inviting viewers to taste the creamy coffee, to plunge their hands somewhere warm and wet, to dance and spin with the euphoric, childlike motion of the top.

In their marked presence and in their signification of sex, femaleness, and Latin rhythms, the transitions contribute to *Go Fish*'s poetic discourse on the complex and contingent nature of cultural identification, and this too is part of the film's utopic and thus unifying foundation. The quirky and artful transitions energize *Go Fish* and heighten our view of the characters' capacity to act on their own behalf and ours, even during the film's one scene of street hostility. In a grainy daylight exterior, shot in slow motion, Kia keeps a steady pace on foot while looking over her shoulder to shout "fuck you" to a man, off-screen, who has just called her a "fuckin' dyke." The harassment is routine but the unafraid response is triumphant, the stuff of both plausibility and fantasy for a beleaguered audience of lesbians—and others—attuned to the daily indignities of public contempt.

## Cultural difference

In the liberal utopian spirit of cultural diversity, the *Go Fish* women are an appealingly multicultural group: Kia is African-American and Evy is Latina, and although the national origin of Evy's family is not declared, director Troche's own Puerto Rican background moves me to think of Evy's mother as Island-born as well. Daria, Max, and Ely are all European American. Among the lead characters, class positions, if not origins, level off at lower- and middle-income upward mobility, marked by apartment settings that are attractive (but not cinematically plush) and come equipped with such pleasures as appliances, sound systems, and good kitchen knives. College experience also suggests relative cultural and economic capital; all the leads have some, and Kia, a college teacher, has presumably been through graduate school.[11] Finally, sequences of nongenre style in *Go Fish* mark its address, in part, to college-educated audiences with relatively specialized tastes in cinema. The women dress stylishly and inexpensively, making and remaking their looks through a charming assortment of thrift-shop retrogarb, denim cut-offs, wool blazers, Doc Martens, baseball caps, and the occasional leather jacket. *Go Fish* presents styles reminiscent of the subtle variations that come with a group of women whose ages, in the early 1990s, span the half-generation from mid-twenties to mid-thirties and whose sexual identities roughly align with fem or butch.

In this lively cultural universe, difficult questions and conflicts about gender run parallel to romantic caution and intrigue. Indeed, some of *Go Fish*'s most compelling moments broach these questions, including an anti-genre montage sequence about halfway through the film that shows Max seated to write and then visually interprets her prose. In the sequence, leads and extras don jeans, then bridal gowns and veils set atop the conspicuously sharp edges of lesbian hairstyles. They face the lens, line up behind each other, and then step out of line, move toward and away from the camera, trade perfunctory kisses in various combinations, and drop wedding lace off their shoulders, revealing bare breasts, all to the accompaniment of Max's poetic voice-over, which ends with the statement, "I'm not waiting for a man, I just hate this eerie feeling that a man's waiting for me." Throughout the sequence, Max voices her fear of waking some day to discover herself heterosexual and married to an honest and devoted man who likes the fact that she has "tried everything and still has chosen him." What if she can't quite weather the concealments so often imposed on lesbian life or their flip side, the risks of exposure? What will become of her desire for an unselfconscious kiss in the supermarket or of the unambiguous use of gendered pronouns and phrases such as "really good friend"? The scene evokes the delicate, creeping ambivalences still inscribed on lesbian identification by heterosexual dominance, ambivalences many of us feel but find awkward or painful to acknowledge for fear of personal failure and community betrayal. The non-narrative style of the sequence, moreover, suits its thematic queries, pulling the film away from romantic comedy and into gender and sexual critique.

*Go Fish*'s poignant lesbian insights raise other questions about cultural identity, particularly around race, ethnicity, and interracial attraction, but these questions are not so directly addressed. They are present (if not as markedly for the white characters) in the Latin score and the very fact of Evy and Kia's romance, first signaled by a languorous close-up of two pairs of naked feet—Kia's dark ones and Evy's lighter ones—standing face to face. They are also present in the unsubtitled uses of Spanish, first by Evy, her mother, and Evy's ex-husband, Junior, and again in the reflective voice-over conversation as an angry and worried Evy makes her way back from her mother's apartment to Kia's. But unlike the sex-gender queries made explicit in voice-over and on screen, racial and ethnic identification are dealt with subtly in Go Fish, not in the narrative but in the film's mise-en-scène (see Rich, "Difference," 326). There, racial and ethnic difference is visible, but the characters do not speak it, at least not directly. It is as though there is no room, in a movie about lesbians, for taking on other social and cultural positions despite their simultaneity in everyday life. It is also as though Evy and Kia, the only lead characters who are not white, are presumed to understand each other as women of color, setting aside the cultural tensions that might well surface amid their love and solidarity "in the very house of difference" (Lorde). The genre boundaries of romantic comedy and the film's utopian narrative of community-as-sanctuary limit direct expressions of dissent or antagonism among the five leads.[12]

There is, however, ethnic difference and interethnic tension in the film's gender dialogues, for example, when Evy arrives at Kia and Max's apartment, fresh from her fight with her mother and Junior. Junior outed Evy, whose mother then told her to leave the house and never come back. Hearing the news, Max frames Evy's problem as gender war. Of Junior, she says "the guy's a jerk, let's get him, let's take him out," little recognizing that, at the moment, Junior is the least of Evy's worries. It is her mother who concerns her, and she just wants the nattering Max to shut up. "Don't worry," says Max, "we can be your family now." The comment is well intended but ill considered, a failure to understand Evy's anger and confusion in losing her mother's respect and support. Inter-generational conflict, moreover, is made particularly complex in Evy's expressively Catholic and partly immigrant family, a scenario that exposes the WASPish impulse in Max's response. Max may not be wrong, perhaps, but her one-dimensional gender critique goes too short a distance toward understanding Evy's anxiety.

The relegation of race representation and interracial antagonism to the mise-en-scène perhaps spares Go Fish's many white lesbian fans the discomfort of complicity, the sense that we too participate in a social world that consistently imposes white dominance while denying or underrating its historical and everyday effects. Evy's fight with her mother, moreover, relocates the most pointed and visible moment of antagonism away from the film's interracial lesbian community, depositing it instead in the intraracial milieu of an "ethnic" and working-class family. Like many typifications, the scene is plausible and may even resemble some viewers' experiences—but that does not wholly transform its stereotypical meanings.

I do not offer this analysis to deny the multicultural character and value of (some) nonfictional lesbian communities, including the one that produced *Go Fish*. Perhaps that is where Turner, Troche, and their collaborators worked through some of the likely struggles that are utopically absent from the film. Nor must every text accomplish all narrative and cultural possibilities. I do, however, want to query the dangers, for lesbian representation, of romantic comedy's generic pleasures, especially where they subdue race and class critique. In *Go Fish*, the humor relies on the film's utopian sensibility, its image of "how things could be" in a lesbian-identified community that is at once multicultural (marked by visible and audible difference) and racially and economically unconflicted. This is perhaps a necessary strategy in a film so fondly regarded by many for its representation of a historically invisible character type: the happy lesbian in love. In the very gesture of presenting that type, though, *Go Fish* becomes a political text, and thus it makes sense to ask a political question: How, in an alternative scenario, might race and class critique openly reframe lesbian humor and romance?[13]

## Sexual conflict, sexual practice

Not all forms of community conflict, however, are evacuated from *Go Fish*; indeed, such conflict moves into high relief in a scene I call "Sex Cops." The scene opens with an aerial medium shot of Daria naked in bed with someone whose face and torso are identifiable as male. The two kiss, stroke, and press against each other, and then the film cuts to Daria, dressed, walking through her neighborhood. Almost immediately, she is accosted in slow motion by two figures, who cover her mouth and pull her to the scene of an interrogation. In a pointed reversal of who poses a threat to a lone woman on the street at night, the captors and inquisitors are themselves lesbians (though not Max, Ely, Kia, or Evy, preserving solidarity among the five leads), and almost all hold Daria in contempt for sleeping with a man and still calling herself a dyke.

Here again, *Go Fish* isolates conflict in nonrealist style. In a swirling and tightly edited five minutes of hand-held head shots (which some viewers read as Daria's bad dream), the scene delivers a thick wash of lesbian sexual polemic. One by one, the women voice a string of accusatory questions and one-liners, each coming sharp on the heels of the one before, and Daria responds with matched verve and clarity amid the high-contrast surveillance of the interrogation spotlight:

COP 1: What do you think you're doing?

COP 2: It makes me sick.

DARIA: Does it make you sick, or does it just scare you?

COP 3: Just don't call yourself something that you're not.

DARIA: If you're talking about me calling myself a lesbian, that's what I am.

. . .

COP 1: You mean you want to go out and get some dick?

DARIA: I'm not talking, like, commitment here. I'm talking about sex.

COP 2: There is no such thing as just sex.

. . .

DARIA: I had sex with one man. You know, if a gay man has sex with a woman, he was bored, drunk, lonely, whatever, and if a lesbian has sex with a man, her whole life choice becomes suspect. I think it's bullshit, I think you all are giving men way too much importance.

. . .

COP 1: She's cute enough, but if I thought she would have a sudden urge to have sex with a man while I was dating her, I'd say forget it.

DARIA: If you and I were in some committed relationship, I wouldn't be having sex with anyone but you.

COP 5: But who's to say this little whim won't pop up again?

DARIA: I don't cheat on people.

The Sex Cops dialogue offers a virtual inventory of lesbian sexual conflict, each objection teetering on the shaky ground of sexual difference: phallic desire versus antiphallic contempt, sexual autonomy ("just sex") versus sexual dependency ("no such thing"), libertinism versus community standard, pleasure versus attachment, purity versus contamination, identity versus practice.

The scene preserves Daria's faith in herself and her commitments to women despite the contradictions of what it means to be a lesbian ("I'm a lesbian who had sex with a man"). Though some among the sex cops are skeptical of the interrogation ("Why is everyone acting like it's the end of the world?"), most weigh in against Daria, and some are prepared to banish her from their circle. The scene also speaks to the raw materials of lesbian identity: sexual practice and resistance, ideation, women's solidarity, and love. There is a queerness in it, a sensitivity to contradiction that leaves room for those devout lesbians whose pasts and fantasies are impure, with no regrets, and whose political wariness is pricked by the voice of a sexual Big Sister.

At the same time, the Sex Cops conflict is never resolved, which is as it must be. The interrogation ends, and Daria, a little rattled, leaves the group to return to her place in the aerial chorus. It was neither puritanism nor simple gender repression that moved the Sex Cops to question Daria's choices in the first place or that made this stylized, sometimes disturbing scene believable to me. Instead, I read in its address some of the same anxieties voiced in the bridal sequence: How and where does one find the clarity and conviction to claim rather than refuse the contingencies and insecurities of life outside the mainstream? To survive the pressures and impositions of sexual domination and the still more imposing voice of Big Brother? Some might find a haven in an impermeable lesbian identity, but, in refusing to settle its own questions, *Go Fish* offers a more "postmodern" (or perhaps just more realistic) vision of living with contingency, irresolution, uncertainty, even conflict, of seeing them too as lesbian raw material, the stuff and strength of which queer lives are made. And in the end, it is Daria whose response offers what I consider the most radical potential. Amid her recuperation of serial monogamy and her defensive (if implicit) valuation of "romance" over "cheating," Daria calls lesbianism a "life choice"—not genetic destiny and asserts that the others are "giving men way too much importance." Her statement resists sexual essentialism (in which lesbianism enforces a unilateral sexual attraction to women) while also claiming the specificity and thus autonomy of lesbian desire and identification, which can be neither defined nor dislodged merely by sexual play with men.[14]

The mixed valences of the Sex Cops sequence work for me because they are not the sum total of sexual discourse in *Go Fish*. They arise alongside the film's ample (if tame) depictions of lesbian sex. Some, like nail clipping, are allusive, while others are more explicit, if still vanilla. But the film does make room for sleeping around, for having sex apart from making love, for sweet and arousing close-ups of pierced nipples, open mouths, and tangled tongues, for that lightness of step that comes from finally getting laid, and for lots of fascinated talk about sex, though it may be more gushy than hot. There are bare crotches, backs, and asses, and even some sexy and silly crosscutting between breaking bread and spreading thighs, as Ely prepares dinner while Daria goes down on a lover. Though there is compelling eroticism in the image of insatiability, there is also some sexy relief in *Go Fish*'s quirks, its easy sexual variation, and its musical and kinetic rhythms. It is against this sultry ground of eroticism that the Sex Cops sequence acquires its comic effect. The peremptory one-liners become auto-ironic—self-parodies of lesbian high-mindedness and sexual control (to wit, "I don't think she's strong enough to be a dyke" and "You just can't stay away from that dick." Ouch!). This is one of the strengths of *Go Fish*: to take on, not eschew, the sexual-political overdeterminations of lesbian life. It is a strategy that further aligns *Go Fish* with *Comedy in Six Unnatural Acts*, its cinematic ancestor of some twenty years earlier. Richard Dyer writes of Oxenberg's film,

There is no fixed strategy in *Comedy*. It plays equally with movie images, traditional sub-cultural styles and lesbianfeminist ideals; it is equally prepared to appropriate movie styles to celebrate lesbianism ... or to mock straight perceptions. The self-confidence of affirmation politics makes such an assured examination possible, so much so that there is no need to roundly condemn anything or assert unproblematically positive alternatives. What is positive about the film is its assumption that lesbians are strong enough to be able to work with and against definitions of themselves, strong enough to have humor, even at their own expense.

(*Now You See It* 280–81)

Framed in Dyer's terms, humor becomes a political resource, not in the simple sense of self-recognition through targeted comedy but as a powerful mix of engagement and detachment that enables members of nondominant groups to live, observe, and potentially transform (not merely endure) the rigors of subaltern life (Mindess 49).

## Conclusion: contingent communities

My reading of the coordinates of story, style, and extrafilmic discourse that animate *Go Fish* as lesbian romantic comedy and connect it to lesbian-identified audiences starts from the idea that the boundaries of community are permeable. These boundaries are imagined in the film partly through bids for comic recognition—the cachet and currency of in-jokes, of visual, verbal, and gestural references that, when they appear at all in mainstream sources, are likely to be both underdeveloped and overendowed with stereotypical significance. While it would be tempting to imagine a unitary and unifying model of community in lesbian cinema that could be a rallying point for lesbian audiences, filmmakers, and other cultural producers at a particular moment, I do not think it could stand as an autonomous model of a form. Subaltern representations and meanings emerge in relation to the sticky conditions of domination, acquiescence, resistance, and struggle among nondominant groups. This is a historical relation that demands a historical analysis of what articulates texts and audiences in a given time and place.

Go Fish has its lesbian detractors, women who find the film juvenile, trivial, and insufficiently serious about women's oppression, who see in it no narrative reflection of their own lives, who are neither amused by it nor happy about its crossover potential. "This," they ask, "is us? Hardly."[15] Still others have been annoyed by the film's stylized and self-conscious moments. Such reactions, juxtaposed with the positive reception of *Go Fish* in print and in art houses and malls in several countries and many regions, are reminders that claims and appeals to an "authentic" lesbian subject are fraught. Such claims have a strategic place—in some (though not all) moments of social, cultural, and political mobilization; in recognition of the tax that heterosexist societies still levy on queerness each and every living hour; and in attempts to make space for new cultural repertoires, new producers, and new audiences. To project that strategic truth as an essential one that fixes the contours of lesbian life and identity, however, is to trade an old fiction (lesbians are bad, ill, damaged, lost) for a new one (lesbians are good, healthy, natural, the wave of the future for women). Such a counternarrative may be appealing in some contexts, but it is ultimately no less prescriptive, no more open, progressive, or sensitive to the contingency of lived practice and history (Hall).

Lesbian communities *and* lesbian cinema both would be well served, I think, by following the lead of *Go Fish*'s recognition of solidarity as a spatial and temporal condition (people coming together at certain places and times), of conflict as a producer of clarity and even good faith along with its agonies (in contrast to the faux alliances and limited comfort that so often emerge from effaced or evaded conflict), of the power of conjoining humor at one's own expense and the rare joy of lesbian address. Such conditions do not promise that something will be funny to anyone in particular, nor do they guarantee an image of a community that all lesbians would want to join. Rather, they demonstrate how representation can be contextualized to accomplish social and political insight, to connect it to the urgency of everyday life, and to set it in motion in the world beyond the text. This, for me, is the promise—incomplete, but real—of *Go Fish*, as one moment in the ongoing struggle over interpretation, a struggle that those of us with nondominant subjectivities depend on for our survival.

## Notes

This essay is reprinted from *Signs: Journal of Women in Culture and Society*, Vol. 25, No. 1. (Autumn, 1999), pp. 37–64. © 1999 by the University of Chicago.

My thanks to the many people who have responded to this essay at conferences and invited lectures, particularly Carole Spitzack and Kathryn Cirksena. Thanks also to Linda Schmidt at the Samuel Goldwyn Company for the script and videotape of *Go Fish*, to graduate students in my seminar on the politics of sexual representation at the University of Massachusetts, and to the following friends and colleagues for their readings, comments, anecdotes, and one-liners: Marty Allor, Carolyn Anderson, Dianne Brooks, Mary Conway, Norman Cowie, Barbara Cruikshank, Richard Dyer, John Emi, Steven Feld, Jocelyn Geliga-Vargas, Lynda Goldstein, Larry Gross, Janice Irvine, Leola Johnson, Eugene Michaud, Michael Morgan, Cindy Patton, Deborah Porter, Deidre Pribram, Pamela Sankar, Hannah Schwartzchild, Scott Tucker, Sharon Ullman, and Nan Woodruff. Thanks, finally, to the *Signs* editors and editorial staff for their careful assistance and to two anonymous reviewers for their insights.

1  Only a minority of queers have easy access to film festivals; thus theatrical distribution remains as important a concern as production in discussions of the range of portrayals available to different audiences. For an introduction to writings about the new queer cinema, see Halberstam; Rich, "New Queer Cinema"; Gever, Greyson, and Parmar; and White, "Queer Publicity." For a longer view of the history of lesbian and gay cinema, see Dyer, *Now You See It*, and for comment and reflection on the work (including *Go Fish*) of executive producer Christine Vachon, see Abramovitch.

2  For a discussion of lesbian typification in *Comedy in Six Unnatural Acts*, see Rich, "Goings and Comings."

3  Shortly after *Go Fish*'s release, the *New Yorker* described writer/actor Guinevere Turner's skepticism about the film's crossover potential: "Her uncertainty, she says, has to do with a lot of the jokes, which she sees as lesbian in-jokes—one about female anatomy and about how lesbians never break up. And then there's the scene in which Max comments on the ragged state of Ely's fingernails. 'The average person doesn't get that,' Ms. Turner said. 'Lesbians use their hands a lot, so bad fingernails—that's a really terrible thing'" (41).

4  On *Laverne and Shirley*, see Doty. On *Cagney and Lacey*, see D'Acci.

5  A Jewish friend and colleague recently pointed out that "inside" responses to film humor are also matters of degree. He described attending Woody Allen's *Radio Days* (1987) with a non-Jewish date in a university town with a small Jewish community. His date laughed at the jokes, but he laughed bigger and sooner and ended up feeling, he told me, like he was wearing a neon yarmulke in a sea of affectlessness.

6  *Go Fish* does include one scene of family hostility to lesbianism, in which Evy has a fight with her ex-husband and her mother (and which I discuss in a later section). However, Evy's relationship with Kia is not the central romance of the film; Max and Ely's is, and toward them there is none of the usual family conflict. On the relative absence of images of lesbian communities in cinema, especially in films organized around coming out stories and lesbian romance, see Straayer, esp. chap. 2. Straayer cites *Go Fish* as an exception to this trend (294, n. 23).

7  Indeed, extending its reflexive consciousness, *Go Fish* directly takes up the discourse of positive and negative images of queerness in a pointed conversation between Max and Ely following their first date at a queer film. In the conversation Max is impatient with the image of neurosis she has just witnessed, though Ely notes that indeed there are unhappy gay people, so filmmakers should be able to tell their stories too. Reflecting discursive politics in many extrafilmic queer settings, the positions are laid out but not resolved.

8  For a useful, if dismaying, inventory of lesbian and gay pathology in Hollywood cinema, see Russo.

9  For two excellent studies of narrative, gender, and spatiality, the first about the early twentieth-century films of Italian filmmaker Elvira Notari and the second about butch lesbians in literature, see Bruno and Munt.

10  For more on the history of lesbian and gay urban communities, see Franzen; Kennedy and Davis; Newton; Beemyn; and the film *Forbidden Love* (a 1992 documentary [with dramatic sequences] by Aerlyn Weissrnan and Lynne Fernie, from Studio D of the National Film Board of Canada). For a comprehensive study of the relationship between gay men and urban space, see Chauncey, esp. chaps 7, 9, and 12.

11  For a discussion of how class positions and mobility are signaled through nondialogic conventions in cinema, see Anderson. See Bettie for a provocative

analysis of where class tropes may be found in popular texts that appear not to address social class questions.

12 The film's race discourses are also expressed, implicitly, in the character of Kia. She is a somewhat maternal figure—older than the others and wiser, schooling her friends both in the classroom and in affairs of the heart. She is a wonderful and patient friend, but as the only African-American woman, and as a voluptuous and affectionate character as well, Kia is also reminiscent of the Hollywood mammy, which in some instances becomes an overtone of her role in *Go Fish*. This is least true, I think, in her interactions with Evy, and most true in those with Max, her younger, smaller, white, and more conspicuously feminine friend, whose romantic ambitions and tactics Kia nurtures without ever being nurtured in return. I'm not sure whether to regard the mammy overtones as troubling or as a send-up, or both.

13 A similar critique has been made of the 1995 summer release *The Incredibly True Adventures of Two Girls in Love*, in which one member of the protagonist teenage couple is African-American and the other is white. It is part of that film's strategy to present but not problematize the racial difference between the two characters, except to reverse the stereotypical class positions of each: the white woman is working class and the black woman upper middle class. A more sustained attempt to raise race and class questions is made in *Forbidden Love*, which mixes documentary and dramatic sequences. Its articulation of racial difference and hierarchy, however, comes through only in the documentary testimony. Finally, for discussions and examples of how humor is constituted through race, class, and gender idioms, see Jewelle Gomez and the comedy performances of Marga Gomez, which explore national, ethnic, gender, class, and sexual identification among New York Puerto Rican lesbian characters. Cheryl Dunye's independent feature *Watermelon Woman* (1997) may also be a place to return to these questions in narrative fiction film.

14 For a theoretical exploration of how lesbianism can be disarticulated from male norms of definition and representation, see de Lauretis.

15 I would like to be able to cite published accounts of such responses to *Go Fish*, but I have encountered them only in various spoken exchanges among lesbians discussing the film. At a presentation of this paper at the 1996 annual meeting of the International Communication Association in Chicago, however, feminist scholar Kathryn Cirksena mentioned that she had not liked the film, which she found precious and remarkably unaware of its own cinematic and political history. Cirksena's comments reminded me that generation—and the historical valences attached to it—has been the most consistent factor in negative responses to *Go Fish*. It isn't quite a matter of young dykes liking the film and middle-aged ones disliking it (at 41, I am myself middle-aged, and I liked the film very much). But to the extent that it appears that way, I, like Cirksena, locate the difference in the film's treatment (or nontreatment) of history, especially feminist history.

## Works cited

Abramovitch, Ingrid. "Godmother to the Politically Committed Film." *New York Times*, 21 July 1996: 18.

Anderson, Benedict. *Imagined Communities: Reflections on the Origin and Spread of Nationalism*. London: Verso, 1983.

Anderson, Carolyn. "Diminishing Degrees of Separation: Class Mobility in Movies of the Reagan-Bush Era." In *Beyond the Stars*, Vol. 5, *Ideology in American*

*Popular Film*. Ed. P. Loukides and L. K. Fuller. Bowling Green, Ohio: Popular Press, 1996: 141–63.

Becker, Edith, Michelle Citron, Julia Lesage, and B. Ruby Rich. "Lesbians and Film." In *Out in Culture: Gay, Lesbian, and Queer Essays on Popular Culture*. Ed. Corey K. Creekmur and Alexander Doty. Durham, NC and London: Duke University Press, 1995: 25–43.

Beemyn, Brett (ed.). *Creating a Place for Ourselves: Lesbian, Gay, and Bisexual Community Histories*. New York: Routledge, 1997.

Bettie, Julie. "Class Dismissed? *Roseanne* and the Changing Face of Working Class Iconography." *Social Text* 45 (1995): 125–50.

Bruno, Giuliana. *Streetwalking on Ruined Map: Cultural Theory and the City Films of Elviva Notari*. Princeton, NJ: Princeton University Press, 1993.

Certeau, Michel de. *The Practice of Everyday Life*. Berkeley: University of California Press, 1988.

Chauncey, George. *Gay New York: Gender, Urban Culture, and the Making of the Gay Male World, 1890–1940*. New York: Basic, 1994.

D'Acci, Julie. *Defining Women: Television and the Case of "Cagney and Lacey."* Chapel Hill: University of North Carolina Press, 1994.

de Lauretis, Teresa. *The Practice of Love: Lesbian Sexuality and Perverse Desire*. Bloomington: Indiana University Press, 1994.

——"Sexual Indifference and Lesbian Representation." In *The Lesbian and Gay Studies Reader*. Ed. Henry Abelove, Michele Aina Barale, and David M. Halperin. New York: Routledge, 1993: 141–58.

D'Emilio, John. *Sexual Politics, Sexual Communities: The Making of a Homosexual Minority in the United States, 1940–1970*. Chicago: University of Chicago Press, 1983.

d'Erasmo, Stacey. " 'Go Fish' Lands a Big One." *Out* 13 (June 1994): 47–48.

Doty, Alexander. *Making Things Perfectly Queer: Interpreting Mass Culture*. New York: Routledge, 1993.

Dyer, Richard. "Entertainment and Utopia." *Movies and Method*. Vol. 2. Ed. Bill Nichols. Berkeley: University of California Press, 1985: 220–32.

——*Now You See It: Studies on Lesbian and Gay Film*. New York and London: Routledge, 1990.

Franzen, Trisha. "Differences and Identities: Feminism and the Albuquerque Lesbian Community." *Signs: Journal of Women in Culture and Society* 18 (1993): 891–906.

Gever, Martha, John Greyson, and Pratibha Parmar (eds). *Queer Looks: Perspectives on Lesbian and Gay Film and Video*. New York and London: Routledge, 1993.

Gomez, Jewelle. "In the Telling." *Forty-Three Septembers: Essays*. Ithaca, NY: Firebrand, 1993.

Halberstam, Judith. "Some Like It Hot: The New Sapphic Cinema." *The Independent* 15 (1992): 26–29, 43.

Hall, Stuart. "New Ethnicities." In *Stuart Hall: Critical Dialogues in Cultural Studies*. Ed. David Morley and Kuan-Hsing Chen. London: Routledge, 1996: 44–49.

Kennedy, Elizabeth Lapovsky, and Madeline D. Davis. *Boots of Leather, Slippers of Gold: The History of a Lesbian Community*. New York: Penguin, 1993.

Kuhn, Annette. *Women's Pictures: Feminism and Cinema*. London: Routledge & Kegan Paul, 1982.

Lorde, Audre. *Zami: A New Spelling of My Name*. Trumansburg, NY: Crossing, 1982.

Mayne, Judith. "Lesbian Looks: Dorothy Arzner and Female Authorship." In *How Do I Look? Queer Film and Video*. Ed. Bad Object Choices. Seattle: Bay, 1991: 103–43.

Mindess, Harvey. *Laughter and Liberation*. Los Angeles: Nash, 1971.

Munt, Sally. "The Lesbian Flaneur." In *Mapping Desire: Geographies of Sexualities*. Ed. David Bell and Gill Valentine. London: Routledge, 1995: 114–25.

Musser, Charles. "Ethnicity, Role-Playing, and American Film Comedy: From Chinese Laundry Scene to Whoopee (1894–1930)." In *Unspeakable Images: Ethnicity and the American Cinema*. Ed. Lester D. Friedman. Champaign: University of Illinois Press, 1991: 39–81.

Neale, Steven, and Frank Krutnik. *Popular Film and Television Comedy*. New York: Routledge, 1990.

*New Yorker*. "A Couple of Lesbians, Sitting around Talking (Mostly about Their Film)." *New Yorker* 9 May 1994: 40–41.

Newton, Esther. *Cherry Grove, Fire Island: Sixty Years in America's First Gay and Lesbian Town*. Boston: Beacon, 1993.

Rich, B. Ruby. "Goings and Comings." *Sight and Sound* 4 (July 1994): 14–16.

——"The New Queer Cinema." *Sight and Sound* 2 (September 1992): 30–34.

——"When Difference Is (More Than) Skin Deep." In Gever, Greyson, and Parmar: 318–39.

Russo, Vito. *The Celluloid Closet: Homosexuality in the Movies*. Rev. ed. New York: Harper, 1987.

Smith, Barbara. "Toward a Black Feminist Criticism." *Conditions* 2 (1977): 25–44.

Stacey, Jackie. " 'If You Don't Play, You Can't Win': *Desert Hearts* and the Lesbian Romance Film." In *Immortal, Invisible: Lesbians and the Moving Image*. Ed. Tamsin Wilton. New York and London: Routledge, 1995: 92–114.

Straayer, Chris. *Deviant Eyes, Deviant Bodies: Sexual Reorientations in Film and Video*. New York: Columbia University Press, 1996.

Wexman, Virginia Wright. *Creating the Couple: Love, Marriage, and Hollywood Performance*. Princeton, NJ: Princeton University Press, 1993.

White, Patricia. "Female Spectator, Lesbian Spectre: *The Haunting*." In *Inside/Out: Lesbian Theories, Gay Theories*. Ed. Diana Fuss. New York: Routledge, 1995: 142–72.

——(ed.). "Queer Publicity: A Dossier on Lesbian and Gay Film Festivals." *GLQ: A Journal of Lesbian and Gay Studies* 5 (1999): 73–93.

——"Supporting Character: The Queer Career of Agnes Moorehead." In *Out in Culture: Gay, Lesbian, and Queer Essays on Popular Culture*. Ed. Corey K. Creekmur and Alexander Doty. Durham, NC, and London: Duke University Press, 1995: 91–114.

# Chapter 9

# Chica flicks

## Postfeminism, class, and the Latina American dream

### Myra Mendible

> Through the pursuit of an ever-changing, homogenizing, elusive ideal
> of femininity . . . female bodies become docile bodies—bodies whose
> forces and energies are habituated to external regulation, subjection,
> transformation, "improvement."
>
> Susan Bordo, *Unbearable Weight: Feminism,*
> *Western Culture, and the Body*

The popularity of the chick-flick phenomenon poses new challenges for
feminist criticism and politics. The genre's commercial success signals
women's increasing clout as both consumers and producers of shared
social meanings. The appeal of woman-as-spectacle is by now a film theory
cliché, but the commercial success of the chick genre attests to women's
influence as paying spectators. It suggests that female subjectivity and
desire are marketable commodities, and that female audiences play a vital
role in the cultural economy. But in a US media culture driven by the
demands of the marketplace, can chick flicks muster the political commitment associated with earlier traditions of women's filmmaking? Critics
debate whether chick flicks reflect women's increasing options and lifestyle
choices or trivialize and de-politicize values associated with feminism. They
note that chick heroines are often white middle-class women who embody
consumer values and the mantra of individualism and self-gratification.
Indeed, the genre is often identified with a "postfeminist" retreat from
social activism and a "return to lifestyle choices and personal consumer
pleasures."[1] Defenders counter that chick flicks revitalize feminism,
positing more playful, ironic subjectivities and resisting claims to any
"authentic" feminist agenda that can bind women across differentials of
sexuality, race, and class.

This essay extends these debates to consider the cultural politics suggested
by chick flicks in which the "chick" is neither white, middle-class, nor
socially empowered. Part of the problem with the moniker *chick flick* is
that critics seem to assume a clearly identifiable chick prototype and

demographic. Yet neither of these presumptions has been adequately examined or contested. Since upwardly mobile, middle-class white chicks are often the subjects of romantic comedies, they frequently serve as the focus of these debates. This dissolves contradictions and differences under a universalizing "whiteness" and relegates variants of this model to the genre's periphery.[2] Thus the charge that chick heroines only aspire toward personal fulfillment, not social equality and community or that they unambiguously celebrate consumerist values is always already compromised by the chick's socially privileged position. The potential virtues and pitfalls of contemporary female-centered films are measured against this standard, skirting more nuanced critiques of the chick flick's multiply inflected relationship with both consumer values and feminist struggle. Just as significantly, the erasure of class from most of these discussions ignores the crucial economic relations and social hierarchies underlying the production and circulation of the genre.

In particular, I hope to comment on the ambivalent construction of working-class, female agency in recent films featuring Latina protagonists. *Maid in Manhattan* (2002), *I Like It Like That* (1994), and *Real Women Have Curves* (2002) incorporate prevailing social anxieties and contradictions, literally "resolving" them on the Latina body. The body is central in the articulation and naturalization of social differences, and the Latina's racially "hybrid" position in US culture (where she is historically represented as neither "black" nor "white") places her in ambivalent, often adversarial relation to dominant narratives of femininity and national identity. The films surveyed here offer a range of visions: *Maid* is directed by a man and qualifies as a Hollywood product; *I Like It Like That* and *Curves* are independent films directed by women. The latter two feature relatively unknown Latina actresses in lead roles, while *Maid* draws on Jennifer Lopez's box office appeal (and sexual allure). Yet all three focus on issues of particular concern to female audiences, emphasizing themes of empowerment in the context of work, family, and romance, in particular, marking domestic spaces identified with "Latino" culture in tense opposition with public spheres of production and consumption. Most notably, all invoke prototypes and settings of earlier "proletarian" films (i.e. maids, sweatshops, ethnic ghettos) thus foregrounding potentially volatile signs of resistance and struggle.

The Latina body has long been a troublesome presence in the US cultural imagination, alternately delighting, enticing, and instructing film audiences. Deployed as a sign of ethnic, gender, and class difference, Latina bodies have invoked a range of diverse and contradictory meanings.[3] Adrienne McLean argues that ethnic stars offer female spectators an opportunity to identify with a figure uniquely privileged to defy the social order of white, patriarchal capitalism. Culturally imbedded associations between ethnic femininity and disruption, unruliness, excess, and innovation, McLean notes, make it more likely that female spectators can enjoy such representations from a safe distance (11). But the status, popularity, and commercial success of ethnic stars often depends on their capacity to embody ideals of whiteness; as Richard Dyer has shown, the marketing of star bodies itself assumes a "white" audience and thus works to "deactivate" threatening racial elements that might impede crossover success (*Heavenly*). Hollywood films, Dyer explains, routinely use various forms of camera backlighting to emphasize female whiteness, while advertisements strive to "whiten" the female face because "to be a lady is to be as white as it gets" (*White* 57).

In today's transnational media markets, this ambivalent signifying role is syncopated to the rhythms of market forces. US Latino/as are a marketable, profitable target audience with a purchasing and spending power of over $500 billion a year; among US minorities, Latino moviegoers outnumber non-Hispanic blacks and represent the fastest growing admissions group in the US ("Loco"). As a result, Hispanic-themed media have emerged as a vehicle for shaping images of and for Latino/as, and for conveying normative ideals of cultural citizenship and "belonging" (Dávila).[4] An iconic Latina femininity, reconfigured to meet the demands of the marketplace, advertises products and lifestyles identified with US consumer society at home and abroad. In the film industry, the usual repertoire of spitfires, bombshells, cantina girls, and drug molls is undergoing revision, though Latina protagonists are still a rarity in Hollywood films. A crop of so-called "crossover" Latina stars—many born and raised in the US—today serve as enticing emblems of equal access and transcultural consumer pleasures. They also embody "Latinness" in the popular imagination, shaping not only external views of Latina/o identity but also enabling various forms of self-identification. Chica flicks participate in this broader socioeconomic process, alleviating underlying "tensions between the myth of American culture as all-incorporating and the reality of a fragmented, divided society" (Negra, *Off-white* 9). Operating through narratives of romance, the chica flick's harmonious matings can assuage racial and class anxieties, reflecting a reassuring vision of racial, gender, and class harmony. It can also, potentially, reveal cracks in the mirror.

This ambivalence and inconsistency exemplifies Hollywood's rocky romance with working-class protagonists generally, who are consistently marked as "ethnic."[5] The nation's self-image as a predominantly classless "free market" economy casts individual will as the measure of success or failure; thus it is no wonder that the "othering" of working-class characters (or the displacement of class on to "race") informs our cinematic tradition. Steven J. Ross reminds us of the interdependency between an incipient film industry and the labor class; working-class people, often immigrants, were not only the frequent subjects but also the main consumers and producers of movies. As a result, Ross points out, labor-friendly filmmakers set their features within the popular form of melodramas, love stories, and comedies, producing movies that were remarkably sympathetic to the working class. While black, Mexican, and Asian audiences were mostly excluded from white theaters, the appeal of movies was compelling enough that patrons of color endured uncomfortable seats in the balconies of segregated theaters or thronged to ethnic-owned movie houses in urban neighborhoods. This created a social space where workers and immigrants "often talked and fantasized about challenging the dominant political order and creating a very different kind of America" (24). The cinema's power to arouse desires and fuel political passion unnerved legal authorities and cultural conservatives, who felt threatened by the prospect of a highly politicized, predominantly foreign-born working-class populace. Thus the post-First World War studio system pushed the politics of American cinema in increasingly non-controversial directions. Studio moguls widened their appeal and increased profits by shifting attention away from class conflict and struggle toward "the pleasures of the new consumer society" (9).[6]

This is not to say that this relationship between mainstream cinema and the working class remained consistent throughout the twentieth century. The intersection where class struggle meets popular entertainment is never stable or predictable. John Bodnar contends that movies are subject to ideological "mood swings" and contradictions, producing ongoing tensions, for instance, between America's ideal of liberalism (with its emphasis on individual rights, freedom, and self-reliance) and participatory democracy (which works through collective action, affiliation, inter-dependence). While early "worker films" often set the individual in the context of collectivist social action (for example, labor unions), films focusing on working-class characters in the post-First World War period have tended to reconcile these tensions by personalizing social conflicts. Rather than endorsing collective activism or political organizing as a means to solve social problems, Hollywood films focus on individual experience—on the protagonist's personal hardships, longings, and triumphs. Films featuring working-class women as powerful leaders of collective action—such as *Norma Rae* (1979), *Silkwood* (1983), and *Places in the Heart* (1984)—emerged in the Seventies and Eighties, but Bodnar contends that even these set the broader issues in relation to the female protagonist's personal development or family concerns. In today's "post-Marxist" cultural climate, however, any references to "class-struggle" in current film discourse seems as passé as bra burning.[7]

This "mood swing" is also apparent in cinematic treatments of feminism as a socially transformative project. The ideological shift away from a collective gender politics corresponds, Barbara Ehrenreich points out, with an era in which feminism's earlier emphasis on social, cultural, and economic inequalities has been succeeded by a "mainstream feminism" that calls "unambiguously for [the] assimilation" of women into existing hierarchies (215–16). Thus women filmmakers in Hollywood today may not be transforming existing hierarchies as much as integrating into them. For example, Christina Lane has noted that in Hollywood women directors tend to become "pigeonholed" in less prestigious genres such as romantic comedy, melodrama, and teen film (37). As Lane points out, "most female directors are restricted to projects with middle range budgets that are 'dependent' upon the box office returns of current blockbusters" (37). These include romantic comedies and teen films—the staple of chick flick success.

In each of the chica flicks discussed here, the Latina body serves as iconic shorthand for the triptych of ethnicity, gender, and class. Given the political mood of the times, however, it is not surprising that Wayne Wang's rags-to-riches tale (specifically, maid's uniform to Dolce & Gabbana suit) starring "Jennie from de block" Lopez is the most commercially viable. The class conflicts and political undercurrents suggested by Kevin Wade's screenplay are mostly smothered in sugar and corn. (There is no spice in this Ralph Fiennes–J. Lo film mating.) Critics have understandably emphasized the film's ludicrous Cinderella plot, "pleasant" and predictable storyline, and of course, J. Lo's ubiquitous booty, the latter almost redeeming the film from the no-man's land of banal romantic comedies. But even as a romance, *Maid* was a miss: "don't look for this one on any future 'Greatest Chick Movies According to US!' list" quips one chick critic website.[8] My aim here is not to contradict these assessments, but to explore how the chica's literal and symbolic re-fashioning in this film reveals underlying political anxieties and social contradictions.

Single mom from the Bronx Marisa Ventura (Lopez) works as a maid in a luxury Manhattan hotel. One day she "borrows" a white Dolce & Gabana suit from a wealthy guest's closet and meets handsome (though stilted) Senate candidate Christopher Marshall (Fiennes), who mistakes her for a well-endowed socialite. The rest is history—film history, that is. *Maid* recycles earlier cross-class fantasy plots, which as Ross's study suggests, helped to shape the belief that participation in consumer society makes class differences irrelevant.[9] It is also worth noting echoes of nineteenth-century "imperial romances" in this post-NAFTA film product.[10] Just as the US's continental expansion produced border tales in which a "whitened" (i.e. "Castilian" looking) Mexican woman became a suitable marriage partner for the Anglo male, so this film allegorizes a happy mating between the growing Hispanic working class and the Republican party. Lopez's iconic body has been assimilated (i.e. "whitened") sufficiently in recent years to make her a privileged site for such mediations.[11] Critics have commented on Lopez's marketable "hybridity" (Valdivia); her "crossover" butt (Beltran; Negron Muntaner); and her visual transformation into a blonded, slimmed down version of pan-Latina femininity (Knadler). In this film, all of these resources come into play.

*Image 9.1* The Latina maid (Jennifer Lopez) gushes subserviently at the white
male senator (Ralph Fiennes)

The opening scenes establish a series of binaries that structure this
"border romance": uptown/downtown, rich/poor, white/others, public/
private. Public transportation ferries Marisa between her working-class
Bronx neighborhood and the ritzy Manhattan hotel where she works,
traversing a space that is more than geographical. But there are signs that
Marisa is socially redeemable: Marisa's bus reading is *The Drama of the
Gifted Child*; her son Ty (Tyler Garcia Posey) is a precocious ten-year-old
who happens to be fascinated with Nixon (Kissinger the year before),
reminding us at one point that Nixon opened "the East" for "the West";
and Marisa is seen by her workmates as potential assistant manager
material. Class differences throughout the film are racially inscribed—a
black security guard, an Asian laundress, all-white hotel guests and
management—but Christopher's description of Marisa as "Mediterranean-
looking" keeps her ethnicity vaguely, alluringly exotic. Even her name—
Ventura—signals adventure. It also brings to my mind the commercial
aims underlying this particular "venture."

As I noted earlier, most critics have underestimated the political undercurrents suggested here, particularly at a time when "compassionate
conservatism" emerges as an appeal to the "working poor," the majority
of whom are immigrants and ethnic minority women. A notable exception
is Stephen Knadler's recent essay, "Blanca from the Block," which merits

closer attention. In his incisive critique of the film, Knadler reminds us of recent attempts by the Republican and Democratic parties "to woo Latina/o voters." Increasing anxieties about the "crisis" posed to the GOP by Latino immigration has fueled nativist rhetoric—eerily familiar to anyone who has read nineteenth-century "sensational" papers and novels about unruly hoards of Mexicans scurrying across the border and undermining "American" culture. Knadler quotes a 1998 *National Review* article warning conservative readers that "without cultural and economic assimilation," Latinos are likely to push "the GOP toward minority status" early in this century.[12] This need to seduce "the Latino vote" (a phrase that assumes a nonexistent unitary Latino/a identity) was clear in the 2004 presidential elections, when both parties' conventions featured token "Latino" supporters on prominent display. But as Knadler aptly points out, wooing the Latino voter involves not just political strategy, but also subject formation: the constituting of a Latino citizenship disciplined into conformity with consumer values and behaviors. Knadler cites Lauren Berlant's argument that citizenship in the democratic nation increasingly translates into "consumerist identification with a set of privatized feelings" rather than a critical voice "that might effect collective action, protest, and social transformation."

Marisa's body is thus a contested site, a body marked by working-class "ethnic" ties (and as Knadler points out, politically neutralized "African" traces), yet potentially assimilable. The plot hinges on this ambivalence, hinting at resolving the social conflicts it poses. Marisa is situated somewhere between those inside the economic and social mainstream and those on the fringes of US society. While personally capable of transformation and improvement, she is also "representative" of her barrio community. For example, when Marshall mentions his upcoming speech on the deplorable conditions in Bronx housing projects Marisa decries his hypocrisy, asking him if he has ever actually been there. Marshall's well-intentioned but unschooled "compassionate conservatism" is set in contrast to Marisa's "authentic" ties to community and place. She is, as Marshall says, "no phony." At the same time, Marisa's link to Latino culture is tenuous and potentially stifling; her mother, who speaks with a heavy Spanish accent, appears in the film as the only real obstacle to Marisa's upward mobility. Not only does her mother's defeatism provide a negative role model, it also points to "culture" as the underlying problem to be overcome. But Marisa does "overcome" (even transcend) her place and community: in a white designer suit, she "passes" long enough to attract the white prince. This figurative cross (class) dressing magically transforms Marisa into a body that matters.

The plot twist hinges on Marisa's singular act of transgression, an act that reflects this ambivalent positioning and its underlying social anxieties. Wearing her maid's uniform, Marisa is docile, invisible, simply another dutiful "Maria." (Both Marshall's aide [Stanley Tucci] and the socialite [Natasha Richardson] repeatedly refer to Marisa as Maria.) But like other domestics, nannies, and workers who tend to the household needs of the affluent, Marisa holds a power rarely verbalized: she has access to the personal space of the elite she serves, cleaning their toilets, changing their bed sheets, literally and figuratively handling their dirty laundry. An element of fear and distrust underlies this social relationship, one that informs a variety of popular stereotypes about and attitudes towards the working class. If this were not a romantic comedy, Marisa's daring could help support such responses; instead, we are made privy to the transformative power of romantic love and designer suits. Marisa looks stunning strolling beside the Republican Senator-to-be in Central Park. In this contemporary "crossover" romance, the figurative mating of labor and capital ostensibly neutralizes the tensions between them.

After her masquerade is revealed, media headlines expose Marisa to the disciplinary gaze of society and employer: she is publicly admonished and shamed for her transgression and fired from her job. Marisa is fortified, however, by the encouraging words of the wise old butler (played with usual grace by Bob Hoskins), who speaks to the "dignity and intelligence" of those who serve and reminds her that, "what we do does not define who we are." Yet it is precisely through what she does—and more precisely, through what she wears—that Marisa assumes value. Marisa is only "seen" when she visually transforms herself from maid to socialite, when any meaningful sign of her difference is displaced and accommodated. More specifically, Chris's "love" casts a legitimating gaze that is gendered, classed, and raced. Marisa's self-affirmation and social "redemption" are intimately bound to Chris's authority: apologizing for her deceit, she humbles herself before him, confessing, "there was a part of me that wanted to see how it would feel to have someone like you look at me the way you did just once." Ironically, Marisa had earlier denounced such deference and deification. In a scene that confirms her mother's role as sign-bearer for a self-defeating and regressive group identity, Marisa accuses "people like her" of making "people like him some kind of God because he's rich, white, he's got things we don't have."

The final moments of the movie publicize Marisa and Christopher's wedding, his Senate win, and her move "up" in the hotel hospitality business through a series of magazine covers. The song "I'm Comin' Up" plays in the background. The final two covers are the most telling: Marisa's photo in *Hotel Management Magazine* proclaims her, "The New Breed of Manager," while Chris's *Newsweek* cover story bears the authoritative title, "Politics and the Working Class." Is this "new breed" signaling the emergence of an empowered Latina working class? Does Marisa's personal achievement "represent" a broader feminist social project? Knadler argues that Marisa's neutralized difference does not "signal an alternative sense of belonging, affiliation, or understanding" nor inspire "resistance to the economic and political status quo." Just as importantly, married to an "ex-maid," Marshall presumably gains direct access to knowledge about the working class. He is now "authorized" to speak on "their" behalf. But consider this: in the "new world order" imagined here, who is still doing the talking and who the cleaning up?

Perhaps, as one critic aptly remarks, "For movies like *Maid in Manhattan* to get much better, the economy may have to get much worse" (Scott). The economic prospects in Darnel Martin's *I Like It Like That* (1994) are much worse. The heroine lives in a cramped Bronx apartment with her man-child husband and three kids. Tight opening shots visualize a maddening sense of physical and emotional entrapment. Lisette (Lauren Velez) locks herself in the tiny bathroom twice throughout the film, blasting music on the radio and dancing away her frustration. The plot revolves around Lisette's efforts to support herself and her kids after her husband Chino (Jon Seda) is thrown in jail for stealing a stereo, a story sweetened by Lisette's undying love for her wayward hubby. Thus a basic romance ideology underscores the narrative, though it is certainly not a fairy tale *à la Maid*. Lisette's assertiveness (or desperation) lands her a job with a white record producer (Griffin Dunne) who needs help marketing Latino music artists. This sets up an uneasy threesome: Lisette is torn between her husband, who doesn't want her to work, a career that legitimizes her, and a relationship with the white boss.

The conflicts posed here are multiply inflected: Lisette's body is racially marked as "mulata," a physical and social status that relegates her "beneath" her lighter-skinned Latino husband, Chino (Jon Seda). Her body is sexualized in the opening frames of the film: her nude body is engaged in a marathon with Chino, who is testing his ability to maintain an erection for eighty-nine minutes. The children are pounding at the door and screaming throughout as Lisette "works" her husband, urging him to "hurry up and come." Chino's evil mother (Rita Moreno) despises the fact that her son married "down." Just as Marisa's mother expresses a regressive, "can't do" attitude that we can blame for her failures, Chino's mother embodies a Latino culture identified with racial and class bigotry. Given this domestic scene, it is no wonder that within the first few minutes of the film Lisette says, "I hate my life."

This sense of entrapment is also played out through the community itself, which is depicted as smothering in its "backwardness." The film is set entirely in a predominantly Puerto Rican ("Nuyorican") neighborhood in the Bronx, except on those occasions when Lisette is at work. It is a community where females fight openly over a man—where Chino's ex-girlfriend, Magdalena, publicly flirts with Chino and insults Lisette. Chino's "homeys" represent a repressive, disciplinary machismo that enforces a "Latino" masculine code by keeping an eye on Lisette while Chino is in jail. They spend most of their time hanging out on the street. When her boss, Stephen, drives her home at 4 a.m. in his red Lamborghini, the homeys tell Chino that his girl was "fucking a white guy" in his car. Later in the film Lisette defends herself against their accusation in another street spectacle, yelling at her nosy neighbors, "I got a job! What the fuck you people have?" Again "you people" suggests a Latino community that is poor, contentious, oppressive, racist, rigidly gendered, and self-defeating.

But Lisette's presumed "knowledge" of Latino style in its popularized, trendy manifestations marks her escape. As mediating body, she brings this knowledge to the world of popular culture, registered here through the music industry. Advising the young Mendez Brothers on how they should dress and pose for pictures, Lisette handles a precious commodity for her boss. This aspect of the film narrative offers a nod of recognition to the economics of popular culture; in particular, it reminds us that Latino music artists are a lucrative business. Lisette's boss woos the Mendez Brothers to sign with his label, telling them that "by some fluke of nature I wasn't born Latino . . . but I have an assistant." Yet the assistant that he originally had in mind was not Lisette, but the buxom senorita he points out in a bar. While Lisette's body doesn't measure up to his desired image, she can still serve as cultural translator; her genuine interaction with the Mendez Brothers and knowledge of a "hot Latino look" makes her hirable. In knowing how to package and market the Mendez Brothers into an image of Latino cool, she represents a behind-the-scenes figure in the booming business of Latino "crossover" success.

Martin's first feature film received positive reviews from critics who praised its "realistic" portrayal of "the concrete rhythm of downtown streets" and its "irresistible" heroine. She received the New York Film Critic's Award for Best New Director and the film earned four Independent Spirit nominations—with Velez winning Best Cinematic Female Lead. An African-American screenwriter, actress, and producer who grew up in the Bronx and previously worked with Spike Lee, Martin does suggest a more complex view of her Latino protagonists than generally available. Despite Chino's stereotypically machista attitude (he wants her to go on welfare rather than work, and he responds to his homey's tale of Lisette's infidelity by moving in with Magdalena after his release from jail), he nevertheless has a gentleness and love for Lisette that hints at a redeemable Latino masculinity. Martin is uncompromising in her depiction of Lisette, whose resilience and spunk challenge the stereotype of Latinas as sexy but helpless victims of a macho culture. Not surprisingly, one critic hails the film's feminism, praising Lisette's "new-found self-confidence and economic independence" and effusing, "it's a joy to see how she changes" (McAlister).

Yet the film avoids broader cultural or economic critique, opting for "crossover" appeal by weaving strands of rebellion into a reassuring national self-image. The class and gender conflicts suggested here remain safely confined to the geographical and cultural borders of the urban barrio. Lisette's self-empowerment is defined in clear opposition to her Latino family and community, which serves as the Other to a more enlightened (though passionless) "American" society. Male domination and bravado have a foreign name, "machismo," deferring "blame" for male chauvinism away from "Anglo" males and masking broader regulatory regimes or mechanisms of control. Stephen's bland sexual performance is contrasted against Chino's virility, but only in Stephen's world does Lisette achieve self-determination and worth. And female friendships seem possible only where there is no competition, as between Lisette and her transvestite brother Alexis (Jesse Borrego). These strategic oppositions have a distancing effect that fosters a guiltless spectatorship; despite the maddening entrapment depicted in the film and the conflictive, volatile space it reveals, *I Like It Like That* is marketed as a comic romance.[13] The complex social conflicts the film poses are tidily displaced and disavowed, resolved through Lisette's personal triumph and potential assimilation into an American consumer society in which she can buy—not steal—her coveted stereo.

Only Patricia Cardoso's *Real Women Have Curves* manages to offer a positive example of feminist resistance fused with ethnic and class empowerment. The film features an eighteen-year-old chica protagonist who refuses to starve her body into compliance with prevailing beauty myths. Ana, warmly captured by newcomer America Ferrera, wants to revise these myths to include less docile bodies; she also rejects full-time work at her sister's garment factory, which Ana recognizes as a sweatshop. Estela (Ingrid Oliu) takes pride in owning her own business, though the gowns she makes and sells for $18 will later retail for $600. Ana defies this social order and refuses to join the ranks of the docile exploited. "You're all cheap labor for Bloomingdale's" she tells the women laboring at their sewing machines. Thus her personal challenge to dominant beauty ideals also hints at collective activism. Ana's right to be "fat" merges into a broader struggle for dignity and rights at the workplace: in the scenes where she rouses female workers at her sister's sweatshop, Ana recalls labor activist figures of early worker films. In this context, however, rebellion takes the form of a collective shedding of clothes; the oppressive heat sparks this defiant gesture, but it is fueled by the women's desire for self-affirmation. Comparing stretch marks and cellulite, the women momentarily forge an alliance that dares anyone, as Ana puts it, "to tell me what I should look like and what I should be."

A recent high school graduate, Ana is smart enough to be offered a scholarship to Columbia, but her "old world" Mexican parents want her to stay close to home. In this film, however, Latino culture is not stripped of complexity; as Desson Howe points out, no one in this film "is easily pegged." Ana's mother, played with dignity by veteran actress Lupe Ontiveros, is not just a "convenient villain." It is clear that she loves Ana

*Image 9.2* Ana (America Ferrera) inspires her co-workers to take a stand
against their sweatshop conditions

and is struggling to reconcile her own life experience with her daughter's. The women workers are admirable without being mere victims of capitalist oppression; like many female laborers around the world, they are invisible cogs in the economic machinery, backroom producers never seen in those glossy fashion ads. But they are not simple props—they are humanized in their resilience, humor, and flaws. Finally, Ana's Anglo boyfriend, Jimmy, genuinely likes and appreciates her. He is neither her "savior" nor her oppressor; in fact, as one grateful male critic points out, "this is a feminist motion picture where men are not demonized" (Berardinelli).

Most reviewers responded favorably to this female empowerment tale with an ethnic twist. "A solid chick flick" notes one (Berardinelli); "liberation cinema on multiple levels" proclaims another (Anderson); "a dyed-in-the-womb female empowerment movie" writes yet another (Howe). The film also received several critical awards and nominations, including Sundance's 2002 Audience Award, Special Jury Prize (for America Ferrera and Lupe Ontiveros); the 2002 Humanitas Prize; the 2003 Independent Spirit Award (Best Debut Performance for Ferrera); and the San Sebastian International Film Festival's 2002 Youth Jury Award (for Cardoso). Unfortunately, reviewers share a need to label and categorize Cardoso's film; in numerous reviews, the film is repeatedly compared to *My Big Fat Greek Wedding* (both were distributed by Newmarket Films, which is targeting the "ethnic" niche market). This not only fuses differences between these films under a catch-all "ethnic" tag, but may also limit the film's broader appeal. Cardosa had tried to get the film made for ten years, and perhaps in an effort to reach mainstream audiences, she ultimately softened the political thrust that characterized Josephina Lopez's play (on which the film is based); Lopez's screenplay (with George LaVoo) tones down the labor angst that fueled the original script and individualizes the conflicts by focusing on Ana's personal development. It nevertheless manages, despite its familiar coming-of-age framework, to glean images of female solidarity and community.

In this brief sampling of contemporary chica flicks, I have tried to suggest some limits and challenges facing the genre. The ambivalent, uneasy political strains I have remarked on in these films no doubt reflect and negotiate existing structural and material conditions. While it is true that a Latina-centered Hollywood film like *Maid in Manhattan* can get wide distribution now, films that present Latina self-representations are still extremely limited in their ability to reach non-Latino audiences. As Chon Noriega points out, "Studios have yet to commit themselves to the grass-roots marketing strategies that ethnic and other specialty films require. And, more often than not, traditional saturation campaigns—especially the television trailers—have played into stereotypes that alienate the films' potential viewers" (147). Although writers, scholars, and filmmakers are making strides in promoting and showcasing Latina self-representations, power differentials affect access and resources. At this writing Latino/a -centered films, like most independent films, do not have the wide distribution networks needed to reach mass audiences; many remain accessible primarily in cosmopolitan areas with "art house" theaters or to students in large urban universities with Latino/a or film studies programs.[14] It is notable, for example, that Cardoso's film opened in the US on October 20, 2002 on only 55 screens. Neither "newcomer" Ferrera nor veteran Ontiveros had mainstream name recognition. By contrast, Wang's *Maid in Manhattan* featuring "Latina" icon Lopez in the lead opened December 15, 2002 on over 2800 screens in the US alone; it was seen by almost nineteen million viewers during its opening weekend, and within six months had been seen by almost 60,000 Argentines, one and a half million Germans, and over a million Spaniards. There is also a gendered component to these equations: while the emergence of Latinos as a viable niche market has facilitated their entry into corporate mass media, it is still a male-dominated industry. Vicki Mayer's intriguing work, for instance, reveals the near invisibility of Latina writers for mass media and the scarcity of US Latinas in directorial positions and shooting crews.[15]

In closing, I would note that the foregrounding of career success and self-empowerment narratives for women accompanies an era of down-sizing, outsourcing, budget cuts, and underemployment. Indeed, the much-heralded mobility of professional women in recent years obscures the enduring status of working-class women generally, whose real wages have actually declined.[16] Latinas' symbolic power in consumer tales also belies their embodied status as citizens: US Latinas are over-represented in high school dropout and teen pregnancy rates, and foreign-born Latinas comprise a majority share of low-wage factory or domestic jobs. For many women, the struggle for self-respect, dignity, and social justice is far from over. There is clearly a need for films that can challenge—not merely accommodate—our most comforting illusions and myths. This involves women at all levels of the film industry, from conception, to production, to distribution, and reception—the last marking one of the most contested, unpredictable, and yet accessible of "political" arenas. After all, female spectators help shape film tastes and values; let us begin by refusing to buy into self-help philosophies and better wardrobes as the panacea for what ails us.

## Notes

1 *Cinema Journal* recently devoted an In Focus section to examining the emergence of a "postfeminist" film and television culture in which "feminism is no longer relevant." See, in particular, Chris Holmlund's "Postfeminism from A to G" and Yvonne Tasker and Diane Negra's useful overview on the "postfeminizing" of cinema. Negra has also analyzed recent films featuring female leads that persistently stage "retreatist" fantasies in which a well-educated white female professional displays her "empowerment" by withdrawing from the workforce (and symbolically from the public sphere) in favor of domesticity. Here the rhetoric of "choice" works to mask and thus sustain structural inequalities ("Quality").

2 This tendency calls to mind Barbara Ehrenreich's remark that when Americans think about class, they "see the middle class as a universal class, a class which is everywhere represented as representing everyone" (4).

3 Extended analyses of this film and media history include Beltran, Lopez, Mendible, Noriega, Rios Bustamente, and Valdivia.

4 Dávila's use of the term "Hispanic" calls attention to its depoliticized and official status in the US, as opposed to "Latino," which stems from negotiations between an imposed and a self-generated identity grounded in activism and struggle. My practical application of the latter term in this essay refers generally to US inhabitants, both native and foreign-born, of Latin American and Hispanic Caribbean descent. Despite the homogeneity implied by such labels, however, "Latinos" in the US remain a diverse people whose histories, language usage, and circumstances may differ significantly and who may not speak Spanish or share other identifying criteria.

5 It's notable that the historical working class "ethnics" in film were so-called "white ethnics" (i.e. Irish, Italian, Jewish, Eastern as opposed to Western Europeans). The former have been generally assimilated into the cultural mainstream, with echoes of this past heard only in names such as "Brockovitch."

6 Ross found that by 1926, film censorship boards, each employing different standards, all found films dealing with class struggle even more threatening than displays of sex and violence.

7  For recent texts that critique the dwindling interest in "class" as a subject of inquiry, particularly in cultural studies, see Cevasco, Ebert, McLaren and Farahmandpur, Milner, and Munt.

8  Interestingly, these "movie chicks" criticize the film for including "too much preachy stuff" and being "too much *Norma Rae* and not enough *Pretty Woman*." See <http://www.themoviechicks.com/dec2002/mcrmaidmanhattan. html>.

9  Following the decline of labor films in the 1930s, working-class characters no longer improved their lot through unionization or organized effort, but through miraculous strokes of luck, Ross found. For instance, in *The Millionaire* (1921), a bookkeeper inherits $80 million; in *A Daughter of Luxury* (1922), a homeless girl discovers she is really a wealthy heiress.

10  Amy Kaplan has shown that mid-nineteenth century "narratives of domesticity and female subjectivity" were "inseparable from narratives of empire and nation-building" (583). Shelly Streeby's investigation of popular fictions such as Charles Averill's *The Mexican Ranchero, or, The Maid of the Chapparal* (1847), Harry Hazel's *Inez, the Beautiful* (1846), Ned Buntline's *Magdalena, the Beautiful Mexican Maid* (1847) and *The Volunteer* (1847) suggests that these "border romances" shaped discourses of imperialist expansion in ways that would significantly influence early twentieth-century films.

11  Jennifer Lopez recognizes her place within this fluid racial category, commenting about her role in *Money Train*: "They wanted a Latina . . . somebody who could be with Wesley, and with Woody. Apparently in Hollywood, brown is some kind of mediating color between black and white" (Murray 72).

12  Also see Morris.

13  The trailers and video blurbs emphasize Lisette's "marital problems" and the "amusing" interference of the nasty mother-in-law and Latino neighbors. I should also note that Martin's original title for the film was "Black Out," but according to the IMDB website, Columbia Pictures insisted on a name change. I leave it to my readers to speculate on their reasons.

14  There are several excellent volumes committed to showcasing Latino/a self-representation in a variety of independent and non-commercial venues. See de Alba, Flores, and Habell-Pallán and Romero.

15  The pinch is also felt by Latino/a actors, who are still underrepresented in mainstream films: a recent Screen Actor's Guild survey found that acting roles for Hispanics in Hollywood actually fell 10.5 percent in 2003 ("Screen").

16  Census analysis shows that only incomes for the top 5% of the population experienced real income gains in 2004, while incomes for the other 95% of households were flat or falling. Between 2001 and 2003, poverty levels in the US increased from 32.9 to 35.9 million. It rose again in 2004 by 1.1 million (Kerr). In the field with the highest proportion of female workers—kindergarten and preschool teachers (98% women), men had median earnings of $22,000, $5,000 more than women ("Census"). As for the dream of upward mobility: Jennifer Johnson's study suggests that women who grew up middle-class tended to stay that way, while the majority of those who grew up working-class had difficulty overcoming the setbacks imposed by lack of education, low-wage jobs, and low self-esteem.

# Works cited

Anderson, John. "Real Women Have Curves." *Newsday*, 18 Oct. 2002. <http://www. newsday.com/entertainment/movies/ny-womenhavecurves,0,966395.story>.

Beltran, Mary C. "The Hollywood Latina Body as Site of Social Struggle: Media Constructions of Stardom and Jennifer Lopez's 'Cross-over Butt.'" *Quarterly Review of Film & Video* 19 (2002): 17–86.

Berardinelli, James. *Real Women Have Curves*. Online Review. <http://movie-reviews.colossus.net/movies/r/real_women.html>.

Bodnar, John. *Blue-Collar Hollywood: Liberalism, Democracy, and Working People in American Films*. Baltimore: Johns Hopkins University Press, 2003.

"Census Study Finds That Men Earn the Most." *The New York Times* March 25, 2003: A13.

Cevasco, Maria Elisa. "Whatever Happened to Cultural Studies: Notes from the Periphery." *Textual Practice* 14 (3): 2000.

Dávila, Arlene. *Latinos Inc: The Marketing and Making of a People*. Berkeley: University of California Press, 2001.

de Alba, Alicia Gaspar (ed.). *Velvet Barrios: Popular Culture and Chicana/o Sexualities*. New York: Palgrave Macmillan, 2003.

Dyer, Richard. *Heavenly Bodies: Film Stars and Society*. Basingstoke, UK: Macmillan, 1986.

——*White*. New York: Routledge, 1997.

Ebert, Teresa L. *Ludic Feminism and After*. Ann Arbor: University of Michigan Press, 1999.

Ehrenreich, Barbara. *Fear of Falling: The Inner Life of the Middle Class*. New York: Pantheon, 1989.

Flores, Juan. *From Bomba to Hip Hop: Puerto Rican Culture and Latino Identity*. New York: Columbia University Press, 2000.

Habell-Pallán, Michelle and Mary Romero (eds). *Latino/a Popular Culture*. New York: NYU Press, 2002.

Holmlund, Chris. "Postfeminism from A to G." *Cinema Journal* 44.2 (Winter 2005): 116–21.

Howe, Desson. "On 'Real Women' and Feisty Daughters." *Washington Post*, 15 Nov. 2002: WE42.

Johnson, Jennifer. *Getting By on the Minimum*. New York: Routledge, 2002.

Kaplan, Amy. "Manifest Domesticity." *American Literature* 70.3 (September 1998): 581–606.

Kerr, Jennifer C. "Poverty Rate Rises to 12.7 Percent." *Washington Post* 31 August 2005.

Knadler, Stephen. "Blanca from the Block: Whiteness and the Transnational Latina Body." *Genders* 41 (2005). 30 Sept 2005. <http://www.genders.org/g41/g41_knadler.txt>.

Lane, Christina. *Feminist Hollywood From Born in Flames to Point Break*. Detroit, MI: Wayne State University Press, 2000.

"Loco for Hollywood." *Hispanic* 11.6 (June 1998): 16.

Lopez, Ana M. "Are all Latins from Manhattan? Hollywood, Ethnography, and Cultural Colonialism." In *Unspeakable Images: Ethnicity and American Cinema*. Ed. Lester Friedman. Chicago: University of Illinois Press, 1991: 404–23.

Mayer, Vicki. *Producing Dreams, Consuming Youth: Mexican Americans and Mass Media.* Piscataway, NJ: Rutgers University Press, 2003.

McAlister, Linda Lopez. "The Woman's Show." WMNF-FM Tampa, FL (88.5), 29 October 1994.

McLean, Adrienne. "I'm a Cancino: Transformation, Ethnicity, and Authenticity in the Construction of Rita Hayworth." *Journal of Film and Video* 44.3–4 (Fall/Winter 1993): 8–26.

Maltby, Richard and Ian Craven. *Hollywood Cinema.* Oxford: Blackwell, 1995.

McLaren, Peter and Ramin Farahmandpur. "Critical Pedagogy, Postmodernism, and the Retreat from Class: Towards a Contraband Pedagogy." In *Postmodernism in Educational Theory: Education and the Politics of Human Resistance.* Ed. D. Hill, P. Mclaren, M. Cole and G. Rikowski. London: Tufnell, 1999.

Mendible, Myra (ed.). *From Bananas to Buttocks: The Latina Body in Popular Culture.* Austin: University of Texas Press, 2006.

Milner, Andrew. *Class.* London: Sage, 1999.

Morris, Dick. "Hispanics: Key to GOP's Future." *New York Post,* 15 January 2004.

Munt, Sally (ed.). *Cultural Studies and the Working Class: Subject to Change.* London: Cassell, 2000.

Murray, Y. "Jennifer Lopez." *Buzz* 69 (April 1997): 72.

Negra, Diane. *Off-White Hollywood: American Culture and Ethnic Female Stardom.* New York: Routledge, 2001.

——"Quality Postfeminism? Sex and the Single Girl on HBO." *Genders* 39 (2004). <http://www.genders.org/g39/g39_negra.html>.

Negron Muntaner, Frances. "Jennifer's Butt." *Aztlán* 22.2 (1997): 181–94.

Noriega, Chon A. "Between a Weapon and a Formula: Chicano Cinema and Its Context." In *Chicanos and Film: Representation and Resistance.* Ed. Chon A. Noriega. Minneapolis: University of Minnesota Press, 1992.

Rios Bustamante, Antonio. "Latino Participation in the Hollywood Film Industry, 1911–1945." In *Chicanos and Film: Representation and Resistance.* Ed. Chon A. Noriega. Minneapolis: University of Minnesota Press, 1992: 18–28.

Ross, Steven J. *Working Class Hollywood: Silent Films and the Shaping of Class in America.* Princeton, NJ: Princeton University Press, 1999.

Scott, A. O. "Puttin' Down Mop, Puttin' On the Ritz." *New York Times,* December 13, 2002.

"Screen Actors Guild says Hispanics, Asians Losing Acting Roles." 8 October 2004. <http://www.tampabaylive.com/entertainment/stories/0410/041008guild.shtm>.

Streeby, Shelley. *American Sensations: Class, Empire, and the Production of Popular Culture.* Berkeley: University of California Press, 2002.

Tasker, Yvonne and Diane Negra (eds). "In Focus: Postfeminism and Contemporary Media Studies." *Cinema Journal* 44.2 (Winter 2005): 107–33.

Valdivia, Angharad. *A Latina in the Land of Hollywood.* Tucson: University of Arizona Press, 2000.

——"Latinas as Radical Hybrid: Transnationally Gender Traces in Mainstream Media." *Global Media Journal* 2.4 (Spring 2004).

# Chapter 10

# Chic flicks

## The new European romance

*Mallory Young*

It's no surprise to hear that Britons and Americans—especially women—frequently associate European countries, traditions, and men with romance. It might be surprising however, given that association, to consider the body of European film and find that romance—at least romance as most Anglo-Americans define it—is not a prominent feature. This is particularly true when it comes to romance directed toward female viewers. For most of the history of European film, the notion of a romantic "chick flick" has been as untranslatable in concept as in language.

To those familiar with European culture, this curious lack might be easily explicable. For Americans—along with our romantically inclined cultural ancestors, the British—the romantic ideal is clear: boy meets girl, boy loses girl, boy gets girl. But this ideal does not translate easily into French or Italian or Swedish or German. Check the French standard for romance as an example, and you'll find something more like boy meets girl, boy loses girl, boy spends rest of lonely and miserable life longing for girl. The French romantic hero *par excellence*, after all, is not Prince Charming but Cyrano de Bergerac.

We can add to this divergent view of romance the European proclivity to treat film as a serious art form. Indeed, a clear split has always existed in the fundamental views of film: the dichotomy between European art and American entertainment. Theirs are films, ours movies. Theirs thrill scholars and critics, ours play to ordinary folks. Theirs focus on cultural enrichment, ours on financial. Thus an even slightly serious French or German film that ended happily was, until recently, as unlikely as a light, comic work by Kafka or a fairly-tale ending from Flaubert. The prevailing mood, if not the explicit framework, of European film from the 1950s to the century's end identifies it as a first cousin of literary naturalism, in its oppressive, inescapable fatalism. From the dark, mirror-gazing, suicidal films of Luis Buñuel and Rainer Werner Fassbinder in the Sixties and Seventies to the dark, mirror-gazing, suicidal films of Erick Zonca and Michael Haneke in the Nineties, European film has generally followed a naturalistic path.[1]

This is certainly not to say that comedies—and even romantic comedies —have been missing from the European film canon. But such films have traditionally focused on male central characters. Most recently, for example, note the spate of French films featuring Daniel Auteuil as the bumbling-but-lovable male lead, films such as *The Closet* (*Le Placard*, 2001) and *Après Vous* (2005). Before Auteuil, Gérard Depardieu played the same role in similar films: romantic films, yes; chick flicks, no.

As for the large body of European films focused on women, most of these are not directed *toward* women. Rather they tend to explore what might be termed "women's issues" from men's perspectives. It's easy enough, of course, to ridicule the Hollywood model of romance put forward in the "woman's film." From the classic love stories of the Thirties and Forties to the modern Cinderella stories of the present, the typical Hollywood formula offers no stronger models of feminism than does Harlequin romance. The romantic Hollywood ending typically has the heroine rejecting any extra-marital ambitions in favor of parking herself happily-ever-after in a suburban bungalow. From *Miracle on 34th Street* (1947) to *Raising Helen* (2004), the model has remained the same. On the other hand, most European films haven't actually provided women substantially better options. True, the women of European films don't fall for handsome strangers and find themselves whisked off to the suburbs. They're far too busy humiliating themselves (think of Pedro Almodóvar's *Women on the Verge of a Nervous Breakdown* [*Mujeres al borde de un ataque de nervios*], 1988), mutilating themselves (Ingmar Bergman's *Cries and Whispers* [*Viskningar och rop*], 1972), or killing themselves (Buñuel's *Belle de jour*, 1967).[2]

Even European films by women writers and directors have been more likely to explore the dark sides of women's psychology or sexuality than to satisfy romantic desire. As Emma Wilson explains, this focus goes back to Marguerite Duras' groundbreaking screenplay to the 1959 film *Hiroshima mon amour*. According to Wilson, "Duras' work, and other recent films and texts by women in France, have worked to raise crucial issues about female sexuality, violence and masochism. Such works take crucial risks that are potentially degrading, painful and humiliating" (145). The same can be said for the work of other women filmmakers across the continent. Surely no one could describe Lina Wertmüller's *Swept Away* (*Travolti da un insolito destino nell' azzurro mare d'agosto*, 1974) or Catherine Breillat's *Romance* (1999) as a chick flick.

In the beginning years of the new millennium, however, evidence has appeared of a certain *rapprochement* in the divergent cultures, perhaps even a marriage—whether one of romance or convenience, it would be hard to say. Anglo-American and European films—and audiences— are inching closer together. Thanks to such no longer unprofitable ventures as the Sundance Film Festival and to the baby-boomer-friendly home-video market, independent films have become a prominent influence on the American film industry (Ahearn; Kelly, "Independent Films" E7). At the same time, Hollywood influences have begun to seep into European tastes and sensibilities, becoming as omnipresent as McDonald's or Mickey Mouse. A sizable number of French, German, and Spanish actors are being lured from Western Europe to Southern California. And a surprising number of European and other foreign films are receiving widespread and successful distribution across the *heart*land, so to speak, of America.

In line with this transatlantic intermingling, a number of European films have begun to portray a more typically Anglo-American—if not precisely Hollywood-esque—view of romantic love. Some of these, such as the recent Italian film *Bread and Tulips (Pane e Tulipani*, 2000) or the French *Happenstance (Le Battement d'ailes du papillon*, 2000), recast well-worn American formulas, simply transferring them to a continental setting. But others might actually be contributing to the development of a new European version of the romantic film focused on—and aimed towards—women. Three recent films suggest that a new film genre deserving the title of European chick flick—or "chic flick"—has indeed come into being. All three films follow the Anglo-American prescriptions for chick-flick romance while contributing an unexpected element drawn from traditional European film: the element of naturalism.[3]

The French romantic comedy *Amélie (Le Fabuleux destin d'Amélie Poulain*, 2001), the German romantic drama *The Princess and the Warrior (Der Krieger und die Kaiserin*, 2000), and the German-Italian romantic comedy-drama *Mostly Martha (Bella Martha*, 2001) exemplify the new ideal of romance being portrayed in contemporary European film. Darker and edgier than mainstream American romantic movies, they nonetheless provide their audiences a far more sanguine view of romantic love than did their European forebears, all the way to their surprisingly feel-good endings. And notably, all three films achieved favorable reviews as well as some measure of financial success on both continents.

A comparison of *Amélie* and *The Princess and the Warrior* reveals striking similarities, so I will begin by considering these two films. Each involves an obsessive, lovable, wide-eyed heroine with no "normal" family connections. Each heroine devotes herself to helping others in a closed community of colorful, quirky characters. Both films focus on the loneliness and emptiness of the heroine's life as well as the lives of those around her. Both heroines, while not entirely inexperienced sexually, retain a childish innocence with respect to sex. In each film, as the plot develops, the heroine is fatefully confronted with a somewhat mysterious, slightly unsavory loner. In both films, the heroines choose to promote the ultimate union. Finally, both films invoke literary naturalism, above all in their emphasis on fatalism. But in both, fate suddenly takes a turn towards happy-ever-after. The films' titles are revealing in this regard. The original title of *Amélie—Le Fabuleux destin d'Amélie Poulain* (*The Fabulous Destiny of Amélie Poulain*)—tells us that the story is, literally, fabulous, that is, a fable, and that destiny is clearly the focus.[4] And *The Princess and the Warrior*—Tom Tykwer's English version of his original title, *Der Krieger und die Kaiserin*—is a clear reference to fairy tale.

*Amélie*, the most lighthearted of the three films I treat here, is also the most popular. In the US, it ranks as the highest-grossing French film ever ("Amélie Receives"). In 2004, the film was ranked twenty-fifth among the top 250 movies of all time, according to popular votes gathered by the Internet Movie Data Base (IMDB). Only one foreign-language film, *The Seven Samurai*, is ranked higher, at five. For films made after 2000, *Amélie* ranks an amazing sixth ("Top 250"). *Amélie*'s impact on American popular culture is also unprecedented. Frequent mentions in the popular press and allusions in advertising make clear how fully entrenched it had become in the popular imagination. During *Amélie*'s American run, for example, a reference in a department store catalog credited this "modern-day fairy tale" with inspiring "the resurgence of red" (*Marshall Field's* 4). About the same time, a newspaper article lamented the upcoming demise of the Mobylette "recently immortalized in the hit movie *Amelie*" (Leicester). These are hardly typical references to a foreign-language film in American pop culture.

Perhaps even more surprisingly, the film fared equally well with its home audience. According to the French movie magazine *Première*, it finished 2001 as the most viewed movie of the year in France, ahead of such box office winners as *A. I.: Intelligence Artificielle* and *American Pie 2* ("Entrées France" 171). (It is revealing that *Le Journal de Bridget Jones* also finished in the year's top ten.) In the international market (all markets excluding the US), *Amélie* ranks among the highest grossing films ever ("Box Office"). And according to an article in *USA Today*, "The film's locations, such as Amélie's grocery stand, street (rue Lepic) and workplace (the Café des Deux Moulins, which now has a perpetual waiting list) are crowded with tourists—French and otherwise" (Bell). Clearly, *Amélie* struck a chord that managed to resonate with both American and European audiences.

Although definitions of a chick flick vary considerably, few would exclude *Amélie*. The central focus on a young, sympathetic female character, the explicit emphasis on romantic love, the familiar obstacles postponing the feel-good resolution all qualify as typical romantic chick-flick elements.

Still, in spite of the film's allegiances to the Anglo-American chick flick, it does manage to evoke the bleak world of naturalism through both diegetic (that is, narrative) and non-diegetic elements. Along with the film's emphasis on fate, the characters' isolation most clearly demonstrates this naturalistic bent. All of those quirky, lovable characters in Amélie's world are, in fact, desperately lonely models of alienation. Amélie's neighbor, an isolated old man separated from the world by his brittle bones; her landlady, a sorrowful woman abandoned by a once loving, now dead husband; her father obsessed with building a shrine to her dead mother; the young mentally deficient man working in the open-air produce market, tormented by his heartless boss; the boss himself, a lonely apartment dweller; Amélie's co-workers and café clients—all are single, alone, estranged from family members, lovers, friends. This is a Paris not of lovers, but of loners. Frequently Amélie's efforts to benefit her fellow loners only make the sadness of their lives more palpable. The false letter Amélie sends the landlady, for example, a supposed last and long-lost assurance of her husband's love, brings the lonely woman joy—but simultaneously makes clear the pathos and depth of her solitude.[5]

The film's non-diegetic elements, particularly the camera work, contribute further to an underlying sense of sadness and alienation. On an initial viewing, the opposite might seem to be the case. The film's director, Jean-Pierre Jeunet, readily admitted to having digitally spruced up his Parisian setting. Litter, graffiti, and even racial diversity were removed from Amélie's Paris (Hoberman). The film's digitally enhanced colors are intentionally cartoon-like: outdoor scenes are less washed in sunlight than painted in bright Jello tones. As numerous reviewers pointed out, this is a fancifully non-existent Paris, a Paris of dream and fantasy. Still, the apartments of Montmartre, the café, the train station, the subway are rarely portrayed as cheerfully bustling. The camera closes in on its subjects, isolating them from the surrounding world; it backs away to show a character alone in a larger empty space. In one such scene even the

*Image 10.1* Amélie's (Audrey Tautou) isolation is emphasized by the film's camera work

*Image 10.2* Amélie framed against an empty Paris metro station

normally frenetic Gare de l'Est is devoid of commuters, leaving Amélie framed against the background of an empty metro station.

Yet the film lets us know from the beginning that what we are watching is indeed comedy. Or the film's narrator tells us so. His playful and ironic commentary directs our response. The events that traditional naturalism would exploit for their tragic gloom—the accidental death of Amélie's mother, the remoteness of her father, the loneliness of her childhood—are presented by the narrator in comic terms:

> Amélie is six. Like all little girls, she'd like to be hugged by her Daddy. But he never touches her, except for a monthly checkup. The thrill of this rare contact makes her heart beat like a drum. As a result, he thinks she has a heart defect. Declared unfit for school, Amélie is taught by her mother. . . . Deprived of playmates, slung between a neurotic and an iceberg, Amélie retreats into her imagination.
>
> ("The Script")

Amélie's dream world is exploited for comic effect. The neighbor's comatose wife has, in Amélie's imagination, simply "chosen to get all her life's sleep in one go." Her sole friend, her goldfish Blubber, is described as "suicidal" as he leaps from his bowl. As "Blubber's suicide attempts destroy Mother's nerves," he is released into the nearest creek. To fill the void, "her mother gives her a used Instamatic." Then

> One day, tragedy strikes. Amandine takes Amélie to Notre Dame, to pray for a baby brother. Minutes later, heaven sends, alas, not a baby

boy, but Marguerite, a tourist from Quebec, bent on ending her life. Amandine Poulain dies instantly.

("The Script")

This is black comedy, but the comedy clearly outweighs the blackness. Jeunet is well known for his "astonishing visual invention" (Ebert) and wildly surrealistic elements; in *Amélie* these too are used for comic effect. Lamps converse with paintings, photos provide commentary, and Amélie literally melts into a puddle on the café floor. And then there is that classic, American-style feel-good ending. Fate, with a little help, has succeeded in bringing boy and girl together. In the meantime, the film has brought together European naturalism and American romanticism to create a new and satisfying blend.

As one of the leaders of Momentum Pictures, the film's British distributor, said, "Often, foreign films are about inaccessible, dark subject matter like child abuse or obscure philosophers or are too arty for regular moviegoers, but *Amélie* is a brilliant film for both sides of your brain" (quoted in Bell). In a question-and-answer session filmed in California, director Jeunet made a distinction between new French directors including himself and New Wave French directors such as Louis Malle, noting that he and his peers make films for the audience, not just for themselves ("Q and A").

This is not to say, of course, that everyone was satisfied. A few serious critics on both sides of the pond were outraged with what they viewed as Jeunet's sell-out. Following his more extreme, experimental films co-directed with Marc Caro, *Delicatessen* (1991) and *City of Lost Children* (*La Cité des enfants perdus*, 1995), *Amélie* appeared to these critics as a shameless pandering to American audiences—and American money. The French leftist *Libération* accused the film of "spurious populism," "an example of an idiot globalization that transposed the 'fake magic' and inane gaiety of EuroDisney to Montmartre" (Hoberman). One American reviewer claimed that the film "felt more like a wanna-be unique American film dubbed in French" ("Amelie"). His final assessment is telling: "Unless you like *both* the sappy sensationalism of most romantic comedies *and* funky French flicks, pass on this one."

Most notably, *Amélie* was passed over for Official Selection at the 2001 Cannes Film Festival, according to some sources because of its lack of seriousness (Ebert). As it turned out, the resulting scandal probably helped the film more than any advertising could have. The overwhelming majority of journalists and critics at Cannes loved the film and turned on Gilles Jacob whose lukewarm response had prompted director Jeunet to withdraw it from the competition ("Intimate Chat"). According to director Jeunet—with perhaps a bit of Gallic exaggeration—the film eventually garnered some 450 rave reviews to half a dozen negative ones ("Intimate Chat"). Indeed the film went on to win the 2002 César Awards for both best picture and best director, after receiving thirteen nominations, more than any other film in history ("Amélie Receives"). Still, the initial rejection suggests that, at least until recently, in the European cultural mindset, chick flicks from either side of the Atlantic were not worthy of critical respect. Jeunet himself explained the phenomenon in a single sentence, noting that what above all fuels the French mind is cynicism ("Intimate Chat"). No wonder then that chick romance in general has been a hard sell.

German director Tom Tykwer's film, *The Princess and the Warrior*, was less subject to complaints of sweetness. Unlike *Amélie*, which announces its comic intention, Tykwer's films tend to play against audience expectations. In his previous film, *Run Lola Run* (*Lola Rennt*, 1998), he played with three possible plot developments, first providing the dark versions, then concluding on a happy note. In each case, the different outcome, in spite of the heroine's similarly brave and desperate efforts, was determined by fate alone. One critic describes the typical Tykwer film, in fact, as "a long journey into the hands of fate" (Kelly, "Heaven" 9). In *The Princess and the Warrior*, Tykwer again plays with naturalistic convention. But this time he dangles the dark ending in front of us, then in a quick sleight-of-hand, suddenly switches it for the happy one. The film apparently wants us to believe that we are—or might be—watching a conventional piece of European naturalism. Again and again, we expect the film to take a tragic turn. But each time, it surprises us by landing somewhere else entirely.

Fate enters by way of an accident in which the heroine Simone ("Sissi"), a lonely young mental hospital worker, is seriously injured. Even the last-minute, lifesaving act performed by a handsome stranger, an emergency tracheotomy, is a violent one. The film's setting in the starkly beautiful German town of Wuppertal also suggests the bleak world of naturalism more than the frothy fairyland of romance.

Recovered from her injuries, Sissi sets out to find her mysterious rescuer. Fate has, she now believes, linked them inextricably. Although she manages to identify and locate the man more easily than we could have hoped, her real difficulties, it turns out, are just beginning. Not only is her intended mate, Bodo, a brooding loner involved in criminal activity, but he has no intentions of linking up with Sissi or anyone else. Having lost his wife in a freak accident, he spends a good part of each day pondering committing suicide—and the rest committing crimes equally likely to lead to his death. Sissi's persistence pays off, however, and she eventually convinces Bodo to accept her help in hiding him from the police.

In this film, too, a flashback is provided of the death of the heroine's mother. We discover, through a black-and-white scene of the past, that her mother's accidental electrocution in a bathtub wasn't accidental at all. A mental patient in the same institution where Sissi now works, believing himself betrayed, had thrown a plugged-in hair dryer into the tub. And now that same patient, once again sensing betrayal, slips into the bathroom

*Image 10.3* Sissy (Franka Potente) and Bodo (Benno Fürmann) prepare to leap
to their fate in *The Princess and the Warrior*

where Bodo soaks unsuspectingly. Bodo notices the man's entrance, but
a toaster is already flying through the air. We cringe in fearful expectation
—only to see Bodo reach out his hand to catch the toaster.

The same reversal of expectation operates when the young lovers,
pursued by the police, look searchingly at one another, join hands, and
take a running leap from the hospital roof. We watch in painful dread as
the camera follows their downward plunge. But at the moment of impact,
we are once again treated to surprising relief: the two lovers have landed
with a splash in a previously unseen lake. The camera now follows their
graceful glide through the water and their gradual reemergence at the
surface. By the film's end, Sissi and Bodo have escaped their pursuers and
joined an old friend who lives in a remote and idyllic seaside castle—a
fairy-tale ending indeed.

Again, not everyone got the point. The review in *USA Today* accused
the film of being "weighed down by the almost giggle-inducing moroseness
without which even the greatest of German cinema could not exist"
(Clark). The reviewer is clearly aware of the naturalistic gloom typical of
German film. But he doesn't notice that Tykwer, rather than simply forging
on through that gloom, has emerged into a new vision—one that another
critic more perceptively described as "Deeply whimsical beneath its poker
face" (Holden).

Of course, fairy tales themselves do not always end happily: sometimes
the red shoes dance away with the heroine's feet leaving her maimed, and
the grandmother, eaten by the wolf, stays dead. But in his "amazingly

fractured fairy tale of fate" (White), Tykwer, like Jeunet, gives us happily ever after, after all. And again, the blend of the dark conventions of naturalism with a boy-gets-girl—or actually girl-gets-boy—romanticism works.

In the German–Italian film *Mostly Martha*, many of the same elements reappear. Once again we have an alienated heroine who lacks normal social ties; once again she is fatefully confronted by a potential mate. In this film, however, the heroine is the main obstacle to the inevitable union. In line with this variation, the film proves to be less susceptible to the typical Hollywood version of romance. As a result, it provides a more balanced and nuanced fusion of the two traditions of romance and naturalism. It is worth noting as well that *Mostly Martha* was both written and directed by a woman.[6]

The film can be placed in another recent film subcategory, the food flick—or more specifically the food romance—a group that includes both American and international offerings such as *Like Water for Chocolate* (1992); *Eat, Drink, Man, Woman* (1994) and its Mexican-American remake *Tortilla Soup* (2001); *Chef in Love* (1997); *Chocolat* (2000); and *Woman on Top* (2000).[7] Martha Klein, a first-class chef in the northern industrial town of Hamburg, is isolated both by her lack of friends and family, and her fanatically obsessive approach to cooking. Her life is focused entirely on the kitchen of the upscale restaurant where she works. Her goal is not to satisfy the customers—whose tastes are not necessarily trustworthy—but to satisfy her own inflexible demand for perfection. As a result, the restaurant owner has required her to make regular visits to a psychiatrist, but Martha has nothing to talk about aside from food.

Once again in line with naturalistic convention, a violent accident propels the plot. Here it isn't the heroine's mother who dies suddenly, but her sister. When Martha's world is, as a result, fatefully invaded by her morose, orphaned niece and a charming Italian sous-chef, the predictable story line begins its progress toward the ice queen's inevitable meltdown. But while the romance is predictable, the very human fears and emotions and relationships surrounding it are not. This film traffics less than the others in surreal fatalism, opting instead for emotional depth. The movie's sublime culinary realism is easily matched, in fact, by its perceptive psychological realism.

When the heat—emotional and physical—of the restaurant kitchen becomes unbearable, we see Martha escape alone to the cold-food locker. When Martha's stubbornly mourning niece Lina refuses to eat, we realize she has hit upon the ideal passive-aggressive approach to wounding her apparently unemotional aunt, exactly as a child in her situation could be expected to do. The scene in which the Italian chef Mario gradually wins Lina over, finally inducing her to eat from a bowl of pasta flavored with savory basil, is both touching and convincing. Later in the film, Martha

*Image 10.4* Martha (Martina Gedeck) escapes to the restaurant cold-food locker in *Mostly Martha*

has made enough emotional progress to allow Mario to cook for her, something she has never allowed anyone else to do. But she still hyperventilates when she sees the destructive effects on her neatly organized kitchen.

Along the same lines, Martha's psychiatrist spends the entire film trying to break her of the habit of cooking for their sessions rather than talking. At the film's end, Martha has agreed to taste a flan prepared by the psychiatrist himself. She can't help noting that something is wrong. "Did you use the Belgian sugar?" she asks suspiciously. "You can tell what sugar I used?" he responds, incredulous. And she replies, "No. I can tell what sugar you didn't use." Martha might have undergone an emotional sea change, but she hasn't become an entirely different creature. Notably, Martha, the sole professional of the three romantic heroines considered here, is not called on to give up her profession. While she must, in line with the Hollywood formula, admit romance (that is, love, marriage, and children) into her life, that won't, the film suggests, require a move to the suburbs. Martha has by this time left her position as head chef. But as the credits roll, the final montage makes clear that Martha and Mario will marry, celebrate joyously with friends and family in the Italian countryside, adopt Lina, and open their own restaurant (whether in chilly Hamburg or sunny Italy isn't revealed). As the ensuing scenes suggest, Martha's obsessive nature remains intact, albeit tempered by Mario's and Lina's good-natured acceptance.

Numerous reviewers noted, with approval, that the film's realism outweighed its romantic inclinations. An Australian reviewer praised screenwriter/director Sandra Nettelbeck for having "the good sense to keep things edgy and unromantic for long enough to hook our interest" (Urban). The reviewer for the *San Francisco Chronicle* noted, along similar lines, that the movie is "not a romance per se. It's just a movie about a woman who's not bubbly, perky or pining in the usual romantic way. She's prickly, distant and fairly content with her regimented life" (LaSalle). And one British critic might have put his finger directly on the pulse of the new European romance when he said that Nettelbeck "has created a film of genuine delight, with a subtlety that could only be European. The feelgood factor, a staple of Hollywood, is binned in favour of emotional truth and the complexities of human nature" ("Mostly Martha Iofilm").

While most American and British critics embraced the film warmly, some German critics were considerably less charmed. One German reviewer charged that while the film would have been suitable for television, it was too light for the moviegoing public ("Bella Martha"). The anonymous critic went on to dismiss the film, although strongly recommending it for all "Hausfrauen" in their forties, who are (presumably by definition) likely to be satisfied by sentimental schmalz. The supercilious tone is abundantly clear. Another German review, while less arrogant in tone, noted the sugary sweet ending, and then voiced a tentative suspicion that it might be ironic (Ammann). No such irony was suspected by any of the American or British critics, nor, I might add, by myself or any other viewer I've questioned. That the reviewer found irony the only acceptable way to explain a typical romantic happy ending does make clear that at least some German critics are not yet fully willing to accept this new breed of European romance. French critics, in this case, were somewhat less harsh, at least one of them citing the film's culinary pleasures as reason enough to accept its predictable plot (Guéret).

The young German screenwriter/director, Sandra Nettelbeck, in any case, apparently had no such compunctions in bringing her first full-length feature to the big screen. Nor, it seems, did the actors, the German actress Martina Gedeck, well known to audiences in her home country, and the equally renowned Italian screen favorite, Sergio Castellitto. Critical concerns also failed to prevent the film's garnering numerous awards, among them the German Film Award in Gold for Outstanding Individual Achievement: Actress and, somewhat surprisingly, the German Film Critics Association Best Actress Award for Martina Gedeck ("Awards"). It is also worth noting that the film won the Best Actor, Best Actress, Best Screenplay, and Grand Prize for 2002 at the Mons International Festival of Love Films ("Awards"). Through its psychologically realistic garb, *Mostly Martha* was recognized in the end as a quintessential romance.

I'm not suggesting here that most European films—not even most of those focused on women—have suddenly veered toward sweetness and light. Not to worry: for every *Amélie* there is a *Piano Teacher*; for every *Princess and Warrior*, there are several takes on *The Dreamlife of Angels*. Nor have those European films that qualify as "chic" flicks adopted all of the characteristics of Anglo-American-style chick flicks. One element missing from all three films considered here is the focus on a close-knit group of female friends, an essential element according to some definitions of the chick flick. Indeed all three of the romantic heroines presented here are clearly portrayed as loners, lacking both friends and close family members. The idea of female bonding is apparently not one that has infiltrated European conceptions of films for women. Still, something new is quietly going on in European cinema. Insofar as a new compromise has been effected, I cannot claim that all American and British audiences have embraced it; many of those drawn to European films prefer the traditional emphasis on doom and gloom. I can see their point: I would be sorry to see a chipping away at the distinctive aesthetics and divergent perspectives of European and Anglo-American cinema. Still, what viewers are getting in this case, I would argue, is not the loss of serious European film, but an increase in the options we're offered. Compromise, after all, is not always a bad thing—and sometimes strange bedfellows make good friends.

## Notes

1   This is, admittedly, a rather grand generalization. In the case of French film, for example, the 1980s and 1990s were marked by the development of the *cinéma du look*, a group of films "characterized by their preoccupation with striking stylistic effects, and their improbable plots usually based on permutations of the thriller genre" (Smith 39). And comedy, particularly social comedy, has always had a major place in the European canon. Still, as an overall assessment of the major distinctions between American and European film, it's fair to speak in these terms. As Hollywood can be distinguished by a partiality for the action-adventure blockbuster and the syrupy-sweet romance, so European film can be identified through its association with the darkness of naturalism.

2   See Molly Haskell's chapter "The Europeans" in *From Reverence to Rape* for a complete look at the views of women in European film from its beginnings through the early 1970s.

3   I don't mean to suggest that these films are limited—either in directorial intention or actual viewing public—to women. All three films procured an audience of both women and men. However, the prevailing ethos of these films makes them of primary interest to a female audience and garners for them, whether in praise or condemnation, the label of chick flick.

4   In the Special Features accompanying the DVD, director Jean-Pierre Jeunet comments on the title's significance given the role of destiny not only in the film itself but also in its making ("Intimate Chat").

5   In her essay on the 1996 French film *Chacun cherche son chat*—a film that might well be added to the group of films discussed here—Lucy Mazdon identifies the theme of alienation as the central focus: "This move from isolation to community, from fragmentation to solidarity, is perhaps the film's key theme" (100).

6   Indeed, I admit I would like to think that Nettelbeck's gender accounts for the more realistic portrayal of romance in her film. I also have to admit, however, that most film romances by Anglo-American women—films such as Nora Ephron's *Sleepless in Seattle* (1993) or Nancy Meyer's *Something's Gotta Give* (2003) and *The Holiday* (2006)—have not, in this respect, diverged significantly from the mostly male-created models of earlier years. A few, however, such as Gurinder Chadha's *Bend It Like Beckham* (2002), might suggest a new direction.

7   A *New York Times* article by Steve Chagollan noted that major American studios are beginning to compete with foreign filmmakers in the creation of food films. In fact, an American remake of *Mostly Martha* titled *No Reservations* and starring Catherine Zeta-Jones and Aaron Eckhart, is due for summer 2007 release. This crossover potential of European "chic flicks" might also support the idea that mainstream American audiences are now more willing to accept the darker European vision—sans subtitles.

## Works cited

Ahearn, John. "Selling the Authentic: American Independent Cinema Marketing in the 1990s." Presentation given at Tarleton State University, Stephenville, TX, 28 Mar. 2003.

Ammann, Corinne. "Kühle Meisterköchin." Cineman. 12 July 2004 <http://www.cineman.ch/movie/2001/3Sterne/>.

"Amelie." *Dave's Somewhat Weekly Reviews* 11 Dec. 2002. 18 March 2003 <http://www.davesreviews.com/reviews/a/amelie.htm>.

"Amélie Receives 13 César Nominations." *StudioBriefing* 4 Feb. 2002. 21 July 2004 <http://imdb.com/title/tt0211915/news/sb/2002-02-04#film4>.

"Awards for Bella Martha (2001)." Internet Movie Data Base. 16 July 2004 <http://imdb.com/title/tt0246772/awards>.

Bell, Carrie. "'Amélie' Capturing World's Fancy." *USA Today*, 1 Nov. 2001. 17 March 2003 <http:// www.usatoday.com/life/movies/2001-11-01-amelie.htm>.

"Bella Martha." Cineclub 5 June 2002. 12 July 2004 <http://www.cineclub.de/filmarchiv/2002/bella_martha.html>.

"Box Office for Amélie." Internet Movie Data Base. 21 July 2004 <http://us.imdb.com/boxoffice/alltimegross?region=non-us>.

Chagollan, Steve. "Eat Drink Make Movie—Hollywood's Next Course." *New York Times*, 9 July 2006. <http://www.nytimes.com/2006/07/09/movies/09chago.html?ex=1310097600&en=66406ea46519c973&ei=5088&partner=rssnyt&emc=rss>.

Clark, Mike. "Languid Plot Dethrones 'Princess.'" *USA Today*, 21 June 2001. 12 April 2003 <http:// www.usatoday.com/life/movies/2001-06-22-the-princess-and-the-warior review.htm>.

Ebert, Roger. "Amelie." *Chicago Sun-Times*, 9 Nov. 2001. 17 March 2003 <http://www.suntimes.com/ ebert/ebert_reviews/2001/11/110901.html>.

"Entrées France mi-octobre / mi-novembre." *Première*, décembre 2001: 171.

Guéret, Olivier. "Bella Martha." *Cinopsis*. 12 July 2004 <http://www.cinopsis.be/rev_main.cfm?lang=fr&ID=2602&rr=1>.

Haskell, Molly. *From Reverence to Rape: The Treatment of Women in the Movies.* 1973. 2nd ed. Chicago: University of Chicago Press, 1987.

Hoberman, J. "Toy Stories." *Village Voice*, 31 Oct.–6 Nov. 2001. 17 March 2003 <http://www. villagevoice.com/issues/0144.hoberman.php>.

Holden, Stephen. " 'The Princess and the Warrior': The Fairy Tale as Surreal Brainteaser." *New York Times*, 22 June 2001. 12 April 2003 <http://www. nytimes.com/2001/06/ 22/arts/22PRIN.htm>.

"An Intimate Chat with Director Jean-Pierre Jeunet." *Amélie* DVD Special Features. 2002.

Kelly, Christopher. "Independent Films Left Out in the Cold." *Fort Worth Star Telegram*, 17 Jan. 2003: 1E+.

——"Heaven." *Fort Worth Star-Telegram*, 18 Oct. 2002, *Star Time*: 9.

LaSalle, Mick. "Mostly Martha." *San Francisco Chronicle*, 23 Aug. 2002. 12 July 2004 <http://www.sfgate.com/cgibin/article.cgi?f=/c/a/2002/08/23/DD243464/DTL>.

Leicester, John. "France Is Bidding Adieu to a Beloved Moped." *Fort Worth Star-Telegram*, 15 Feb. 2003: 1B.

*Marshall Field's Direct*. Spring 2002: 4.

Mazdon, Lucy. "Space, Place and Community in *Chacun cherche son chat*." In *France on Film: Reflections on Popular French Cinema*. Ed. Lucy Mazdan. London: Wallflower, 2001: 95–105.

"Mostly Martha Iofilm Review." Iofilm. 12 July 2004 <http://www.iofilm.co.uk?cgi-bin/printer_friendly.cgi?filename=mostly_martha_2001.shtml>.

"Q and A with Director Jean-Pierre Jeunet." *Amélie* DVD Special Features. 2002.

Smith, Alison. "*Nikita* as Social Fantasy." In *France on Film: Reflections on Popular French Cinema*. Ed. Lucy Mazdan. London: Wallflower, 2001: 27–39.

"Top 250 Movies as Voted by Our Users." Internet Movie Data Base. July 2004. 12 July 2004 <http://us.imdb.com/chart/top>.

"The Script." TUGC's Fabulous Shrine to *Amélie*. 21 July 2004 <http://hom.smart-popcorn.com/amelie/bonus.php>.

Urban, Andrew L. "Mostly Martha." Urban Cinefile. 12 July 2004 <http://www. urbancinefile.com.au/home/view.asp?Article_ID=6869&p=y>.

White, Dave. Quoted from IFILM review of *The Princess and the Warrior*. 12 April 2003 <http://www.rotten tomatoes.com/m/princess_and_the_warrior/>.

Wilson, Emma. "Deforming Femininity: Catherine Breillat's *Romance*." In *France on Film: Reflections on Popular French Cinema*. Ed. Lucy Mazdan. London: Wallflower, 2001: 145–57.

# Chapter 11

# The "babe scientist" phenomenon

## The illusion of inclusion in 1990s American action films

*Holly Hassel*

John Rambo, the Terminator, Indiana Jones, Martin Riggs, John McClane: tough, resourceful, authoritative males stoically making the world safe from futuristic terrorists, drug lords, Teutonic mercenaries, Nazis, small-minded rednecks and small-town sheriffs. As this litany of protagonists and antagonists from action-adventure films of the 1980s suggests, the American action film has long been the province of the burly, muscle-bound hero, as well as one of the most commercially successful genres in American cinema. What, then, does this historically male-dominated genre have to do with chick flicks? A spate of action-adventure films dating from the early 1990s has sought to co-opt female viewers by including a "partner" for the muscular male protagonist: the female scientist or, in Internet Movie Database parlance, the "babe scientist."

The female partner's function is to reveal the complex plot devices, usually scientific in origin, that have catalyzed the film's conflict. As such, she appears to have equal narrative significance to her male counterpart. By creating a plausibly sympathetic female character, producers and writers have transformed or, at the least reshaped, what Philippa Gates has called the "male melodrama" into a quasi-"chick flick."

However, the babe scientist phenomenon presents three narrative and gender problems for female viewers. First, her role as co-protagonist is undermined in the films because she is often presented as overly invested in science at the expense of "intuition." Second, her over-reliance on science diminishes her ability to vanquish the threat. Third, she hood-winks female audiences who initially identify with what appears to be a strong, female character but who turns out to be weak and in need of "re-education."

Despite her drawbacks, the babe scientist may offer hope for transforming the action genre in the twenty-first century. She is the precursor to an emerging brand of heroine who appropriates the qualities of the male action hero, while retaining qualities typically associated with chick-flick heroines. Emotionally sensitive, she is trained in martial arts and thus bridges the mind–body gap between the traditional chick flick and the traditional action film. Her presence may foreshadow more central female action heroines and even the birth of the chick action flick.

## Introducing the babe scientist

As romantic interest or buddy (or a combination of the two), the babe scientist is a ubiquitous presence in the 1990s action film.[1] She is established early on as both a "babe" and a scientist. Often she first appears using complex technical jargon to show her scientific credibility, while the hero or other male characters comment on her sexual appeal. The introduction of Dr Sheila Casper (Dina Meyer) in *Bats* (1999) is typical. We see her in the depths of a cave in Skull Valley, Arizona, in dialogue with her assistant Jimmy, who is above ground while she spelunks, gushing about "chiroptera" and "medium roosts." After Jimmy confesses his dislike for bats and caves, she wonders, "If you hate bats and caves so much, what the hell are you doing with me?" He responds, "for one, I ain't gonna lie. You're kind of cute." When *The Peacemaker* (1997) opens, Nicole Kidman is doing laps in a swimming pool, certainly a visual cue as to her "babeness." Her scientific credibility, like Dr Sheila Casper's, is confirmed by her mastery of technical vocabulary. As she rushes in to meet with a presidential advisor, offering her theory that a nuclear explosion was no accident, she says that "SS18s pencil out at 1 point safe." The line has to be translated from "science-ese" by another advisor. The film validates her both as the object of sexual interest to the main character (and heterosexual male moviegoers) as well as ostensibly worthy of admiration from female audience members. While such a filmic move suggests "chicks" are welcome at this flick, this is only partly true.

*Image 11.1* A flock of giant, mutated bats terrifies Dr Sheila Casper (Dina Meyer) in 1999's *Bats*

## You don't bring science to a gun fight

At first glance, we might believe that the 1980s action genre has shifted away from its masculinist origins. If, as Latham Hunter has argued, the genre emerged as "a corrective response to the feminist boom of the 1970s," the babe scientist's inclusion may be a corrective response to its hypermasculinity. At least, her feminine influence tempers the male hero's masculinity and her alignment with rational thought counters his reliance on action. Ironically, however, while science has traditionally been coded masculine, her attachment to science actually undermines her in the film. The action film privileges an anti-empirical, intuitive "animal instinct" or "primitivism" over study and scholarship. Thus, aligning the female co-protagonist with science marks her as out of place in the film.

The babe scientist, in fact, often clings to science, appearing cold, dispassionate, and blindly faithful to the ability of reason to unravel all mysteries she encounters. Because science often fails (despite her best efforts) to explain the threat—in contrast with the hero's intuitive grasp of the problem—she takes on the role of the "resistant" buddy who needs to be convinced of the correct path by the male protagonist. This could be called the Mr Spock—or, perhaps, Ms Spock—phenomenon. In *Deep Blue Sea* (1999) and *I, Robot* (2004), for example, the babe scientist is "seduced" away from her reliance on logic and empiricism to the male protagonist's way of seeing things.

Cold and focused, Dr Susan McAllister (Saffron Burrows) in *Deep Blue Sea* conducts genetic research on sharks at an underwater medical lab called Aquatica, formerly a Navy station for submarine loading and refueling. The work, involving "reactivation of the human brain cell," is ostensibly geared toward curing Alzheimer's disease. Yet, her drive to get her research approved creates the film's tension. The film opens with two scenes that illustrate McAllister's faulty science: first, a raft of teens is nearly eaten by one of the super-smart sharks that has escaped from the facility; second, she is marched into the office of the company funding her research to defend her slipshod research techniques.

McAllister's status as a babe is established when Carter, a shark wrangler played by Thomas Jane, expresses interest in her.[2] After Carter comments flirtatiously, "one day you'll take me up on that beer," she responds, "it's all work for me, Carter." She is constructed as physically attractive but inaccessible and out of touch with the "true" purposes of life.

This single-minded focus on scientific research at the expense of concern for human life contrasts with the action hero's commitment to preserving it. The babe scientist, with her skewed and bungled attempts at scientific solutions to human problems, needs to be re-educated in the ways of the human spirit. In fact, Carter spends the film counteracting the threat produced by McAllister's bad science: she has skipped "three rounds of preliminary trials" to avoid being shut down. McAllister initially rejects his concerns:

CARTER: They're hunting in packs. Like wild dogs. They'll only eat other sharks.
MCALLISTER: You're reading too much into it.
CARTER: That Gen I attacked a 25-foot boat. Am I reading too much into that, too?
MCALLISTER: Did you tell Franklin?
CARTER: I'm just the fishkeeper, lady, but bringing in the shark ahead of schedule was a bad idea.

Carter's practical knowledge as the "fishkeeper" trumps McAllister's "theoretical" and scientific knowledge of the shark brain. His heroism is validated by his demonstrated prowess, courage, and skills as the shark wrangler. He literally rides them like dolphins underwater, ventures into dark waters to feed them, and captures the escaped shark.

McAllister ultimately receives her comeuppance during the harvesting of the shark brain tissue she has been genetically engineering. After outwitting the increasingly cannibalistic, aggressive, and intelligent sharks to capture one and bring it to the wetlab, Carter steadies the shark while McAllister uses her technological expertise (and gadgets) to extract the tissue. The shark is uncooperative, however, and bites off the arm of Jim Whitlock (Stellan Skarsgård), setting into motion a chain of events that leads to typical action fare. The communication center explodes, flooding several floors of the facility, forcing the small group of survivors to flee to the surface, while avoiding the bloodthirsty and vengeful jaws of the three sharks loose in the facility.

The blame falls on Dr McAllister's misplaced values. Franklin asks, "just what the hell did you do to those sharks?" She responds, "Their brains weren't large enough to harvest sufficient amounts of the protein complex, so we violated the Harvard compact. Jim and I used gene therapies to enlarge their brain mass. Larger brain means more protein. As a side effect, the sharks got smarter." Her crimes against nature are exposed and her allegiance to scientific advancement at all costs begins to crumble almost immediately when one character yells, "you stupid bitch!" Carter more articulately schools McAllister on the error of her ways:

CARTER: Exactly how many sticks of dynamite would you have to set off in your ears before your head cleared?
MCALLISTER: You wouldn't understand.
CARTER: I wouldn't, huh? Dumb old Carter. Wouldn't understand that you used us? That you used me? Someone on the water who wouldn't make waves. Someone who wouldn't ask too many questions because he had something to lose.

MCALLISTER: You don't see what we've done here.

CARTER: What you've done is taken God's oldest killing machine and given it will and desire. What you've done is knocked us all the way to the bottom of the goddamn food chain. It's not a great leap forward in my book.

Only after the deaths of many of the central characters, her own attack by one of the sharks (which she kills by electrocution in a water-filled room when she strips to her underwear and stands on her wetsuit as insulation[3]), and the increasing likelihood that they will not survive does she admit, "Carter, what you said down there. Maybe you were right."

Finally, as the largest shark attempts to escape the facility into the "deep blue sea," McAllister converts to the "cowboy way" embodied by the last two survivors, Carter and Preach (LL Cool J), the chef who earlier killed a third shark by gassing up the oven in his kitchen and lighting a match. McAllister no longer defends her rigorous adherence to science at all costs. She admits, "We have to kill her," to which Carter responds, "Now that's the first real smart thing you've said all day." Significantly, for her crimes against the human spirit, she offers herself up as a Christ-like blood sacrifice, cutting deep wounds in her hands to lure the largest shark away from the fence to keep it from escaping. She is eaten by her own creation, but not before—and because—she has seen the light. She has at last learned the power of self-sacrifice and been schooled in the appropriate ways to invest in humanity.

A more recent example of the too rational babe scientist appears in Will Smith's 2004 summer blockbuster, I, Robot. Set in 2035 Chicago, the film follows techno-phobe Del Spooner (Smith) as he unravels the death of Dr Alfred Lanning, the inventor of the laws that govern the robots produced by US Robotics: "1) A robot may not injure a human being or, through inaction, allow a human being to come to harm. 2) A robot must obey orders given it by human beings except where such orders would conflict with the First Law. 3) A robot must protect its own existence as long as such protection does not conflict with the First or Second Law." Despite the apparent logical certitude of these laws, Spooner's intuitive dislike of robots leads him to suspect that all is not right in Dr Lanning's suicide. He relentlessly pursues the truth even when dissuaded by his superior, Lt Bergin (Chi McBride).

As Spooner arrives at US Robotics, where Lanning died, he is assigned an "escort" through the building, Dr Susan Calvin (Bridget Moynahan), who introduces herself: "Lawrence told me to accommodate you in any way possible." Spooner responds lasciviously, "Really?" establishing his sexual interest in her. His query, "so what exactly do you do around here?" is met with an icy and emotionless litany of her academic credentials, to which he responds mockingly, "so what exactly do you do around here?"

She finally quits speaking "science-ese," and says simply, "I make the robots seem more human." After Spooner cracks a joke, she states mirthlessly, "I'm sorry, are you trying to be funny?" Dr Calvin is so scientific she can't even be funny. As the babe scientist, Calvin serves as a foil to Spooner's reckless pursuit of justice and his seemingly irrational suspicion of robots. Even as a robot suspected in the death of Dr Lanning persistently refuses to obey her commands and appears to threaten her with bodily harm, she insists, "it cannot break the rules; they're unbreakable."

Dr Calvin's overly scientific persona validates the audience's identification with Spooner, as the tension escalates between them. Spooner's fears of an impending robot revolution contradict Calvin's avowal that all is well. When he arrives at her apartment after being nearly crushed by a demolition robot in Lanning's house, ranting about the deliberate attempt on his life, she undermines his beliefs: "this is bordering on clinical paranoia!" and "this is a personal vendetta." As a trained psychologist, it is fitting that she can only conceptualize Spooner's concerns in psychological terms, but, in the context, her diagnosis only underscores her professional blindness and the futility of her formal education in making sense of the situation. Her resistance has to be overcome by Spooner's personal charisma and advocacy of the humane. He values human life above all, while Calvin adheres to corporate principles of efficiency, convenience, and cold logic.

Ultimately, just as Dr McAllister comes to see the error of her ways, so does Dr Calvin, as she is persuaded by Lawrence Robertson, US Robotics president, to destroy Sonny, the unique robot whom Lanning enabled to violate the three laws in service to a higher cause: the salvation of humanity. Robertson insists that Sonny must be destroyed. Dr Calvin balks, clearly influenced by Spooner's insistence that Sonny is the key to the mystery, to their pursuit of the truth, while Robertson considers only the bottom line: "Susan, just be logical—your life's work has been the integration of robots." Convinced by his appeal to her logic, she agrees to destroy the robot, but as a reversal later reveals, only because she wishes to free him. She has been converted from her "life's work"—logic, science, technological advancement—to value the heart and spirit. In the end, the traitor to the human race is VIKI, the giant robot consciousness that has masterminded the robot revolution. VIKI is summarily destroyed by Spooner and Calvin, while Spooner instructs Sonny the robot that human choice in deciding life's purpose is "what it means to be free."

The female scientist contributes to the narrative by literally generating the conflict: creating giant, super-smart sharks or sentient robots who attempt to take over the world. She adheres faithfully to her creation, thus erecting another obstacle the hero must overcome. He must eliminate the threat and convert the babe scientist to the ways of humanity and intuition.

## This is no place for a woman

The extermination of the threat depends not on scientific knowledge, which the babe scientist has in spades, but rather on brute physical force—quick reflexes, powerful muscles, and combat skills, characteristics only male protagonists possess. Several films illustrating this vividly include *Tremors* (1990), *Species* (1995) and *Species II* (1998).

In *Tremors*, seismologist Rhonda LaBeck becomes a romantic interest but does not directly vanquish the threat—giant underground worms. Unlike the previous babe scientists, she is not enlisted into the male protagonist's world view directly but instead discovers that action films are no place for women, so to speak. The movie's heroes, Earl Bassett (Fred Ward) and his affable partner, Valentine McKee (Kevin Bacon), are two shiftless but likable roustabouts in the deserted small town of Perfection, Nevada. The inexplicable appearance of underground behemoths who gradually eat several of the town's fourteen residents provides the impetus for the plot—and a standard monster-film ploy: an ensemble cast is stranded in a small place by the imminent threat posed by, usually, a monster of some sort.[4]

The destruction of the "graboids," as they are quickly dubbed, becomes the central tension in the film. While Rhonda offers scientific hypotheses about the creatures, in the end they fall short, and Val destroys the last graboid through cleverness, courage, and swiftness. In a key scene in Walter Chang's store, the limits of scientific knowledge are revealed to the other characters, who represent the public looking for scientific solutions but not receiving them:

WALTER: What's the name you call those things? Where do they come from?
RHONDA: I don't know!
WALTER: You're a scientist, aren't you?
MELVIN: Yeah, aren't you supposed to have a theory or something?
RHONDA: Look, these creatures are absolutely unprecedented.
NESTOR: Yeah, but where do they come from?
MIGUEL: Yeah!
RHONDA: [blank look]
EARL: It doesn't matter where they come from.

Earl's rescue of Rhonda from the demands for scientific answers only reinforces her inadequacy in the *Tremors* diegesis.

In the end, Val and Earl's quick thinking and physical stamina outwit the giant worms. They go "fishing" with homemade bombs from Bert and Heather Gummer, the local survivalists, and blow the worms to smithereens. They finally propel the last one off a cliff as Val lures it after him

*Image 11.2* In 1990's *Tremors*, geologist Rhonda LeBeck (Finn Carter) escapes her pants and the underground monsters, later dubbed "graboids," with the help of handyman Valentine McKee (Kevin Bacon)

and then plays a game of chicken that leads to its demise. Thus, brawn beats brains. This holds true in the sequel as well, where the babe scientist, Kate Riley (Helen Shaver), a geologist for an oil company plagued by a recurrence of the worm infestation, explains the creature's behaviors, providing needed intel for the hero's ultimate goal: the destruction of the threat (predictably, through explosives).

In *Species* (1995), Marg Helgenberger plays Dr Laura Baker, a molecular biologist whose brain is again trumped by the hero's brawn. She is part of an ensemble put together by Fitch (Ben Kingsley), an oily, corporate shill, to trace an escaped alien-human hybrid in the guise of an attractive Aryan-looking female named SIL (Natasha Henstridge). While the film would have us believe that the team members are equal contributors to the enterprise, Preston Lennox (Michael Madsen) takes on the role of the protagonist.

From the beginning, the film plays with gender roles, as when Fitch, the project coordinator who engineered the hybridization, informs the clean-up crew, "We decided to make it female so it would be more docile and controllable." During his delivery of the line, the camera lingers on Dr Baker, even while Lennox jokes, "more docile and controllable? I guess you guys don't get out much." Despite its playfulness, the film nonetheless subscribes to the active hero/passive babe scientist arrangement throughout.

Lennox serves as the catalyst for the film's action. He tracks SIL's moves and follows his instincts, even when SIL cleverly outmaneuvers the team by crashing a car with another body and leaves one of her severed thumbs to make them think she's dead. Baker asserts, "It was her. The tests on the thumb prove it was her." Lennox resists, "Well you've got your tests and I've got my gut, and I just don't buy it." This exchange is quintessential action-film logic: the hero's intuitive grasp of the threat is validated over the empirical evidence Baker provides. In the end, Lennox's "male" heavy artillery (big guns, literally) not Laura's "female" scientific knowledge or any strategies derived from it, eliminates SIL, resolving the conflict.

## Bait and switch

A more significant problem in this sub-genre is the "bait and switch" played on female audience members. They are encouraged to identify with the babe scientist who is presented initially as a "buddy" and/or "romantic interest" character who will play as significant a role in the film's plot as the male protagonist. But then she is shown to be weaker than her male counterpart. Frequently, the babe scientist emerges as an emotionally over-wrought woman who undermines her own authority by turning into a "girl" when the going gets tough.

Were the babe scientist truly functioning as the action film protagonist, she might be entitled, as the male protagonist is, to violent and vigilante behavior. Because the action hero is typically a renegade and in a position to dole out justice whether institutional or personal, personal tragedies often justify retaliation. By contrast, the babe scientist's losses and flaws fuel her scientific investigations and thus compromise her credibility as a rational authority. Stereotypically female emotionalism proves she is unsuited for empirical, masculine pursuits.

Personal tragedy shapes—and thus controls—several babe scientists. In *Twister* (1996), Dr Jo Thornton-Harding (Helen Hunt), a meteorologist, is exorcising the loss of her father when she was a young girl. Jo's borderline-hysterical obsession with finding the tornado that will absorb Dorothy IV, the instrument pack she and her husband have developed for studying tornadoes, is rooted in an irrational belief that the twister sought her out in her youth. "You've never seen it miss this house and come after you," she cries to her estranged scientist husband (Bill Paxton), after a failed attempt to launch the new sensor device. Similarly, Dr Susan Tyler, entomologist, struggles with infertility in *Mimic* (1997). Her own failure to conceive is linked thematically with Judas Breed, her creation, a genetically engineered insect which refuses to remain sterile (George). Her barrenness, rather than her scientific resolve, drives her quest to eliminate the threat. The biochemist character in *Sphere* (1998), Dr Beth Halperin (Susan Stone), has suicidal tendencies and an addiction to prescription drugs. Her past relationship with the team leader Norman (Dustin Hoffman), her former psychologist and lover, undermines her credibility. The military supervisor grills Norman about her stability: "What does that say, Norman? Does it say suicide attempt? Does it say electroshock therapy? [. . .] We're 160 fathoms down and now we've got a nutbag down here who can flip out and crack up." For some of these women, their losses drive their research, a deviation from the scientific ideal of detached objectivity that earns them disapproval from both the audience and their fellow characters. For others, deviation from the scientific ideal leads to complete discrediting.

What it means, then, to be a female viewer of these action flicks is to be in some ways hoodwinked. The babe scientist is a misleading invitation to female viewers to see themselves in a central role in this historically male genre.

## The future of action chick flicks

Despite the drawbacks to the babe scientist's role, she has laid the groundwork for the recently developing "chick action flick": a film featuring a canny, powerful, and victorious female action hero. Can the action flick become a "chick flick"? I would like to argue that this is a distinct possibility, given the trajectory of Hollywood action-adventure blockbusters. One precursor is *The Relic* (1997), starring Penelope Ann Miller as evolutionary biologist Dr Margo Greene, whose scientific knowledge (rather than police detective co-star Tom Sizemore's weaponry) defeats a mutated monster. What Dr Margo Greene lacks in formidable brawn in the face of bodily harm, she makes up for in scientific deduction and direct application of her chemical knowledge to eliminate the threat facing Chicago's National History Museum. A fellow researcher at the museum has returned from South America with a crate full of hormone-laden leaves. His arrival corresponds with the gruesome murder of several of the ship's crew and the security guard at the museum, who had their hypothalamuses ripped from their heads. While the film relies on action-film formulas, it frames Dr Margo Greene as capable of facing the threat not simply through violence but science.

One could do a feminist analysis of Greene's representation in the film and certainly find her lacking the stereotypical qualities of the action-film hero. She personalizes and becomes defensive when her scientific cool should take over. She reacts with hysteria when faced with dead bodies. She is lost in the bowels of the museum for a chunk of the film. More important than her personal qualities, though, is her successful elimination of the threat. This, after all, is the ultimate measure of the action hero's competence and agency. In the film, Lieutenant D'Agosta (Tom Sizemore) has been arguing to postpone an expensive fundraising opening attended

*Image 11.3* Dr Margo Green (Penelope Ann Miller) brings science to a monster-fight in 1997's *The Relic*

by New York glitterati at the museum until the case of the mutilated bodies can be soundly resolved. Despite his protests, the show goes on. At the hands of a rival scientist, Greene is locked in the lab area while dolling up for the festivities. Meanwhile, D'Agosta and a hoard of police comb the museum seeking out a suspect. When the police detective and the scientist finally do meet, she uses her recently invented device, the dubiously named "interpolator," to identify the creature responsible for the attacks. She discovers John Whitney, her research colleague, has evolved into a horrific reptilian predator.

Greene's scientific resolution to the narrative cracks open the action genre, for it flies in the face of formula: the babe scientist supersedes the male hero—a cop, no less—in regaining control over the crisis. In the concluding scene, the "Kothoga" as the creature is called, faces off with Dr Greene, in an expected chase scene where she has to outrun a creature that is far better genetically suited to pursuit than she is to evasion. Dashing up a stairwell into the bowels of the museum's storage areas, a labyrinth of wire shelving and chemical jars, she frantically smashes containers of various chemicals on to the floor. Her actions seem harried and purposeless, but when she arrives at a work area and begins deftly mixing specific chemicals, the deliberateness behind her plan is made obvious. Albeit hysterically and sobbing, she confronts the Kothoga and escapes via a small elevator, tossing the chemicals to the floor, initiating a chemical reaction that produces the requisite action-film out-of-control explosion, and then escapes to safety by jumping into the fireproof tank used to strip flesh from the bones of specimens. Her scientific machinations are spliced with shots of Lieutenant D'Agosta pounding angrily on and shooting ineffectually at the iron door blocking the lab area from the hallway, subverting even more obviously the action-film convention that increasingly privileges technology, weaponry, and bigger, better explosions over intelligence and ingenuity.

However, *The Relic* accomplishes a victory for science and intellect within the genre rather than for feminist action-film achievement in its own right. If the recipe for a commercially successful action-adventure film means striking the balance between intellect and combat, then *The Relic* doesn't quite accomplish that balance. For example, the ever-popular Indiana Jones's archeological knowledge becomes a weapon in the elimination of the threat (Nazis, Voodoo priests, or mercenary treasure seekers) as frequently as he physically resolves a conflict. Dr Greene, by contrast, is neither physically imposing, nor does she retain the stoic toughness that might characterize her either as a macho action hero or truly scientific. In this way, Dr Greene is not a totally successful protagonist within the action-adventure genre.

A contrast might be *Lara Croft: Tomb Raider*, a movie based on the buxom video-game heroine who is known for her adventuring and amateur archaeology.[5] While the film clearly highlights Croft's physical form, this objectification is not significant enough to completely dismiss the film's promise for the chick action flick. It would be difficult to argue that the cinematography in the film does not exploit Angelina Jolie-cum-Lara Croft's ample assets. Even in the opening scene where she makes short work of a killer robot using double-barreled semi-automatic weaponry and enviable combat skills, the camera lingers a little too lovingly over her crotch, breasts, and thighs. This cinematic fragmentation of Lara's body pervades the film. Further, as Steven Poole has claimed, "Because the film has abandoned the notion of a Lara with brains as well as looks—the sledge-hammer action never stops long enough to show Lara thinking her way out of a situation" (46). The more cerebral potential of Lara Croft—the video game's character relies upon her education and puzzle-solving abilities as well as her handiness with a weapon—is left underused in the film.

To its credit, though, the film endows Croft with the qualities of the prototypical male action hero. She is stoic and tough, always ready for the threat that comes her way (animated statues of Shiva, rival tomb raiders, time storms, secret societies). But she is still allowed emotional investment in the work she does. Sherrie Inness, in her analysis of tough women in popular culture, has defined the tough girl as one who can "endure tremendous physical and emotional suffering and still emerge the victor. She has the tight emotional and physical control that has been traditionally associated with men, not women" (13). Croft's alternate scenes of emotional and physical power certainly ground her in Inness's definition of toughness. She shows reserve when her love interest is shot by the bad guy and drowned in a pool, despite her failed attempt to rescue him. She engages in sword and spear combat while fellow tomb raiders rely on impersonal semiautomatic rifles. In the end, she defeats her rival through physical combat. Lara Croft demonstrates her physical prowess and resiliency, while retaining a greater emotional depth than that usually allotted to male protagonists. Intellect, emotion, and body merge as equal elements of her character.

## Conclusions

Films such as *Lara Croft: Tomb Raider* gesture toward a shift from the babe female scientist to the babe female action hero, who is accompanied by a nebbish male scientist who aids and abets her adventuring. Television shows such as *Next Action Star* in which "charismatic men and women from across the country compete against one another to become America's next high-powered male and female action heroes, winning not only a cash prize, but the chance to star in the NBC movie" (NBC.com) suggest a growing public acceptance of the female action heroine. Films such as *Kill Bill, Volumes I* and *II*; *Charlie's Angels*; or the *Resident Evil* series featuring Milla Jovovich kicking zombie ass, reveal a surge of popularity for the empowered female. The feminist and cultural implications of the heroines of these films are more complex than can be discussed here; but clearly questions regarding the use of violence, the possibility of rejecting traditional roles, and the values of emotion and logic hang perilously in the balance.

But what is already changing—changing significantly—is the scope and trajectory of American action films. The evolution in the last decade suggests that chick flicks may no longer be defined by stereotypical melodrama, romance, or weepiness. Female viewers may, at long last, be able to get some "girlie action."

## Notes

1   For a clear definition of the action-adventure film, see Welch 170.
2   Carter's character resembles *Die Hard*'s John McClane, who is described by Peter Parshall as an "ordinary American, working class by speech and dress, uncomfortable in the cosmopolitan world, his only assets guts and determination and a quick mind."
3   Certainly this functions as a reminder that she is a "babe" scientist, but also echoes Ripley, one of the early action-adventure heroines in the archetypal monster film, *Alien*, whose underwear scene finale has befuddled feminist critics.
4   Compare to the *Alien* trilogy.
5   Steven Poole describes it as "a rotting corpse sewn together from the gangrenous limbs of *Indiana Jones* films" (46).

## Works cited

Brown, Jeffrey A. "Bullets, Buddies, and Bad Guys." *Journal of Popular Film and Television* 21.2 (1993): 79–87. *Communication and Mass Media Complete*. Ebscohost. University of Wisconsin-Marathon County. Wausau, WI. 28 June 2004. <www.epnet.com>.

Gates, Philippa. "The Man's Film: Woo and the Pleasures of Male Melodrama." *Journal of Popular Culture* 35.1 (2001): 59–79.

George, Susan A. "Not Exactly 'of Woman Born': Procreation and Creation in Recent Science Fiction Films." *Journal of Popular Film and Television* 28.4 (2001): 176–83.

Hunter, Latham. "The Celluloid Cubicle: Regressive Constructions of Masculinity in 1990s Office Movies." *The Journal of American Culture* 26.1 (2003): 71–86.

Inness, Sherrie. *Tough Girls: Women Warriors and Wonder Women in Popular Culture*. Philadelphia: University of Pennsylvania Press, 1999.

NBC.com. "About the Show." *Next Action Star*. 1 August 2004. <http://www.nbc.com/nbc/Next_Action_Star/about.shtml>.

Parshall, Peter. "Die Hard and the American Mythos." *Journal of Popular Film and Television* 18.4 (1991): 134–44. *Communication and Mass Media Complete*. Ebscohost. University of Wisconsin-Marathon County. Wausau, WI. 5 July 2004. <www.epnet.com>.

Poole, Steven. "Headache or Hard-on?" Review of *Lara Croft: Tomb Raider*. *The New Statesman*, 23 July 2001: 46.

Schleiner, Anne-Marie. "Does Lara Croft Wear Fake Polygons?: Gender and Gender-Role Subversion in Computer Adventure Games." *Leonardo* 54.3 (2001): 221–26.

Welch, James M. "Action Films: The Serious, the Ironic, the Postmodern." In *Film Genre 2000: New Critical Essays*. Ed. Wheeler Winston Dixon. Albany, NY: SUNY, 2000: 161–76.

# Chapter 12

# Babes in boots

## Hollywood's oxymoronic warrior woman

### Kate Waites

Although the warrior woman has become a popular mainstay in contemporary Hollywood films, with such recent incarnations as Lara Croft (*Lara Croft: Tomb Raider*; *Cradle of Life*), Charlie's three Angels (*Charlie's Angels*), and Beatrix Kiddo (*Kill Bill: Vol. 1, Vol. 2*), her representation has had a relatively short celluloid life.[1] Indeed, not until the 1980s when Ripley (Sigourney Weaver) and Sarah Connor (Linda Hamilton) took up arms against alien-enemies in *Alien, Aliens*, and *Terminator I, II*, have audiences of the conventional action genre witnessed the unleashed might and fury of warrior women. They are, one might argue, female heroes come of age in Hollywood action flicks in a postfeminist era. Intelligent, resourceful, tough, and competent, women warriors appear to be the equal of their male counterparts, as they brandish swords and guns and engage in kung-fu style combat to overcome villainy.

Hollywood's female warrior may be construed as a distant cousin of the notorious screen *femme fatale* of earlier decades, as Carol M. Dole argues, since she is the "archetypal Hollywood figure of female violence" (126). But her origin may actually be traced back much further, first to prehistory, then to antiquity and the mythical Amazons, and later to the iconic Judith of the Old Testament Apocrypha. Like their foremothers who were born of patriarchal mythology, today's screen warriors owe their life to a masculinist ideology, fueled, ironically, by feminism. Constructed to titillate an adolescent male audience as much as to appeal to women looking for female models of heroism, Hollywood's women warriors manage to accommodate extreme notions of conventional femininity, even as they go about their business of kicking enemy butt. They have generated as much critical discussion as they have audience attention, as film buffs and theorists alike wrangle with their growing popularity and significance for advancing the cause of equality by granting women more central roles in film. The argument pits those who see the female action hero as symbolically male, and therefore regressive, versus those who view her as upsetting "traditional gender conventions" through parody, and hence, as progressive (Brown 54–55). Typically, female heroes are drop-dead gorgeous and outfitted in costumes that emphasize sexuality rather than muscle—thus mitigating the suggestion of power and strength. Exceptions here are 1990s warriors Sarah Connor in *Terminator II*, Mace in *Strange Days*, and Demi Moore in *G.I. Jane* (who require a separate discussion altogether). They are also directed by a (sometimes absent) male authority figure: Lara Croft gets her orders from her deceased father; Charlie's Angels are commanded by the god-like Charlie and his "earthly" representative, Boswell; and Beatrix Kiddo reports to Bill, the head of the "Deadly Viper Assassination Squad." Otherwise, they are provided with maternal motives so that the preeminent objective in their warrior-ing is framed as mother-ing: Ripley assumes the maternal role with Jonesy, the cat in *Alien* and then becomes Newt's substitute mother in *Aliens*; Sarah Connor fights to protect her son and his future role in the war against the machines in the *Terminator* films; and Beatrix Kiddo in *Kill Bill* is not only commanded by Bill, but she is also framed as the bride-mother on a mission to protect and ultimately reclaim her offspring. Even the names of the warrior women under discussion here, *Lady* Lara Croft, Charlie's *Angels*, and Beatrix *Kiddo*, function symbolically to diminish them and to demonstrate their subordinate place within the conventional system. In this way, the warrior woman is shackled to the conventions or masquerade of femininity even as she takes on the guise of the traditionally male warrior.[2]

Although many agree that the inclusion of chicks in Hollywood action flicks represents a welcome expansion of the male bastion and signifies women's advances in the realms of power on one level, their origin and construction problematize their narrative significance. Like Frankenstein's monster, women warriors must have an inferiority complex, suffering, as they do, from being cast by and in the large image of a male creator. Yvonne Tasker refers to these "phallic women" as perverse because, even as they "turn away from" the "father," they are "nonetheless thoroughly oedipalised" (31). Simultaneously representing male hubris and an unconscious dread of women—the babe that they crave and the boot that they fear—the woman action hero functions as a parody of her "maker." A strange hybrid of over-determined masculine and feminine qualities, she is the monster-other whose existence challenges, and even wrestles with, male power. Ultimately, she reveals less about women or femininity and more about the disguise of masculinity.

The list of female screen warriors grows every day, but they share a common source: male myth-making. In their examination of the nature and origins of the mythical archetypes of the woman warrior, Richard J. Lane and Jay Wurts conclude that—based on archeological and anthropological findings—an authentic warrior woman may be traced back to primitive societies and the "female Scythian and Hycanian warrior-hunters" whose existence gave rise in part to the legendary Amazons (xiii). Ironically, however, the predominant archetype of female strength in Western culture came to be "fabricated almost entirely by Greek patri-archs" who had only disdain for the women among them (second-class citizens) as well as a terror of foreign, more egalitarian and matriarchal cultures and their "strong female-hunter warriors" (40). Accordingly, the Amazons were conceived of as strong, fierce, and decidedly *unwomanly*: they exiled or killed their male infants and cut off their right breast so as to better shoot their bow and arrow. But they were also beautiful, and on the battlefield these "ravishing beauties" deliberately bared their other breast, thus effectively using their sexuality to distract male enemies (41–42). An aesthetic fault in Greek culture, they were depicted as beautiful yet irregular in terms of gender, and distorted in terms of their sexuality, and so the image of the Amazon warrior tells us more about the male mythmakers' ambivalence and insecurities *in relation to* women than it does about strong women acting heroically. Gorgeous yet threatening, desirable but dangerous, the Amazon appeals to a mix of male hubris and uncertainty about women, and forms the prototype for the image of women warriors that follows. Confined to the cage of the monstrous-feminine within phallic ideology, they reflect men's use of hypermasculinity to cloak their fear and manage the paradoxical longing for and rejection of the "other" who challenges their identity.

A descendant of the Amazons, the Hebrew Judith is, similarly, the product of male mythology, as she appears in the *Apocrypha*, a book that is "most central to Judaeo-Christian patriarchy" (Stocker 2). Also described as extraordinarily beautiful, Judith uses her sexuality to seduce and then slay Holofernes to save, single-handedly, her town, Berthulia, and her people, the Israelites, from being conquered by the pagan invaders. Despite her act of heroism, her legacy is mixed; having slain Holofernes with her sex as well as her sword, she has come to represent the notoriously threatening *femme fatale* in popular culture (Stocker 3). After all, in the male imagination, warrior-ing is a masculine enterprise, and so the gender and sexuality of the female must be the defining and qualifying element when *she* engages in an act of heroism. Most importantly, however, Judith is more an instrument of male authority than an autonomous agent. According to Margarita Stocker, the *Book of the Apocrypha* in 16:6 emphasizes the fact that it was "not Judith but God" who vanquished the hand of the enemy "by the hand of a woman" (8). So, let's get this straight: men (patriarchs) wrote this story about a heroic woman who seduces a man with her beauty to save her people, but really, God *gave* her great beauty so that *he* could make her a warrior for his people and the male myth-makers could celebrate it. However outstanding her actions—and cutting off a man's head and displaying it for the entire town to see is pretty courageous—Judith's is the story of a woman, told by a man, using her sex to do the bidding of God, who is himself construed to be male.

This image of a male-created female warrior consistent with ancient archetypes, whose femininity is the defining element of her masculine enterprise, points up the contradiction that continues to plague the contemporary female screen warrior. Jane Caputi argues: "Popular culture serves as a repository of ancient and contemporary mythic [. . .] images and narratives [. . .] and archetypes" (4), and however much woman's role progresses, her image remains tied to the paradigm in which she was originally conceived, which is, in turn, tied to the mind of the male creator. The Lara Croft films were both directed and written by men, and the character is derived from Toby Gard's 1995 video-game character (Poole 1–2). The male-originated TV series *Charlie's Angels* spawned both male-directed film versions, and although there is one female contributor (of three) to the screenplay of *Charlie's Angels: Full Throttle*, the story and writing credits on both films go to men (IMDB). Like its predecessors, the *Kill Bill* films bear the indisputable stamp of male auteur-director Quentin Tarantino. Indeed, the action film, which tells the story of the exercise of hypermasculinity as a camouflage for male insecurity, remains dominated by male writers and directors.

Thrust into this hypermasculine milieu is Hollywood's woman warrior who comes in a variety of manifestations, from the classic representation of the seductive and dangerous *femme fatale* of the 1940s (and revived in the 1980s), to the contemporary version of the abused woman-turned-warrior (*Thelma and Louise*, 1991; *Enough*, 2001). Although these women use their ingenuity and take up arms (and sometimes fists) against men, they tend to be victims who are motivated by survival. Worthy as this motive might be—and who can blame Thelma or Louise for wanting a self-actualized life free from abusive and exploitative relationships with men?—such action heroes cannot be construed as traditional warriors, since they are framed first as domestic and sexual victims. Traditional warriors, by contrast to these female screen versions, whether male or female, according to Lane and Wurts, customarily act out of a "higher purpose" that enables them to "look beyond the immediate [. . .] battle [. . .] and see the larger implications of the struggle" (9). This moral imperative catapults the warrior to a more elevated status, and whether the hero is Spiderman or the Rock, the stakes are high and represent the age-old battle for justice that, typically, involves the good warrior versus the evil villain. As trite and overly simplified as these binary categories may be, they are the bread and butter of the high-grossing, ever-popular action film genre that continues to be dominated by male heroes.

However, given the economic advances of women and a revised view of "womanhood" in recent decades, Hollywood is more willing to put a female in action films as the hero-warrior, the characteristic violence notwithstanding (King and McCaughey 5). And, according to reviewer Bronwen Hruska, "Hollywood's most in-demand actresses are muscling in" on male terrain (6). As a result, the likes of Hollywood A-list babes, Angelina Jolie, Cameron Diaz, and Uma Thurman, are sharing the warrior-stage with prototypical he-man Sylvester Stallone, who has passed his legacy on to Arnold Schwarzenegger, Steven Segal, and, most recently, the Rock and Vin Diesel. And it's an interesting stage to share, in view of the fact that action films, according to Jeffrey Brown, work "within a narrative space that presents masculinity as an excessive, almost hysterical performance" (52).

So what is an audience to make of a hyperfeminine woman warrior enlisted to this over-determined masculine enterprise? More to the point: in a narrative space that is "almost exclusively male" (Brown 52), what do her construction and representation signify?

## Lady Lara Croft

Angelina Jolie's Lady Lara Croft, based on the hugely popular video game, embodies traditional femininity, even as she exhibits the excessive masculinity that typifies the male "warrior" of Hollywood action films. In *Tomb Raider*, for instance, her endeavor to save the world from Manfred Powell and the Planetary Alliance, which seeks to locate the two pieces of the secret triangle of light and thus to control time and the world, originates in her desire to carry out the wishes of her father. In a clearly Oedipal gesture, Lara identifies with her deceased father (rather than with her mother) who appears to her in a dream and directs her to a hidden clock containing instructions regarding her mission. Thus, consistent with the image of Judith who receives her directives and powers from God, the warrior Lara also defers to a male authority figure, having inherited from him the means of accessing the most advanced technology and of developing the martial arts and other skills necessary to mete out justice. Just as Judith's God provided her with the beauty to seduce and slay Holofernes, Lara's father passes on a birthright of status and wealth. Moreover, in a casting coup that is tellingly and ironically symbolic, Jon Voight, Jolie's real-life father from whom she is estranged, plays Sir Croft in the brief scene in which Lara dreams about herself as a young child under the tutelage of her father, who teaches her about the secrets of the universe. The "awful burden" he places "on her shoulders" requires her to defend her father's legacy and castle single-handedly—when it comes under attack from the legion of mercenaries. They are no match for her acrobatic talents and martial arts skills, as she swings trapeze-like from a ceiling harness and picks off her gun-toting foes one by one. The fact that they abscond with the coveted key is secondary to her display of fierceness (reminiscent of Neo from *The Matrix*) and resourcefulness (very like Harrison Ford's Indiana Jones) that looks forward to the ultimate showdown in a cave in Cambodia in the climactic scene.

Although Lara appears to fit the male warrior tradition as the quintessential loner, *Tomb Raider* hints at a prior romantic relationship with fellow geologist and turncoat Adam West, who has sold his services to the enemy. A side-tracking romantic subplot is developed further in *Cradle of Life*, when Lara convinces British Intelligence to release former lover, Marine, and mercenary, Terry Sheridan, from jail to assist in her effort to, once again, save the world. In this faster-paced, stunt-driven, and thrill-packed follow-up to the debut film, Lara must recover the orb (key) to the box containing the "anti-life" hidden thousands of years before by Alexander the Great, who recognized its potential harm if placed in the wrong hands. In this version, Lara receives her marching orders from two representatives of British Intelligence (MI6), which is ironically implied when Lara quips, "so the Queen has given me the authority, has she?" Although her sarcasm suggests that she answers to no one but herself, this assignment from the bastion of British power and imperialism—of which the Queen is merely a figurehead—echoes her deployment by her father in the previous film. In this case, she must now recover the coveted orb from corporate terrorist Jonathan Reiss, who plans to sell the deadly and incurable virus to the highest bidder for use as the penultimate biological weapon. The fact that she must rely on the help of a man who was also her lover weakens Lara's warrior status, and it frames her as a romantic and sexualized figure, particularly in the scene on the boat after they parachute off a skyscraper together, having escaped from Reiss's men. Newly showered and outfitted in a suggestive and strapless white wrap, Lara succumbs to a moment of passion with Terry in her stateroom. The scene is shot in hazy lighting that emphasizes the charged, sexual atmosphere, as Lara slides from beneath his prone body to sit astride him, pinning his hands and permitting the camera a partial view of her ample breasts. It becomes evident that Lara has used this moment of vulnerability to handcuff Terry to the leg of the bed, having doubted his trustworthiness after he declined to "shoot Reiss" when he had the opportunity. Even though she assumes the "masculine" position as the aggressor, the scene effectively slows the action and frames her as "feminine." Moreover, in addition to the gratuitous exposure of her breasts, in the scene Lara must resort to using the weapon of her sexuality in order to seduce and contain her untrustworthy former lover.

This sexualized framing of Lara persists throughout the film, speaking to a much-debated point raised in the ground-breaking work of feminist theorist Laura Mulvey. The representation of "woman" in Hollywood film, she argues, serves as erotic spectacle for the presumed male viewer; hence she is sexualized and defined as passive, consistent with her secondary value or "to-be-looked-at-ness," in contrast to the male's image as active and powerful. In many respects this reductive argument fails to recognize the fluidity of gendered identities and reinforces the traditional polarities of femininity and masculinity. For instance, male action heroes from Sylvester Stallone in *First Blood* to Brad Pitt in *Troy* are designed to some degree as spectacle, with their ultra-muscular, sweaty bodies and revealing outfits. However, in contrast to female warriors, their power is never mitigated and their sexuality does not weaken them. Nor do they have to use sex as a weapon. In fact, their power and strength are never questioned, in part because they are contextualized differently, as they are invariably surrounded by other mighty male cohorts or else villains of nearly equal power. Typically, women—if present at all in male action films—are secondary, romantic figures that serve to distract and sometimes endanger the male hero. (Consider, for example, Jamie Lee Curtis alongside Schwarzenegger in *True Lies*.) When the woman warrior is feminized and forced to deploy her sexuality as a weapon, it distracts her and the viewer from her mission, even when it is rationalized as a part of her plan. Her status is further reduced because, unlike her male counterpart, she is depicted as an anomaly. Indeed, neither in *Tomb Raider* nor in *Cradle of Life* is there another woman whose power equals Lara's. In fact, there are no notable women at all, and in contrast to Jeffrey Brown's

*Image 12.1* Lara Croft (Angelina Jolie) arrives via jet ski

argument that the "cinematic gaze of the action film codes the heroine's body in the same way as the muscular male hero's, as both object and subject" (56), Lara Croft has a voluptuous rather than a "hard" body, and her image as a female warrior is an isolated and unsupported one.

What undermines Lara's warrior status in *Cradle of Life* most, however, has to do with the plot. The film opens with Lara jet-skiing to a Greek fishing vessel following an earthquake that has shifted the underwater world allowing access to the ruins of the Lunar Temple, which Lara has discovered. Dismissing the captain's doubts, Lara reminds him that "everything lost is meant to be found," and so she sets her sights on the long-lost map to the origins of life. Lara is unaware, however, that the villainous Reiss has recruited the Che Ling gang to follow her and secure the orb. Echoing Greek mythology in which Pandora, Eve's sister-in-original-crime, is charged as the culprit for unleashing evil into the world, Lara's quest for knowledge actually aligns her with naïve and silly Pandora. In contrast to the quintessential action warrior, Rambo (Sylvester Stallone) in *First Blood* who vows to win a war that he "never started," Lara must contend with the ramifications of her own *feminine* misbehavior. Although she poses as a tough, intelligent, and resourceful warrior figure, the narrative frame highlights her essentially female nature, as viewed through the eyes of a male creator.

Like her screen precursor, Ripley, whom Philip Green sees as a "phallic woman" who finds herself "ultimately recuperated by family ideology," Lara may be viewed as a fetishized and "sublimated attempt" by contemporary male myth-makers "to confront a changing reality in the sexual division of labor that highlights the putative change every bit as much as the fetish" (187). Green is pointing up the essential contradiction reflected in the construction of the contemporary warrior woman: fetishized and thereby reduced, even as she embodies the traits of the empowered postmodern woman. The warrior woman's image, which is packaged in regressive conventions, reflects the uneasy attempts of Hollywood creators/writers to accommodate women in both real and symbolic realms of power.

## Charlie's Angels

*Charlie's Angels* and *Charlie's Angels: Full Throttle* derive from the 1970s TV series of the same name, which reflected a similar attempt by the culture to accommodate social changes in the wake of the second-wave feminist movement. Besides making original Angel Farrah Fawcett into a sexual icon, whose signature hair, face and body looked out from posters plastered on almost every teenage boy's wall, the series mirrored the culture's unease with women coming of age and taking it to the men on their home turf (which was just about everywhere except in the home). Hence, although they brandished guns and caught the bad guys, the three female private detectives' actions were overshadowed by their beauty and sex appeal. Or, as *Rolling Stone*'s Peter Travers more aptly describes it, "Back then, the joke was that, given the dumb plots, you could watch the show with the sound off and focus on how Farrah Fawcett, Kate Jackson and Jaclyn Smith fought crime in various states of undress" (1).

The *Charlie's Angels* film remakes do little to change this image, even as they reveal more pugnacious Angels, reflecting the culture's heightened ambivalence about even more capable women. Clearly, Alex (Lucy Liu), Natalie (Cameron Diaz), and Dylan (Drew Barrymore) are portrayed as brainier, tougher, fiercer, and much more highly skilled than their predecessors. On par with contemporary male warriors, they throw punches and kicks and perform death-defying kung-fu acrobatics, *à la* Jackie Chan. In fact, even though they do not employ firearms in their game plans, physical aggression is their carrying card. But their performance is not only far fetched, it is also silly, bathed, as it assuredly is, in persistent signifiers of emphasized femininity.[3] The original film opens with an action-packed scene in which Alex, in mid-air, overtakes a bad guy with a bomb and then safely lands on a boat that is captained by Natalie, who wears a revealing bikini. Alex sports a tight, black outfit and her long, black hair spills out from under her helmet, so it is not too much of a stretch to equate the phallic-like bomb with the fetishized woman (that, in a matching closing scene, is recuperated when she actually sits astride the bomb). Moreover, there are more costume changes than set changes in both razzle-dazzle, scene-driven (rather than plot-driven) films, from barely-there underwear to skin-tight leather pants and slinky dresses, all of which serve as an importunate reminder to the viewer that these are *babes* first and that their butt-kicking is a bit of a ruse.

The flimsy plot in the first film revolves around a twin conspiracy by a team of criminals—John Knox and partner Vivian Wood—to infiltrate the mainframe of Red Star Satellite Network to gain control of its global positioning network, then locate and kill Charlie Townsend (the Angels' boss, whom Knox holds responsible for his father's death). Besides working undercover in sexually suggestive outfits to re-secure the mainframe and save both Charlie and Bosley, the Angels also pursue romantic relationships, thus shoring up their feminine identity. Natalie flirts with bartender Pete (Luke Owen), while Alex sustains an exclusive relationship with Jason (Matt LeBlanc). Consistent with her weak-minded character, however, Dylan falls for the seductive charms of bad guy Knox—whom she is assigned to guard—who has deceived the team of investigators into believing that *his* life and software are in danger. In a pivotal scene in which he reveals his true, criminal intentions after sleeping with her, Dylan's vulnerability is exposed, and it is clearly connected to her sexuality as well as to her gender. After sleeping with her, Knox ridicules the towel-clad Dylan, referring to her as a clueless detective who has "no idea what's going to happen"; then he shoots at her, causing her to crash through a picture window and land on the ground naked.

In the sequel, these mitigating, genderized factors in the Angels' warrior status are intensified. As they track the thieves who stole the valuable ring with coded information identifying members of the Witness Protection Program, they juggle warrior-ing alongside their relationships with men, as if to convince the audience that these are, indeed, women masquerading in combat boots. Natalie considers co-habitation and puppy-adopting with Pete; Alex tries on the domestic role for Jason while entertaining a visit from her doting father; and Drew must contend with her vindictive ex-con-lover, Seamus O'Grady (Justin Theroux) as well as with the unsolicited attentions of the "Thin-Man"/Assassin (Crispin Glover). A fallen Angel, Madison Lee (the curvy and hard-bodied Demi Moore) even makes an appearance in this film to tempt Natalie to abandon (father? God?) Charlie and follow her to the dark side, thereby suggesting the age-old duality of Woman: good (Mary/angels) or evil (Eve/*femme fatale*).

Whereas Lara Croft's sexuality, like Judith's, is at least employed as a mechanism or strategy to wield power, the extremely sexualized and feminized Angels are posed merely as erotic spectacle, which serves only to diminish their strength. In a review of the first film, critic Chris Vognar quotes communications professor, Christopher Sharrett, who confirms that such pseudo "girlpower" films "are in fact crafted for adolescent boys" (2C). While the undue attention to the female warriors' sexuality and feminine identity is, by all measures, over the top, their construction is consistent with the majority of movies in the female action-adventure genre, according to Philip Green, because even though female heroes appear to be empowered, "Glamour still rules" (78). One might also argue that femininity, that is, weakness and corruptibility, rule right alongside glamour.

But the over-determined display of conventional femininity and sexuality is but one facet in this not-so-covert vehicle of gender performance in women's action films. For instance, both *Charlie's Angels* and *Charlie's Angels: Full Throttle* open with a male voice-over announcing the story of "three very different little girls" who "grew up to be three very different women. They are brilliant and beautiful, and they work for me. My name is Charlie." Voice-over is a standard device in film that is used to establish authority or control of the narrative, according to film theorist Kaja Silverman, since the god-like voice speaks from outside the narrative frame and suggests omniscience (52–53). Fittingly, the Angels/private investigators take orders from Charlie, whom they communicate with only through telephone and via his point-man, Bosley (Bill Murray in the first film and Bernie Mac in the sequel). Consistent with the images of warrior-predecessor, Judith, and counterpart, Lady Lara Croft, the Angels are cast primarily as women who fight fiercely and heroically at the bidding of an all-powerful, obscure male authority figure. Like Sir Croft who speaks "from the grave" (suggesting supernatural power), Charlie issues directives from an elusive space, thus framing him as an omniscient and godlike figure. Having made a dent in the male citadel of action films, therefore, women warriors are reduced to playing a role in a farce that re-inscribes their feminine place within the phallic system, even as it inadvertently exposes the pretense of hypermasculinity.

## Beatrix Kiddo: the bride/the mother

At first glance, Quentin Tarantino's *Kill Bill: Vol. I* (2003) and *Vol. II* (2004) appear to subvert this gender charade. Superior to all of the action films previously discussed, in terms of their creative plots, muscular camera work, balletic martial-arts fight scenes, and visually stunning direction— they are Quentin Tarantino films, after all—they refrain from exploiting the sexualizing signifiers of the woman-warrior film. Minus the gratuitous nakedness and the superfluous, romantic subplot, as well as the revealing and suggestive costumes, *Kill Bill, Vol. I* and *Kill Bill, Vol. II* feature a woman warrior (Uma Thurman) who "is a near-perfect example of a truly strong female action hero":

> *Kill Bill's* leading lady and her female nemeses stagger instead of prance, sweat rather than preen, and utter pre-kill one-liners that rival those made famous by California's new governor [. . .] *Kill Bill* is one of a small handful of big-screen blockbusters that skips the skimpy skirts and sexual double-entendres generally used to demean the anger or strength of celluloid femmes fatales.
>
> (Raha)

Although the warrior sports a tight, yellow leather motorcycle outfit, and her arch-enemy (Lucy Liu) wears conventionally feminine dress, neither is reduced by Tarantino's less imposing use of these signifiers. And unlike the solitary Lara Croft, the hero (Beatrix Kiddo) is bolstered by comparable female warriors, her former colleagues in the deadly Viper Assassination Squad (Elle Driver, Vernita Green, and O-Ren Ishii), as well as by O-Ren Ishii's exceptionally capable female bodyguards. Moreover, whereas Croft and the Angels remain un-mussed as they engage in less than convincing, video-game-like combat, the *Kill Bill* warriors are portrayed as credible, compelling, highly-skilled martial artists and swordswomen, the campiness notwithstanding. Tarantino, of course, is working in part from a bona fide tradition in kung-fu films, in which the powerful and violent woman warrior is "transgressive"; that is, having established her skills, she has earned her acceptance into the coterie of men (Arons 31), and thus, plays a viable role within the tradition. Perhaps most significantly, by having

Kiddo directly address the camera as well as speak in voice-over in the opening scenes in *Vol. II*, as she introduces her odyssey of revenge and justice in flashback, the film suggests that she has authorial control over her own representation (in direct contrast to the use of voice-over by Charlie, who exercises authority over "his" Angels). In a scene that is beautifully shot in grainy black and white, Kiddo, through the device of voice-over, recounts events leading up to her brutal assault, as she drives a convertible en route to her next target, Bud, Bill's brother and one of the deadly Viper Assassination Squad that left her for dead.

But even as the depiction of the warrior woman in these films appears to sabotage gender conventions, it slyly redeploys them. The plot, Beatrix Kiddo's precarious identity, and pivotal scenes are bathed in cultural signifiers that re-inscribe conventional femininity on a banner of masculine derring-do. *Vol. I* is a near-wordless, thrill-packed and dazzling display of kung-fu acrobatics in which the poetic and dynamic camera becomes a kind of narrator and character at once, since the female hero's name as well as many plot details—the story behind the massacre—remain undisclosed until the second film. But the film and the nameless character's construction within it ultimately tell a tired old tale.

The film opens with a black-and-white close-up of the bloodied, pregnant bride's face, shortly before a man's hand and gun enter the frame; then the gun fires a bullet at close range, leaving the "Bride" (Beatrix Kiddo) for dead. Shots of the comatose woman in a hospital bed reveal that she survived the massacre of seven other participants in the wedding orchestrated by her jealous former lover, "Bill," and his "Viper Assassination Squad." The film then cuts to color in the present and a series of scenes in which the miraculously recovered Kiddo is seen driving up to a house in Pasadena. The front porch of the placid suburban house is strewn with toys, indicative of a conventional domestic arrangement. But this image is instantly shattered when Kiddo engages in hand-to-hand combat with Vernita Green (Vivica Fox), the woman who answers the door, also identified as one of the female assassins responsible for the wedding-massacre in a black-and-white flashback.

At one point, however, the two women freeze, almost tableau-like, in deference to motherhood when, in a deep-focus shot through the picture window and between the two combatants, a school bus is seen pulling up in front of the house, depositing Vernita Green's little girl. In a clearly ironic gesture that appears to mock traditional femininity, the bloodied and discombobulated mother greets her daughter, Nicky, and introduces her to "mommy's friend." Kiddo follows suit, sliding into a solicitous, maternal role, while her rival sends the child to her room and, inexplicably, invites her guest into the kitchen for coffee. During the course of their conversation, in which Vernita apologizes for her part in the massacre and the loss of Kiddo's baby-to-be, she suddenly pulls a gun out of a cereal

*Image 12.2* School bus depositing the daughter of Vernita Green (Vivica Fox) as she fights with Beatrix Kiddo (Uma Thurman)

box and aims it toward Kiddo, who manages to whip a knife out of her boot, killing her enemy. The camera then cuts to the little girl standing in the doorway, having just witnessed the revenge-murder of her mother. Visibly distraught that the child has witnessed the event, Kiddo explains to the little girl that her "mother had it comin'" and: "When you grow up, if you still feel raw about it, I'll be waitin'." (Is this the set-up for *Vol. III*?)

This scene echoes other such scenes in both films, reinforces the problematic plot, and frames the contested site of the warrior woman's construction. On the one hand, the character is accorded all the qualities and signification of her male action-hero counterpart: she is tough, fearless, aggressive to the point of ruthlessness, and more than able to hold her own in battle. Simultaneously, however, despite not being overtly sexualized, the character's name is Beatrix *Kiddo* (an obvious diminution of her identity). Moreover, in *Vol. I*, her identity is relegated to the "Bride" seeking revenge for the murder of her husband-to-be and his family as well as her own unborn child. In *Vol. II*, the film identifies her as "Mother," a role which takes precedence over her warrior role, as reflected in the scene in which she identifies with the "mother" in her enemy, Vernita Green, and with the mother in herself. Or, as reviewer Mark Rahner deprecatingly puts it: "The Bride becomes The Mommy in *Vol. 2*" (13). These identifiers encase her in a box of femininity and maternity that overshadows her warrior status. In addition to being "framed" as the Bride-Mother, Kiddo is not an autonomous agent. Like Lara Croft and the Angels who take directives from a quasi-supernatural male authority figure, Kiddo is but the handmaiden of Bill, who recreated her in his image, a relationship which becomes clear in key scenes in *Vol. II* that depict her worshipfully learning at the feet of her lover.

All non-stop action and little dialogue, the first film leaves many questions to be answered by the sequel: who exactly is this unnamed Bride? Who is Bill and why did he want her dead? And how did she become such a deadly martial arts warrior? Even as Kiddo continues to hunt down her enemies, the second film resolves these questions and fleshes out the plot through flashback: enlisted as Bill's assassin and his mistress, Kiddo is sent to study with Chinese martial arts master, Pi Mei, under whom she excels and learns the mysteries of Kung Fu, including the "five-point exploding palm technique," by which, in the film's climactic scene, she wins revenge and gets the better of her former lover and master, Bill. But the more the viewer gleans about her character and the mystery of the wedding-chapel massacre, the more the film itself devolves into conventional devices. The audience is tipped off to this development in the first film, when Elle (Darryl Hannah) visits the comatose Bride in the hospital disguised as a nurse. Prepared to "finish her off," she makes cellphone contact with the unseen Bill, who rescinds his order to kill her, given her helpless state, implying that such a kill would be unworthy of the Bride's warrior status, and orders Elle to "come home, honey. I love you [Elle] very much." Clearly, Elle acts at his bidding and is entangled in a romantic and protégée relationship with Bill, just as the Bride has been, as we learn in *Vol. II*. This scene also looks forward to the Hatori-Hanzo sword-wielding showdown between Elle and Kiddo in Bud's trailer in the second film, and highlights feminine traits of jealousy and competition that effectively reduce their warrior status and battle to a stereotypical "catfight."

In another telling flashback scene at the chapel where the wedding rehearsal is taking place shortly before the massacre, Bill, inexplicably, appears (*Kill Bill, Vol. II*). He assures Kiddo that his intention is not to interfere with her plans to wed and assume a more unadventurous identity, and at her suggestion he even poses as her father to the groom's family. The Oedipal reference here becomes clear when, of course, the "Father" removes/kills the husband-substitute of whom he decidedly does not approve. Such moments serve to recuperate the warrior for traditional womanhood, and they culminate in the second film when Kiddo tracks down Bill in his home after having eliminated all the assassins implicated in the chapel massacre. Once again, she encounters a domestic scene, but this time Bill is depicted as a paternal figure entertaining and making a sandwich for his five-year-old daughter, recalling the earlier showdown with Vernita Green. Of course, Kiddo is astonished to meet the five-year-old-daughter who was—unbeknownst to her—ripped from her womb during the chapel-massacre by her jealous former lover and father of the child. In her face-off with Bill and under the influence of a paralyzing truth serum, Kiddo recounts, in flashback, the scene in which she first discovered her pregnancy while on a kill-mission for Bill. This scene reveals that she is magically altered by the prospect of motherhood: she discloses this information to her intended target in an effort to call off "the kill" and leave the business as well as Bill so as to make a better life for her child-to-be.

Indeed, her decision to give up her "career" to be a wife and mommy in El Paso, Texas, is the lynchpin of the plot, because it sets the massacre-plan in motion. In addition to resolving all the plot questions posed in the original film, *Kill Bill, Vol. II* also succeeds in putting the fierce, embattled warrior woman back in her proper place, not by punishing her and/or killing her off, *à la* film noir, but rather, by seeing her capitulate to the traditional paradigm of wannabe-stay-at-home mom. This transformation is most evident in the operatic face-off between Kiddo and Bill—her lover, father, god—following which she is depicted as a fawning, protective mother watching cartoons with her newly discovered daughter on a bed in a motel room.[4]

The film as well as the warrior woman that seems most promising at the outset, therefore, proves to be the most reduced, and the choices available to her—warrior *or* mother—are not only clichéd, but also extreme and finally moot, as each cancels the other out. Moreover, like her action-sisters, Kiddo is ultimately directed by, if not created by, Bill, a male, godlike figure, and she is showered in regressive feminine conventions that overtake her transgressive heroic role.[5] Hollywood's warrior woman, then, is but a Pygmalion-like figure, a projection of male fantasy and his need to contain her in a feminine box even as she dons the accoutrements of her male counterpart. Hollywood's prototypical warrior woman is a strange amalgamation of the hypermasculine and emphasized feminine, implying that even our twenty-first-century myth-makers continue to be steeped in the lore—as well as the law—of the father.

## Notes

1   Naturally, women did appear as warriors on screen in early cinema, but typically in B-pictures or lesser known films, including classics such as *Joan of Arc* (1948).

2   Taking a page from Judith Butler, Yvonne Tasker sees the female action hero as "cross-dressing," that is, taking on the body language and appearance of the "butch" stereotype. Her examples include Ripley (*Alien*), Sarah Connor (*Terminator*), Charly (*Long Kiss Goodnight*), and Mace (*Strange Days*). Although she considers the ambiguous construction of the female hero and the ways in which it "poses a challenge to gendered binaries" (69), she emphasizes the hard-bodied, muscular heroine that is the exception rather than the rule, as seen in the films of the new millennium. Moreover, her discussion does not include how the image reflects (male) authorship.

3   For some fans of the original 1970s television series, it may also be construed as an ironic nod to its campiness (see Gough-Yates). However, significant differences between the television series and the film make any argument about its self-reflexivity suspect. For example, feminist elements of the series —the Angels' rejection of the police department's chauvinism and their

choice of career as detectives over marriage or relationships—are glaringly absent. Instead, the romantic and sexual relationships bear equal narrative weight in the film, to the point that such relationships seem to intrude on the action.

4   A postfeminist interpretation might well—as suggested by the review from *Bitch* magazine cited above—see these issues from a different perspective. Beatrix Kiddo's decision to reject her role as assassin in favor of marriage and children, for example, could be framed as an extreme—and somewhat tongue-in-cheek—example of the conflict between career and family, the same issue raised in many recent chick flicks. Such postfeminist films are often read as acknowledging the real difficulties women face in trying to "have it all." These readings, however, fail to acknowledge the regressive and anti-feminist motives at work.

5   More recent action films—*Cat Woman* (2004), *Elektra* (2005), and *Mr & Mrs Smith* (2005)—stack up equally poorly as examples of newly designed and empowered screen warrior women. A box-office disaster, *Cat Woman* seems to be little more than a vehicle for Halle Berry's character to hiss and strut in body-hugging leather. Equally absurd is Jennifer Garner's pouty turn in *Elektra*. Cast as a blood-thirsty assassin and loner who finally "sees the light" and turns her extraordinary sword-fighting skills to domesticity and defense of father, child, and family, Garner is more akin to a *Maxim* cover-girl than a warrior woman. Angelina Jolie's Mrs Smith is the promising equal of her husband (Brad Pitt) in aggression, masterful use of weaponry and, of course, stunning good looks. Like Elektra, she also trades in the assassin market for profit until she turns all mushy with her assassin-competitor-husband. This image-conscious film promises to level the gender playing field by displaying Mr Smith as an equivalent sex object. However, whereas his ruthlessness is tempered by his humanity and desire to avoid actually killing Mrs Smith in defiance of his orders, she is framed as a ruthless and deadly serious—if drop-dead gorgeous—shrew, even as her charming husband behaves with restraint, levity, and humor, providing more notches on his belt of humanity.

## Works cited

Arons, Wendy. "If Her Stunning Beauty Doesn't Bring You to Your Knees, Her Deadly Drop Kick Will." In *Reel Knockouts: Violent Women in the Movies*. Ed. Martha McCaughey and Neal King. Austin: University of Texas Press, 2001: 27–51.

Brown, Jeffrey. "Gender and the Action Heroine: Hardbodies and the Point of No Return." *Cinema Journal* 35 (Spring 1996): 52–71.

Caputi, Jane. *Goddesses and Monsters: Women, Myth, Power, and Popular Culture*. Madison, Wisconsin: University of Wisconsin Press, 2004.

Dole, Carol M. "The Gun and the Badge." In *Reel Knockouts: Violent Women in the Movies*. Ed. Martha McCaughey and Neal King. Austin: University of Texas Press, 2001: 78–105.

Goldstein, Joshua S. *War and Gender: How Gender Shapes the War System*. Cambridge: Cambridge University Press, 2001.

Gough-Yates, Anna. "Angels in Chains: Feminism, Femininity, and Consumer Culture in *Charlie's Angels*." In *Action TV: Tough Guys, Smooth Operators and Foxy Chicks*. Ed. Bill Ogersby and Anna Gough-Yates. New York: Routledge, 2001: 83–100.

Green, Philip. *Cracks in the Pedestal: Ideology and Gender in Hollywood*. Amherst: University of Massachusetts Press, 1998.

Hruska, Bronwen. "Make Her Day: Hollywood's Leading Ladies are Getting in on the Action Genre." *Entertainment Weekly*, 11 June 1993: 6–7.

Inness, Sherrie A. *Tough Girls: Women Warriors and Wonder Women in Popular Culture*. Philadelphia: University of Pennsylvania Press, 1999.

King, Neal and Martha McCaughey. "What's a Mean Woman Like You Doing in a Movie Like This?" In *Reel Knockouts: Violent Women in the Movies*. Ed. Martha McCaughey and Neal King. Austin: University of Texas Press, 2001: 1–25.

Lane, Richard J. and Jay Wurts. *In Search of the Woman Warrior: Four Mythical Archetypes for Modern Women*. Wales: Cygnus Books, 2002.

Mulvey, Laura. "Visual Pleasure and Narrative Cinema." *Screen* 16.3 (Autumn 1975): 6–18.

Poole, Steven. "Tomb Raider History: Lara's Story." 6 April 2005: 1–7. <http://freespace.virgin.net/star.gate/trhistory.htm>.

Raha, Maria. "Smells Like Tarantino Spirit." *Bitch (S)hitlist* 12 November 2003. 17 June 2004 <http:/www.bitchmagazine.org/blog/archives/2003_11.html>.

Rahner, Mark. "Let the Bloddletting Begin." *Sun-Sentinel*, August 22, 2004: 13.

Silverman, Kaja. *The Acoustic Mirror*. Bloomington: Indiana University Press, 1992.

Stocker, Margarita. *Judith: Sexual Warrior: Women and Power in Western Culture*. New Haven: Yale University Press, 1998.

Tasker, Yvonne. *Working Girls: Gender and Sexuality in Popular Cinema*. New York: Routledge, 1998.

Travers, Peter. Review of *Charlie's Angels*. *Rolling Stone*, 30 June 2004. <http://www.rollingstone.com/reviews/movie?id=5948215&pageid=rs.Reviews MovieArchives>.

Vognar, Chris. "'Girl Power' Comes with a Price." *The Miami Herald*, August 18, 2003: 2C.

# Chapter 13

# Afterword

## Once I got beyond the name chick flick

*Karen Hollinger*

### The chick flick and the history of the woman's film

I find it somewhat difficult even to begin talking about chick flicks because it is a label that for a long time I have hesitated to use, considering it a disparaging term that diminished the significance of women-oriented cinema. The essays in this volume, however, are trying to do something quite different. They are trying to reappropriate the term and use it as a positive descriptor for what one might otherwise call contemporary woman's films. Once I got over my disinclination even to use the term in the first place, the next question that came to mind is what exactly is a chick flick anyway? Is it a genre *per se* or rather a loosely defined umbrella term uniting a disparate group of films that have really three things in common: their primary appeal to female viewers, their concentration on issues relevant to women, and their focus on a female protagonist? This is, in fact, a definition with some history, and it raises perhaps one of the fundamental questions that we can ask about these contemporary chick flicks: How do they relate to the history of women's cinema?

As the editors note in their Introduction to this volume, the definition offered above is based on one first proposed in *The Desire to Desire* by Mary Ann Doane, who was writing about the category of films known as the woman's film or woman's picture of the 1930s and 1940s. Notable examples of classic woman's films that still attract substantial attention from critics and viewers alike include *Mildred Pierce* (1945), *Stella Dallas* (1937), *Gaslight* (1944), *Rebecca* (1940), *Back Street* (1932; 1941), and *Dark Victory* (1939). Doane saw woman's films as comprising a distinct Hollywood genre and broke them down into four categories: the love story, the plot of which centers around heterosexual romance; the maternal melodrama, dealing with a mother's affections for and tribulations in regard to her children; the paranoid gothic film, in which a recently wed woman fears her husband may be a murderer; and the medical discourse film, whose protagonist is suffering from a physical or psychological affliction (36).

Maureen Turim in this volume discusses a number of other possible predecessors of the contemporary chick flick. She traces the origins of the chick flick not only to the woman's films of the 1930s and 1940s, but to woman-centered silent films, which she describes as woman's films before there was a label for them. She looks in particular at D. W. Griffith melodramas such as *Way Down East* (1920), *The White Rose* (1923), and *True Heart Susie* (1919) that focus on mother–daughter bonding, female self-sacrifice, and women's betrayal by men. Turim also points to a long filmic tradition of female-centered romantic comedies, action melodramas, and what she calls dramatic comedies (combining serious and comedic elements) that stands as a precursor to today's chick flicks. Turim proposes that thinking about these pre-chick-flick films might be useful to considerations of contemporary films. Notable issues that feminist theorists have debated in regard to earlier woman's films include the negative effects of the intense emotional response they often evoke from female spectators, their ability to address the issue of female desire while at the same time seeming to advocate restrictions upon it, their cross-gender appeal, and their relation to the historical context in which they were produced. All of these considerations could be well applied to the contemporary chick flick.

The chick flicks that other authors in this volume are examining, however, can be said to have moved significantly away from earlier woman's films, but perhaps, as Turim suggests, not so much that all connections are lost. Certainly, romance and motherhood still remain prominent aspects of contemporary chick flicks, but with a difference, and some of this difference I would suggest comes from the influence of later woman's films. The sub-generic divisions of the woman's film that Doane discusses were transformed in the 1970s into what some critics have called the new woman's film. This regeneration occurred after woman's films had fallen into a period of hiatus during the 1950s, when family melodramas, aimed much more at mixed male and female audiences—such films as *Written on the Wind* (1954), *East of Eden* (1955), and *Giant* (1956)— began to predominate. The new woman's films of the 1970s significantly altered the contours of the genre by dealing with two issues initiated by the growth of the woman's movement in this period: the independent woman and female friendship. Films such as *An Unmarried Woman* (1978) and *Alice Doesn't Live Here Anymore* (1974) featured a woman attempting to make it on her own after divorce or the death of her spouse. Female friendship films also proliferated in this decade, notable examples being *Julia* (1977), *The Turning Point* (1977), and *Girlfriends* (1978).

As I argue in my book *In the Company of Women: Contemporary Female Friendship Films*, films focusing on women's friendship clearly came to dominate the woman's film market in the 1980s. While other types of woman's films are still evident in this period, they were not produced in even close to the numbers of female friendship films. Films dealing with independent women actually began to die out in the 1980s, or they transformed pre-existing genres on film and on television, muting the more patriarchally challenging aspects of the 1970s independent woman films, which openly championed female independence. For instance, what might be categorized as independent mother films modify their female protagonist's sense of independence by combining it with her devotion to motherhood, a much more traditionally feminine trait. Examples include *Stella* (1990; the Bette Midler remake of the 1930s maternal melodrama *Stella Dallas*), *Terms of Endearment* (1983), *The Good Mother* (1988), *This Is My Life* (1993), and more recently *Anywhere But Here* (1999). The paranoid gothic film has largely been transformed into the victimized-woman's-revenge film in *The Accused* (1988), *Sleeping with the Enemy* (1991), and more recently *Enough* (2002). The scenario of the abused woman has also become a staple of made-for-television woman-in-jeopardy movies. Other television dramas have continued in the tradition of earlier medical discourse films by focusing on plot formulas that involve a woman's courageous struggle against a debilitating illness.

Of the various categories of new woman's films, however, the female friendship film clearly found the widest audience and the greatest popularity with mainstream production and distribution companies in the 1980s and 1990s. In many ways, these earlier portrayals of women's friendship can be seen as the direct ancestors of today's chick flicks, but interestingly in the late 1990s the subgenre itself with its almost exclusive focus on female bonding seemed to run out of energy. I would suggest two reasons for this decline: first of all, the increasingly conservative climate in the US in the late 1990s and into the 2000s seems to have made the female friendship film, which clearly was inspired by feminist notions of sisterhood, anathema to mainstream filmmaking. Secondly, the 1990s also witnessed a significant rise in women's involvement in the US film industry as producers and directors, as well as an increase in the clout of female stars, who became more involved in production. Despite their foregrounding of female characters and what are generally considered women's issues, Hollywood female friendship films were overwhelmingly the products of male directors and production executives. The entry of women into directorial and managerial roles changed the contours of woman's films in a direction that presages the appearance of the chick flicks that are discussed in this volume.

One of the first changes women's greater involvement in filmmaking brought about was a return to classic woman's literature as a source of female-centered plots and characters. This "return to the classics" movement began in the mid-1990s with the remarkable popularity of the film adaptations of Louisa May Alcott's *Little Women* (1994) and Jane Austen's *Sense and Sensibility* (1995), both of which focus on women's sisterly relationships as drawn by prominent women writers of the past. These

Hollywood box office successes were transitional films between the dying female friendship film cycle and the newly emerging women's return to the classics movement. This new cycle in American women's cinema relied heavily on female filmmakers, stars, and production executives to push not only to get the films into production, but also for a refashioning of their films' nineteenth-century heroines in accord with popular notions of twentieth-century feminist ideas.

Timothy Corrigan, the first to identify this wave and dub it a "return to the classics" movement, associated it with politically conservative trends such as "a therapeutic turn from cultural complexity," "an increasing concern with manner over matter," and a reaction against postmodernist trends in filmmaking that diminish traditional plot and character (72). Corrigan did not recognize that a significant segment of this movement involved the input of female filmmakers and to a large extent was directed to a female audience. Many 1990s classic adaptations represent not only a conservative return to what is presented as a simpler, better past, but also the attempt of female screenwriters, directors, stars, and production executives to recapture for a contemporary female audience the distinctive voices of prominent women of the past, either real or fictional, and to give these voices a vaguely feminist tenor. In addition to *Little Women* and *Sense and Sensibility*, films such as *Clueless* (1995), *The Portrait of a Lady* (1996), *Mrs Dalloway* (1997), and *Mansfield Park* (1999) were all adapted by female screenwriters, and often female directors and producers as well, primarily from novels written by female authors, focusing on female protagonists.

If these films were nostalgic attempts to escape from current "cultural complexity" by returning to an idyllic past, as Corrigan maintains, this past is dominated by female figures who are reshaped in images framed by a contemporary female sensibility, influenced by feminist ideas, and fashioned for a contemporary female audience. This return to the classics movement, however, seems to have very quickly run its course in the late 1990s and, as the essays in this volume suggest, at the time of this writing American women's cinema seems to be swerving off in myriad directions. In a gesture of appropriation, the contributors to this volume have taken the previously pejorative term *chick flicks* and used it positively to describe these new directions in women's cinema that both partake of the history of the woman's film and move substantially beyond that history.

## What is a chick flick then?

Do we want to call the current wave of chick flicks a genre or perhaps more accurately a subgenre of the larger filmic category of woman's films? If it is a subgenre, it certainly is a wide-ranging one. What the chick flick has now come to include is not just the offspring of earlier woman's films and the continuing sporadic revivals of female friendship films and women-oriented literary adaptations, but new categories of women-oriented films. This has caused some uncertainty about exactly how to define the boundaries of the subgenre. As Deborah Barker points out, the chick flick has been defined variously as escapist entertainment for women, simply as films that men do not like, as examinations of capable, independent female characters and their empowerment, as emotional "tearjerkers," as tales of female bonding, and as the antithesis to male-oriented action films. Although really the boundaries of the woman's film always were rather vague, the subgenre of the chick flick seems to have developed even more ill-defined and porous borders and to be constantly expanding in new and previously unexplored directions.

At the core of the chick-flick phenomenon right now, I would place a group of films that, as Lisa Rüll suggests, combine a comedic look at the lives and loves of contemporary young women with an accompanying focus on female empowerment and solidarity. They also add a tincture of old-fashioned sentimentality and a fairy-tale sensibility to the mix. As Carol Dole points out in her essay, the result of this rather odd recipe is films that have a strong connection to third-wave feminism in that they mix feminist ideas with traditional femininity. Films such as *Bridget Jones's Diary* (2001), *Legally Blonde* (2001) and their sequels, as well as the extremely popular television series *Sex and the City* (1998–2004), seem to me to form the core of the chick-flick subgenre. These films appeal to the postfeminist sensibilities of a twenty-to-thirtysomething audience and convey the third-wave feminist notion that women can have it all. They can be whatever they want to be and have whatever they want to have. The films also show a renewed acceptance of traditional notions of femininity that were largely rejected by second-wave feminism but have been revived in this postfeminist era. They combine this acceptance of conventional femininity, however, with feminist calls for female independence and for women's pursuit of success in the public sphere.

Additionally, a notable group of chick flicks are teen pics or maturational female comedies, such as the popular *The Princess Diaries* (2001) and its sequel. These films resemble their more mature counterparts in that they show their adolescent female protagonists entering young adulthood ostensibly with the freedom to select what is right for them from a wide range of life choices. As Dole points out, the problems these postfeminist-inspired films have in fashioning plausible endings that convey their upbeat message suggests a disconnection between the "girlpower" sentiments these films want to propagate and the realities of women's lives. Nonetheless, the idea that women can be whatever they want to be and can do it in pink dresses and stiletto heels is obviously a very attractive one to a wide female audience. That the endings of these chick flicks seem forced, completely implausible, and/or simply ridiculous indicates, however, that the marriage between feminism and conventional femininity may not be quite as happy as these films might want young women to believe.

Many of these teen chick flicks fall into the makeover film category. *The Princess Diaries* and its sequel are paradigmatic examples. They show a young independent woman who does not meet the criteria of conventional beauty experiencing an external transformation that places her much more in accord with mainstream beauty standards. The changes she experiences in terms of her looks not only internally alter her sense of identity and self-confidence but also bring her the external joys of love and/or marriage. As Suzanne Ferriss points out, *The Princess Diaries* is part of a long tradition of films from different periods in film history that center on female protagonists of various ages who experience life-changing transformations from ugly ducklings to beautiful swans. Notable examples of such films include *Funny Face* (1957), *Moonstruck* (1987), *Pretty Woman* (1990), and *My Big Fat Greek Wedding* (2002). Each of these films fashions a narrative that takes its heroine from a femininity that is not accepted by mainstream society to the essence of conventional feminine beauty. Films deliberately invoking the fashion world, such as *Funny Face* and *The Devil Wears Prada* (2006), highlight the role of consumer culture in fashioning femininity, raising additional questions about women's uses of fashion in crafting identity. Significantly, Ferriss can find only one lone parody of the makeover film cycle, the independent 1995 film *Party Girl* directed by female director Daisy von Scherler Mayer. Scherler Mayer's film presents a scathing critique of the makeover film plot as it shows its heroine finding true fulfillment not in female submission within love and marriage but in female autonomy and career accomplishment, not in self-definition through shopping but in forging an identity with both style and intellect.

It would be a mistake to see the focus of all chick flicks as women in their twenties or thirties. In her essay, Margaret Tally points to the prevalence of what she calls the "older bird" chick flick that centers on the sexual awakening of a woman in middle age. As Tally suggests, many of these films, such as *Something's Gotta Give* (2002), *The Banger Sisters* (2002), *Under the Tuscan Sun* (2003), and *Calendar Girls* (2003) make progressive statements about the ultimately enriching effects of a middle-aged woman's reassertion of her sexuality. Again, like their younger chick-flick counterparts, these older birds are shown by the film's end to have it all: a happy family life, a fulfilling career, and good sex. In fact, the life-is-pretty-rosy-for-women-today message might really be the glue that holds the current chick-flick phenomenon together. According to Mallory Young, this happy-ever-after quality has allowed the chick flick to extend its domain to European films. Young suggests that the chick flick has infiltrated Europe in the form of what she dubs "chic flicks," woman-oriented romantic comedies that employ the boy-meets-girl, boy-loses-girl, boy-gets-girl formula so prevalent in American romance films. *Amélie* (2001), *The Princess and the Warrior* (2000), and *Mostly Martha* (2001) mix the characteristics of upbeat romance with a sense of naturalism inherited from an earlier European film tradition. Combined with a comedic tone and a requisite happy ending are isolated, alienated characters, tragic plot elements, and a sense of the inexorable march of fate.

Deborah Barker also points to another category of chick flicks, the "Southern-Fried Chick Flick," which she believes has a wide appeal to both younger and older female viewers. Tracing the history of the southern chick flick back to female friendship films of the late 1980s and early 1990s such as *Steel Magnolias* (1989) and *Fried Green Tomatoes* (1991), both of which strongly emphasized their southern settings, Barker argues that more recent chick flicks set in the South, including *Divine Secrets of the Ya-Ya Sisterhood* (2002), have cultivated their predecessors' wide appeal to both younger and older female viewers. They have done so in two major ways: first, their emphasis on mother–daughter bonding allows them to examine areas of conflict between second- and third-wave feminism. This emphasis on intergenerational female relationships is complemented by the films' southern setting, which as Barker points out, renders the films perfect bridges between feminism and the postfeminist backlash against it. Because the South is commonly seen as a bastion of conservative thought, it furnishes an ideal setting for films that attempt to negotiate between feminist progressivism and the postfeminist backlash's emphasis on traditional values and a return to conventional femininity. In trying to construct a bridge between feminism and postfeminism, however, the southern chick flick incorporates feminist ideas only to depoliticize them and make them acceptable to the patriarchal status quo. Films such as *Steel Magnolias*, *Fried Green Tomatoes*, and *Divine Secrets of the Ya-Ya Sisterhood* personalize feminist issues by reducing them to the level of individual economic empowerment, sexual freedom, and life choices. As Barker notes, the larger social problems of institutionalized sexism and racism are marginalized not only by being reduced to personal dilemmas but also by being relegated to the past. Thus, these southern chick flicks, like other films within the chick-flick category, present a rosy picture of contemporary women's lives in which every road to personal fulfillment is open to every woman if she just can make the right personal decisions.

Similarly, Lisa Henderson shows that this rosy view of contemporary womanhood extends to lesbian-oriented chick flicks. Henderson argues that Rose Troche's low-budget, independent feature *Go Fish* (1994) presents the lives of its twentysomething protagonists as "a modest lesbian utopia." Self-consciously deviating from earlier lesbian films, which Troche described as "agonized tract[s] about coming out" or movies in which women "only have sex under excruciating circumstances" (quoted in Hollinger 170), *Go Fish* presents a lesbian romantic comedy with a happy ending that takes place, as Henderson points out, in "a lesbian identified community that is at once multicultural . . . and racially and economically unconflicted." Like other chick flicks, *Go Fish* reaches out to its female viewers, and notably to its lesbian viewers, to tell them that they too can have it all, this "all" being idyllic lesbian love and utopian lesbian community. They can have it all, as the film's protagonist announces in her concluding voice-over direct address to the audience, if they can just manage to make wise personal choices. Her rather *jejune* advice is:

> Don't fear too many things—it's dangerous. Don't say so much— you'll ruin everything. Don't worry yourself into a corner and just don't think about it so much. The girl you're gonna meet doesn't look like anyone you know, and when you meet her, your toes might tingle, or you might suppress a yawn. It's hard to say. Don't box yourself in. Don't leave yourself wide open. Don't think about it every second, but just don't let yourself forget. The girl is out there.

This passage suggests quite clearly why not all viewers saw the film as a charmingly up-beat representation of "an historically invisible character type: the happy lesbian in love." Those that Henderson describes as the film's "lesbian detractors," and, I might suggest, some non-lesbian detractors as well, found its treatment of lesbianism "juvenile, trivial, and insufficiently serious about Women's oppression."

A bit farther from the center of the genre, one might even say reaching the tentacles of the chick flick out to infiltrate the traditionally male terrain of the action-adventure genre, are what Kate Waites describes as the women warrior films. These films are hybrids that clearly lack the generic purity of the more "girlie-girl" chick flicks described above, and they extend their address to a crossover audience of women seeking hard-bodied female heroes and young men seeking sexy-bodied action heroines. Mixing feminist goals of female strength and independence with a masculinist ideology of violent action, women warrior films within the *Lara Croft*, *Charlie's Angels*, and *Kill Bill* franchises all present kick-ass female protagonists who can hold their own in what had previously been an exclusively male, tough-as-nails action-adventure universe. As Holly Hassel points out, however, the infiltration of the chick flick into the action-adventure domain did not involve immediate acceptance. It required that the transitional figure of what Hassel calls the "babe scientist" first be inserted into the action-adventure film. This figure acted as a female helpmate to the male hero, adding her scientific expertise to the male protagonist's physical brawn to vanquish the threat posed by some terrifying scientific phenomenon, be it mutated sharks, devastating tornadoes, or killer robots.

One might regard the babe scientist as a progressive addition to the action-adventure film, and indeed it was a positive development in that women were finally allowed to enter the genre as more than just helpless victims, but this progress was mitigated, as Hassel suggests, both visually and narratively by the babe scientist's "babeness," her gratuitously sexualized image, and the plot's determination to minimize her importance in vanquishing the film's threat. In fact, Hassel points out that the babe scientist can be seen merely as a bait-and-switch tactic that misled female viewers into thinking they finally had a character in the action-adventure film with whom they could identify. Then, once they were drawn into the film, the narrative condemned the babe scientist as both a bad scientist and a weak warrior who needed to be converted from her cold reliance on intellect to the male hero's more intuitive commonsense grasp of the situation. For Hassel, the move from the babe scientist action-adventure films to the more recent women warrior films, focusing on what she feels are "sensitive female action heroes," such as Lara Croft and Charlie's Angels, is a definite step in the right direction.

## The question of progress

I am not sure I can agree with Hassel that the new female action heroes are really a progressive phenomenon. I think the question of how much progress one can see in all of these new chick flicks remains unresolved. Running through this whole volume of essays is a sense of the deeply ambivalent messages these films convey to their female viewers. Do these new chick-flick representatives of the woman's film really represent a progressive advance over their predecessors? As Maureen Turim suggests, the question comes down to whether chick flicks actually offer their female viewers a different desiring female subjectivity than their predecessors. In some ways the answer to this question is clearly yes, but one must still regard them with a certain amount of caution. Consider, for instance, this chick-flick infiltration of the action-adventure genre, which on the surface seems so progressive. Certainly, it is an important development that women are moving into a filmic space that has been exclusively a male domain, yet is this movement reason for unrestrained celebration? Kate Waites shows that the image of the female warrior, which appears on the surface so transgressive, is actually one fraught with contradictions. As Waites suggests, the woman warrior actually can be seen as an almost monstrous mix of traits that are associated with heroic masculinity and conventional femininity. While she is physically powerful, stoic, and courageous, she is also a motherly, highly sexualized, oedipalized "phallic" woman. Waites even proposes that like the femme fatale of *film noir* before her, the figure of the woman warrior is more a product of male myth-making and a reflection of masculine ambivalence and insecurity about women than of social acceptance of female heroism and strength.

One only has to look at the differing interpretations Waites and Hassel present of Lara Croft to see how ambiguous her representation is and how easily it opens itself up to divergent reading possibilities. For instance, Waites sees Angelina Jolie's Lara Croft as a compromised female action hero, "a hybrid of over-determined masculine and feminine qualities" confined in the "cage of the monstrous-feminine." Hassel, on the other hand, sees Croft as progressively blending together feminine attributes of sexual objectification and heightened emotionality with qualities of narrative agency, stoical toughness, and physical prowess previously only identified with male action heroes. For Hassel, Croft definitely represents a positive direction in the development of the chick action hero, an empowering figure for her female audience, and a powerful presence in the action-adventure genre.

One sees a similar ambiguity in the discussions of other types of chick flicks. For instance, in spite of Dole's support of *Legally Blonde* and other third-wave feminist films, she still feels compelled to discuss the problems the films have constructing satisfying conclusions. While the films propose that women now have a wide range of life choices, they cannot so easily envision to what ends those choices actually might lead, except perhaps for the thrilling possibility of wearing pink for the rest of one's life. Similarly, in spite of her generally favorable reaction to the recent wave of older bird films, Tally also feels they convey a number of problematic messages, the first being the initial assumption that underlies all of these sagas of middle-aged women's glorious rediscovery of their sexuality, namely the idea that women in middle age have lost their sexuality in the first place. This is a dilemma never even remotely suggested for older male stars. Also, as Tally points out, one can ask whether these films really present their female protagonists as sexually free or merely reduce them to their sexuality, a tendency of Hollywood representations of women that is hardly new or progressive. Finally, all of these older bird films are very careful in the end to contain female sexuality within the family and to select as its most salient characteristic the threat or service it poses to the well-being of the family unit. How progressive are these ideas really?

Myra Mendible also sees a decided ambiguity in what she labels "chica flicks," films that extend the plot elements of the chick flick to Latina protagonists. Mendible looks at three examples of this phenomenon: the Jennifer Lopez star-vehicle *Maid in Manhattan* (2002) and two independent films directed by women of color, *I Like It Like That* (1994) and *Real Women Have Curves* (2002). As Mendible shows, each of these films, regardless of their status as independent or Hollywood productions, presents ambivalent images of Latina and working-class women. Their surface narrative works to alleviate racial and class anxieties by offering a reassuring vision of social mobility for those of every race, class, and gender, whereas on a deeper level they reveal below their surface optimism the reality of a fragmented and divided American society. *Maid in Manhattan* is perhaps the paradigmatic example of this ambivalence. Its "border romance" between Ralph Fiennes's Republican senator out of touch with the working class and Jennifer Lopez's Chicana maid with deep roots in her working-class ethnic community shows Lopez's character, Marisa, using fashion and sex appeal to transcend her background and enter into Fiennes's compassionate conservative upper-class life. Elements of the film, however, render this image of social harmony problematic. Marisa transforms herself to become "whitened" enough to merit ascent out of working-class ethnicity. This ascent is presented as a badge of her exceptionality, and her big social accomplishment is not that she finally will be able to speak for herself and her Chicano/a community, but that her presence at her Republican husband's side "authorizes" him to speak on their behalf.

I think one can query the unambiguously progressive nature not just of chick flicks like *Maid in Manhattan* that deal with class and ethnic issues, but of all chick flicks. Do they raise questions that challenge women's prescribed gender roles and the role of female friendship in women's lives or do they ultimately just use these questions to advocate women's submission to long established gender proscriptions? Do they embody the complexities of women's lives or merely reflect male views of women? Do they portray women realistically, and what is a realistic portrayal of women anyway? Do they present positive images of women or is the positive-image approach to popular-culture representations naïve and unduly restrictive? In light of these myriad questions that remain about the chick-flick phenomenon, the effect these films have on their female audience remains highly questionable. The messages offered in these contemporary women-oriented films are just as conflicted as those offered by their woman's film predecessors. Perhaps they are conflicted in different ways, but nevertheless significant ambiguity remains just under the seemingly progressive surface of all of these films. And the ultimate question then becomes the old one that feminists for decades have been asking about woman-oriented cinema: in the final analysis are these films good or bad for women? Or to put it in another way, do they really offer an alternative to male-conceived cinematic representations of women? It seems to me that this determination has yet to be made, but the importance of the question certainly indicates the need for the continuing study of the chick-flick phenomenon. These are films that undoubtedly shape women's thinking about themselves and about women's role in society. That we understand what defines these representations, how their history has evolved, how they relate to male-dominated cinema, and what effects they are having on their female viewers is a project that we must continue to pursue, and this volume makes important contributions to that study.

## Works cited

Corrigan, Timothy. *Film and Literature: An Introduction and Reader.* Upper Saddle River, NJ: Prentice Hall, 1999.

Doane, Mary Ann. *The Desire to Desire: The Woman's Film of the 1940s.* Bloomington: Indiana University Press, 1987.

Hollinger, Karen. *In the Company of Women: Contemporary Female Friendship Films.* Minneapolis: University of Minnesota Press, 1998.

# Selected filmography

*The Accused* (Jonathan Kaplan, 1988)
*An Affair to Remember* (Leo McCary, 1957)
*Alice Doesn't Live Here Anymore* (Martin Scorsese, 1975)
*Alien* (Ridley Scott, 1975)
*Alien 3* (David Fincher, 1993)
*Alien: Resurrection* (Jean-Pierre Jeunet, 1997)
*Aliens* (James Cameron, 1986)
*All about Eve* (Joseph L. Mankiewicz, 1950)
*All About My Mother* (Pedro Almodóvar, 1999)
*Along Came Polly* (John Hamburg, 2003)
*Amélie* (Jean-Pierre Jeunet, 2001)
*Anywhere But Here* (Wayne Wang, 1999)
*Après Vous* (Pierre Salvadori, 2005)
*As Good as It Gets* (James L. Brooks, 1997)
*Back Street* (John M. Stahl, 1932; Robert Stevenson, 1941)
*The Banger Sisters* (Bob Dolman, 2002)
*Bats* (Louis Morneau, 1999)
*Beaches* (Garry Marshall, 1988)
*Beauty Shop* (Bille Woodruff, 2005)
*Because I Said So* (Nancy Meyers, 2007)
*Behind Office Doors* (Melville W. Brown, 1931)
*Belle de jour* (Luis Buñuel, 1967)
*Bend It Like Beckham* (Gurinder Chadha, 2002)
*Better than Chocolate* (Anne Wheeler, 1999)
*The Best Man* (Malcolm D. Lee, 1999)
*Big Business Girl* (William A. Seiter, 1931)
*Birth of a Nation* (D. W. Griffith, 1915)
*Bread and Tulips* (Silvio Soldini, 2000)
*Bride and Prejudice* (Gurinder Chadha, 2005)
*Bridget Jones's Diary* (Sharon Maguire, 2001)
*Bridget Jones: The Edge of Reason* (Beeban Kidron, 2004)
*Bringing Up Baby* (Howard Hawks, 1938)
*Brown Sugar* (Rich Famuyiwa, 2002)
*Calendar Girls* (Nigel Cole, 2003)
*Cat Woman* (Pitof, 2004)

*Caught* (Max Ophüls, 1949)
*Chacun cherche son chat* (Cédric Klapisch, 1996)
*Charlie's Angels* (McG, 2000)
*Charlie's Angels: Full Throttle* (McG, 2003)
*Chef in Love* (Nana Dzhordzhadze, 1997)
*China Syndrome* (James Bridges, 1979)
*Chocolat* (Lasse Hallström, 2000)
*A Cinderella Story* (Mark Rosman, 2004)
*City of Lost Children* (Marc Caro and Jean-Pierre Jeunet, 1995)
*The Closet* (Francis Veber, 2001)
*Clueless* (Amy Heckerling, 1995)
*The Color Purple* (Steven Spielberg, 1985)
*A Comedy in Six Unnatural Acts* (Jan Oxenberg, 1975)
*Congo* (Frank Marshall, 1995)
*Cries and Whispers* (Ingmar Bergman, 1972)
*Crimes of the Heart* (Bruce Beresford, 1986)
*Dark Mirror* (Robert Siodmak, 1946)
*Dark Victory* (Edmund Goulding, 1939)
*A Daughter of Luxury* (Paul Powell, 1922)
*Daughters of the Dust* (Julie Dash, 1991)
*Delicatessen* (Marc Caro and Jean-Pierre Jeunet, 1991)
*Deep Blue Sea* (Renny Harlin, 1999)
*Desert Hearts* (Donna Deitch, 1985)
*The Devil Wears Prada* (David Frankel, 2006)
*Diary of a Mad Black Woman* (Darren Grant, 2005)
*Dirty Dancing* (Emile Ardolino, 1987)
*Divine Secrets of the Ya-Ya Sisterhood* (Callie Khouri, 2002)
*Down with Love* (Peyton Reed, 2003)
*The Dreamlife of Angels* (Erick Zonca, 1998)
*East of Eden* (Elia Kazan, 1955)
*Eat, Drink, Man, Woman* (Ang Lee, 1994)
*Educating Rita* (Lewis Gilbert, 1983)
*Elektra* (Rob Bowman, 2005)
*Ella Enchanted* (Tommy O'Haver, 2004)
*Enough* (Michael Apted, 2002)
*Erin Brockovich* (Steven Soderbergh, 2000)
*The Family Stone* (Thomas Bezucha, 2005)
*Fatal Attraction* (Adrian Lyne, 1987)
*Flashdance* (Adrian Lyne, 1983)
*Footloose* (Herbert Ross, 1984)
*Forbidden Love: The Unashamed Stories of Lesbian Lives* (Lynne Fernie and
    Aerlyn Weissman, 1992)
*Four Weddings and a Funeral* (Mike Newell, 1994)
*Freaky Friday* (Mark Waters, 2003)
*French Kiss* (Lawrence Kasdan, 1995)
*Fried Green Tomatoes* (Jon Avnet, 1991)
*Funny Face* (Stanley Donen, 1957)
*G.I. Jane* (Ridley Scott, 1997)

*Gaslight* (George Cukor, 1944)
*Ghost* (Jerry Zucker, 1990)
*Giant* (George Stevens, 1956)
*Girlfight* (Karyn Kusama, 2000)
*Girlfriends* (Claudia Weill, 1978)
*Go Fish* (Rose Troche, 1994)
*Godzilla* (Rolan Emmerich, 1998)
*Gone with the Wind* (Victor Fleming, 1939)
*The Good Mother* (Leonard Nimoy, 1988)
*The Goodbye Girl* (Herbert Ross, 1977)
*The Graduate* (Mike Nichols, 1967)
*Happenstance* (Laurent Firode, 2000)
*The Heiress* (William Wyler, 1949)
*Hiroshima mon amour* (Alain Resnais, 1959)
*His Girl Friday* (Howard Hawks, 1940)
*Hollow Man* (Paul Verhoeven, 2000)
*Hope Floats* (Forest Whitaker, 1998)
*The Hours* (Stephen Daldry, 2002)
*How to Lose a Guy in 10 Days* (Donald Petrie, 2003)
*How Stella Got Her Groove Back* (Kevin Rodney Sullivan, 1998)
*I Like It Like That* (Darnell Martin, 1994)
*Imitation of Life* (Douglas Sirk, 1959)
*In Her Shoes* (Curtis Hanson, 2005)
*In the Cut* (Jane Campion, 2003)
*The Incredibly True Adventure of Two Girls in Love* (Maria Maggenti, 1995)
*Indecent Proposal* (Adrian Lyne, 1993)
*Iris* (Richard Eyre, 2001)
*It Happened One Night* (Frank Capra, 1934)
*Julia* (Fred Zinnemann, 1977)
*Just Like Heaven* (Mark Waters, 2005)
*Kate and Leopold* (James Mangold, 2001)
*Kill Bill, Vol. 1* (Quentin Tarantino, 2003)
*Kill Bill, Vol. 2* (Quentin Tarantino, 2004)
*A Knight's Tale* (Brian Helgeland, 2001)
*Lara Croft: Tomb Raider* (Simon West, 2001)
*Lara Croft Tomb Raider: Cradle of Life* (Jan de Bont, 2003)
*Last Days of Disco* (Whit Stillman, 1998)
*The Last Kiss* (Tony Goldwyn, 2001)
*Laurel Canyon* (Lisa Cholodenko, 2002)
*Legally Blonde* (Robert Luketic, 2001)
*Legally Blonde 2: Red, White and Blonde* (Charles Herman-Wurmfeld, 2004)
*Like Water for Chocolate* (Alfonso Arau, 1992)
*Little Women* (Gillian Armstrong, 1994)
*The Long Kiss Goodnight* (Renny Harlin, 1996)
*Love Actually* (Richard Curtis, 2004)
*Love Jones* (Theodore Witcher, 2004)
*Lost in Translation* (Sofia Coppola, 2003)
*Love Story* (Arthur Hiller, 1970)

*Lovely & Amazing* (Nicole Holofcener, 2001)
*Madea's Family Reunion* (Tyler Perry, 2006)
*Maid in Manhattan* (Wayne Wang, 2002)
*Mansfield Park* (Patricia Rozema, 1999)
*Marie Antoinette* (Sofia Coppola, 2006)
*The Matrix* (Andy and Larry Wachowski, 1999)
*Mean Girls* (Mark Waters, 2004)
*Mildred Pierce* (Michael Curtiz, 1945)
*The Millionaire* (Jack Conway, 1921)
*Miracle on 34th Street* (George Seaton, 1947)
*The Mirror Has Two Faces* (Barbra Streisand, 1996)
*Mona Lisa Smile* (Mike Newell, 2003)
*Money Train* (Joseph Ruben, 1995)
*Monsoon Wedding* (Mira Nair, 2001)
*Moonstruck* (Norman Jewison, 1987)
*Mostly Martha* (Sandra Nettelbeck, 2001)
*Moulin Rouge!* (Baz Luhrmann, 2001)
*Mr & Mrs Smith* (Doug Liman, 2005)
*Mrs Dalloway* (Marleen Gorris, 1997)
*Mrs Henderson Presents* (Stephen Frears, 2005)
*Music and Lyrics* (Marc Lawrence, 2007)
*My Big Fat Greek Wedding* (Joel Zwick, 2002)
*My Fair Lady* (George Cukor, 1964)
*The New York Hat* (D. W. Griffith, 1912)
*Nine to Five* (Colin Higgins, 1980)
*Norbit* (Brian Robbins, 2007)
*Norma Rae* (Martin Ritt, 1979)
*The Notebook* (Nick Cassavetes, 2004)
*Now, Voyager* (Irivng Rapper, 1942)
*An Officer and a Gentleman* (Taylor Hackford, 1982)
*Once Around* (Lasse Hallström, 1991)
*Party Girl* (Daisy von Scherler Mayer, 1995)
*Passion Fish* (John Sayles, 1992)
*Pat and Mike* (George Cukor, 1952)
*Peggy Sue Got Married* (Francis Ford Coppola, 1986)
*Personal Best* (Robert Towne, 1982)
*Philadelphia* (Jonathan Demme, 1993)
*The Philadelphia Story* (George Cukor, 1940)
*The Piano* (Jane Campion, 1993)
*The Piano Teacher* (Michael Haneke, 2001)
*Places in the Heart* (Robert Benton, 1984)
*The Portrait of a Lady* (Jane Campion, 1996)
*Pretty Woman* (Garry Marshall, 1990)
*Pride & Prejudice* (Joe Wright, 2005)
*The Prince & Me* (Martha Coolidge, 2004)
*The Prince of Tides* (Barbra Streisand, 1991)
*The Princess and the Warrior* (Tom Tykwer, 2000)
*The Princess Diaries* (Garry Marshall, 2001)

*Raising Helen* (Garry Marshall, 2004)
*Rambling Rose* (Martha Coolidge, 1991)
*Real Women Have Curves* (Patricia Cardoso, 2002)
*Rebecca* (Alfred Hitchcock, 1940)
*Romance* (Catherine Breillat, 1999)
*A Room with a View* (James Ivory, 1985)
*Run Lola Run* (Tom Tykwer, 1998)
*Saving Face* (Alice Wu, 2004)
*Sabrina* (Billy Wilder, 1954)
*Secret Beyond the Door* (Fritz Lang, 1948)
*Secrets of a Secretary* (George Abbott, 1931)
*Sense and Sensibility* (Ang Lee, 1995)
*Serendipity* (Peter Chelsom, 2001)
*The Seven Samurai* (Akira Kurosawa, 1954)
*Shall We Dance?* (Masayuki Suo, 1996; Peter Chelsom, 2004)
*She Married Her Boss* (Gregory La Cava, 1935)
*She's All That* (Robert Iscove, 1999)
*She's the Man* (Andy Fickman, 2006)
*Shirley Valentine* (Lewis Gilbert, 1989)
*Shrek 2* (Andrew Adamson and Kelly Asbury, 2004)
*Silkwood* (Mike Nichols, 1983)
*Sleeping with the Enemy* (Joseph Ruben, 1991)
*Sleepless in Seattle* (Nora Ephron, 1993)
*Smouldering Fires* (Clarence Brown, 1925)
*The Social Secretary* (John Emerson, 1916)
*Someone to Watch Over Me* (Ridley Scott, 1987)
*Something's Gotta Give* (Nancy Meyers, 2003)
*Soul Food* (George Tillman, Jr., 1997)
*Species* (Roger Donaldson, 1995)
*Species II* (Peter Medak, 1998)
*Starting Over* (Alan J. Pakula, 1979)
*Stella* (John Erman, 1990)
*Stella Dallas* (Henry King, 1925; King Vidor, 1937)
*Steel Magnolias* (Herbert Ross, 1989)
*Strange Days* (Kathryn Bigelow, 1995)
*Strictly Ballroom* (Baz Luhrman, 1992)
*Sunset Boulevard* (Billy Wilder, 1950)
*Swept Away* (Lina Wertmüller, 1974)
*Tadpole* (Gary Winick, 2002)
*Talk to Her* (Pedro Almodóvar, 2002)
*Tender Comrade* (Edward Dmytryk, 1943)
*Terms of Endearment* (James L. Brooks, 1983)
*Thelma & Louise* (Ridley Scott, 1991)
*These Three* (William Wyler, 1936)
*The Thin Man* (W. S. Van Dyke, 1934)
*Thirteen* (Catherine Hardwicke, 2003)
*13 Going on 30* (Gary Winick, 2004)
*This Is My Life* (Nora Ephron, 1992)

*Titanic* (James Cameron, 1997)
*Too Wise Wives* (Lois Weber, 1921)
*Tortilla Soup* (Maria Ripoll, 2001)
*Tremors* (Ron Underwood, 1990)
*Tremors 2: Aftershocks* (S. S. Wilson, 1996)
*True Heart Susie* (D. W. Griffith, 1919)
*The Truth about Cats & Dogs* (Michael Lehmann, 1996)
*The Turning Point* (Herbert Ross, 1977)
*Twentieth Century* (Howard Hawks, 1934)
*Twister* (Jan de Bont, 1996)
*The Two Mrs Carrolls* (Peter Godfrey, 1947)
*Unconditional Love* (P. J. Hogan, 2002)
*Under the Tuscan Sun* (Audrey Wells, 2003)
*Unfaithful* (Adrian Lyne, 2002)
*An Unmarried Woman* (Paul Mazursky, 1977)
*The Valley of the Dolls* (Mark Robson, 1967)
*Vertigo* (Alfred Hitchcock, 1958)
*Virus* (John Bruno, 1995)
*Volver* (Pedro Almodóvar, 2006)
*Waiting to Exhale* (Forest Whitaker, 1995)
*A Walk on the Moon* (Tony Goldwyn, 1999)
*The Watermelon Woman* (Cheryl Dunye, 1996)
*Way Down East* (D. W. Griffith, 1920)
*The Way We Were* (Sydney Pollack, 1973)
*The Wedding Singer* (Frank Coraci, 1998)
*What Women Want* (Nancy Meyers, 2000)
*When Harry Met Sally* (Rob Reiner, 1989)
*Where the Boys Are* (Henry Levin, 1960)
*White Oleander* (Peter Kosminsky, 2002)
*The White Rose* (D. W. Griffith, 1923)
*The Women* (George Cukor, 1939)
*Women on the Verge of a Nervous Breakdown* (Pedro Almodóvar, 1988)
*Working Girl* (Mike Nichols, 1988)
*Written on the Wind* (Douglas Sirk, 1954)

# Selected bibliography

Adelman, Kim. *The Ultimate Guide to Chick Flicks: The Romance, the Glamour, the Tears, and More!* New York: Random House-Broadway, 2005.

Alexander, Meredith. *The It-Girl's Guide to Video: Sex and Style on the Silver Screen.* London: Penguin, 1999.

Barbas, Samantha. *Movie Crazy: Fans, Stars, and the Cult of Celebrity.* New York: Palgrave, 2001.

Basinger, Jeanine. *A Woman's View: How Hollywood Spoke to Women, 1930–1960.* New York: Knopf, 1993.

Baumgardner, Jennifer and Amy Richards. *Manifesta: Young Women, Feminism, and the Future.* New York: Farrar, 2000.

Bean, Jennifer M. and Diane Negra (eds). *A Feminist Reader in Early Cinema.* A Camera Obscura Book. Durham: Duke University Press, 2002.

Beltran, Mary C. "The Hollywood Latina Body as Site of Social Struggle: Media Constructions of Stardom and Jennifer Lopez's 'Cross-over Butt.'" *Quarterly Review of Film & Video* 19 (2002): 17–86.

Bernard, Jami. *Chick Flicks: A Movie Lover's Guide to the Movies Women Love.* New York: Citadel, 1997.

Berry, Jo and Angie Errigo. *Chick Flicks: Movies Women Love.* London: Orion, 2004.

Blue, Angel. "Chick Movies: The Drinking Game." Lance & Eskimo Dot Com. <http://www.lanceandeskimo.com/angel/chicko.shtml>.

Bodnar, John. *Blue-Collar Hollywood: Liberalism, Democracy, and Working People in American Films.* Baltimore: Johns Hopkins University Press, 2003.

Buhler, James, Caryl Flynn, and David Neumeyer (eds). *Music and Cinema.* Hanover, NH: Wesleyan University Press, 2000.

Buhler, James, Anahid Kassabian, David Neumeyer, Robynn Jeananne Stilwell and Kyle Barnett. "Panel Discussion on Film Sound/Film Music." *The Velvet Light Trap* 51 (2003): 73–91. Project Muse. 6 Jan. 2005. <http://muse.jhu.edu/journals/the_velvet_light_trap/v051/51.1buhler.html>.

Brown, Jeffrey. "Gender and the Action Heroine: Hardbodies and the Point of No Return." *Cinema Journal* 35 (Spring 1996): 52–71.

Bruzzi, Stella. *Undressing Cinema: Clothing and Identity in the Movies.* New York: Routledge, 1997.

Caputi, Jane. *Goddesses and Monsters: Women, Myth, Power, and Popular Culture.* Madison, Wisconsin: University of Wisconsin Press, 2004.

Cevasco, Maria Elisa. "Whatever Happened to Cultural Studies: Notes from the Periphery." *Textual Practice* 14.3 (2000): 433–38.

Cook, Pam. "No Fixed Address: The Woman's Picture from *Outrage* to *Blue Steel.*" In *Contemporary Hollywood Cinema.* Ed. Steve Neale and Murray Smith. London and New York: Routledge, 1998: 229–46.

Dávila, Arlene. *Latinos Inc: The Marketing and Making of a People.* Berkeley: University of California Press, 2001.

de Alba, Alicia Gaspar (ed.). *Velvet Barrios: Popular Culture and Chicana/o Sexualities.* New York: Palgrave Macmillan, 2003.

Denisoff, R. Serge and George Plasketes. "Synergy in 1980s Film and Music: Formula for Success or Industry Mythology?" *Film History* 4.3 (1990): 257–76.

DiBattista, Maria. *Fast-Talking Dames.* New Haven and London: Yale University Press, 2001.

Dicker, Rory, and Alison Piepmeier. *Catching a Wave: Reclaiming Feminism for the 21st Century.* Boston: Northeastern University Press, 2003.

Doane, Mary Ann. *The Desire to Desire: The Woman's Film of the 1940s.* Bloomington: Indiana University Press, 1987.

Donnelly, K. J. (ed.). *Film Music: Critical Approaches.* Edinburgh: Edinburgh University Press, 2001.

Dyer, Richard. *Heavenly Bodies: Film Stars and Society.* Basingstoke, UK: Macmillan, 1986.

——*White.* New York: Routledge, 1997.

Eckert, Charles. "The Carole Lombard in Macy's Window." *Quarterly Review of Film Studies* 3 (Winter 1978): 1–21.

Evans, William and Celestino Deleyto (eds). *Terms of Endearment: Hollywood Romantic Comedy of the 1980s and 1990s.* Edinburgh: Edinburgh University Press, 1998.

Ewen, Elizabeth. "City Lights: Immigrant Women and the Rise of the Movies." *Signs* 5 (Spring 1980): S45–66.

Findlen, Barbara (ed.). *Listen Up: Voices from the Next Generation.* Seattle: Seal, 1995.

Fischer, Lucy. "Greta Garbo and Silent Cinema: The Actress as Art Deco Icon." In *A Feminist Reader in Early Cinema.* Ed. Jennifer M. Bean and Diane Negra. Durham and London: Duke University Press, 2002: 476–98.

——*Shot/Countershot: Film Tradition and Women's Cinema.* Princeton, NJ: Princeton University Press, 1989.

Flores, Juan. *From Bomba to Hip Hop: Puerto Rican Culture and Latino Identity.* New York: Columbia University Press, 2000.

Ford, Elizabeth A. and Deborah C. Mitchell. *The Makeover in Movies: Before and After in Hollywood Films, 1941–2002.* Jefferson, NC: McFarland, 2004.

Frith, Simon, Andrew Goodwin, and Lawrence Grossberg (eds). *Sound and Vision: The Music Video Reader.* London: Routledge, 1993.

Gabbard, Krin. *Jammin' at the Margins: Jazz and the American Cinema.* Chicago: Chicago University Press, 1996.

Gamman, Lorraine and M. Marshment (eds). *The Female Gaze: Women as Viewers of Popular Culture.* London: Women's Press, 1988.

Gaines, Jane. "The Queen Christina Tie-Ups: Convergence of Show Window and Screen." *Quarterly Review of Film and Video* 11 (1989): 35–60.

Gaines, Jane and Charlotte Herzog (eds). *Fabrications: Costume and the Female Body*. New York: Routledge, 1990.

Garber, Marjorie. *Vested Interests: Cross-Dressing and Cultural Anxiety*. New York: Routledge, 1992.

Gates, Philippa. "The Man's Film: Woo and the Pleasures of Male Melodrama." *Journal of Popular Culture* 35.1 (2001): 59–79.

George, Susan A. "Not Exactly 'of Woman Born': Procreation and Creation in Recent Science Fiction Films." *Journal of Popular Film & Television* 28.4 (2001): 176–83.

Green, Philip. *Cracks in the Pedestal: Ideology and Gender in Hollywood*. Amherst: University of Massachusetts Press, 1998.

Harvey, James. *Romantic Comedy in Hollywood, from Lubitsch to Sturges*. 1987. New York: Da Capo, 1998.

Haskell, Molly. *From Reverence to Rape: The Treatment of Women in the Movies*. 1973. 2nd ed. Chicago: University of Chicago Press, 1987.

Habell-Pallán, Michelle and Mary Romero (eds). *Latino/a Popular Culture*. New York: NYU Press, 2002.

Henry, Astrid. *Not My Mother's Sister: Generational Conflict and Third-Wave Feminism*. Bloomington: Indiana University Press, 2004.

Hollinger, Karen. *In the Company of Women: Contemporary Female Friendship Films*. Minneapolis: University of Minnesota Press, 1998.

Hollows, Joanne. *Feminism, Femininity, and Popular Culture*. New York: Manchester University Press, 2000.

Holmlund, Chris. "Cruisin' for a Bruisin': Hollywood's Deadly (Lesbian) Dolls." *Cinema Journal* 34.1 (Fall 1994): 31–51.

——"Postfeminism from A to G." *Cinema Journal* 44.2 (Winter 2005): 116–21.

Hunter, Latham. "The Celluloid Cubicle: Regressive Constructions of Masculinity in 1990s Office Movies." *The Journal of American Culture* 26.1 (2003): 71–86.

Inness, Sherrie A. *Tough Girls: Women Warriors and Wonder Women in Popular Culture*. Philadelphia: University of Pennsylvania Press, 1999.

Kabir, Shameem. *Daughters of Desire: Lesbian Representations in Film*. London: Cassell, 1998.

Kamen, Paula. *Feminist Fatale: Voices from the "Twentysomething" Generation Explore the Future of the "Women's Movement."* New York: Fine, 1991.

Kaplan, E. Ann. *Women and Film: Both Sides of the Camera*. New York: Methuen, 1983.

Karlin, Fred. *Listening to Movies: The Film Lover's Guide to Film Music*. New York: Schirmer-Simon & Schuster Macmillan, 1994.

King, Justine. "Crossing Thresholds: The Contemporary British Woman's Film." In *Dissolving Views: Key Writings on British Cinema*. Ed. Andrew Higson. London: Cassell, 1996: 216–31.

Knadler, Stephen. "Blanca from the Block: Whiteness and the Transnational Latina Body." *Genders* 41 (2005). 30 Sept 2005 <http://www.genders.org/g41/g41_knadler.txt>.

Kuhn, Annette. *Women's Pictures: Feminism and Cinema*. New York: Routledge, 1982.

Lane, Christina. *Feminist Hollywood from Born in Flames to Point Break*. Detroit, MI: Wayne State University Press, 2000.

Lannan, Steve. *Pop Fiction: The Song in Film*. Bristol: Intellect, 2004.

LaPlace, Maria. "Producing and Consuming the Woman's Film." In *Home Is Where the Heart Is: Studies in Melodrama and the Woman's Film*. Ed. Christine Gledhill. London: BFI, 1987: 138–66.

Lopez, Ana M. "Are All Latins from Manhattan? Hollywood, Ethnography, and Cultural Colonialism." In *Unspeakable Images: Ethnicity and American Cinema*. Ed. Lester Friedman. Chicago: University of Illinois Press, 1991: 404–23.

McCaughey, Martha and Neal King (eds). *Reel Knockouts: Violent Women in the Movies*. Austin: University of Texas Press, 2001.

McLean, Adrienne. "I'm a Cancino: Transformation, Ethnicity, and Authenticity in the Construction of Rita Hayworth." *Journal of Film and Video* 44.3–4 (Fall/Winter 1993): 8–26.

McPherson, Tara. *Reconstructing Dixie: Race, Gender, and Nostalgia in the Imagined South*. Durham, NC: Duke University Press, 2003.

Mabry, A. Rochelle. "About a Girl: Female Subjectivity and Sexuality in Contemporary 'Chick' Culture." In *Chick Lit: The New Woman's Fiction*. Ed. Suzanne Ferriss and Mallory Young. New York: Routledge, 2005: 191–206.

Maltby, Richard and Ian Craven. *Hollywood Cinema*. Oxford: Blackwell, 1995.

Mayer, Vicki. *Producing Dreams, Consuming Youth: Mexican Americans and Mass Media*. Piscataway, NJ: Rutgers University Press, 2003.

Mayne, Judith. *Cinema and Spectatorship*. New York and London: Routledge, 1993.

Mendible, Myra (ed.). *From Bananas to Buttocks: The Latina Body in Popular Culture*. Austin: University of Texas Press, 2006.

Modleski, Tania. *Feminism without Women: Culture and Criticism in a Postfeminist Age*. New York: Routledge, 1991.

——*Loving with a Vengeance: Mass-Produced Fantasies for Women*. Hamden: Archon, 1982.

Neale, Steve. "The Big Romance or Something Wild? Romantic Comedy Today." *Screen* 33 (Autumn 1992): 284–99.

Negra, Diane. *Off-White Hollywood: American Culture and Ethnic Female Stardom*. New York: Routledge, 2001.

——"Quality Postfeminism? Sex and the Single Girl on HBO." *Genders* 39 (2004). <http://www.genders.org/g39/g39_negra.html>.

Negron Muntaner, Frances. "Jennifer's Butt." *Aztlán* 22.2 (1997): 181–94.

Noriega, Chon A. (ed.). *Chicanos and Film: Representation and Resistance*. Minneapolis: University of Minnesota Press, 1992.

Projansky, Sarah. *Watching Rape: Film and Television in Postfeminist Culture*. New York: New York University Press, 2001.

Rabinovitz, Lauren. *Points of Resistance: Women, Power & Politics in the New York Avant-Garde Cinema, 1943–71*. 1991. 2nd edition. Champaign, IL: University of Illinois Press, 2003.

Read, Jacinda. *The New Avengers: Feminism, Femininity, and the Rape-Revenge Cycle*. Manchester: Manchester University Press, 2000.

Renov, Michael. "Advertising/Photojournalism/Cinema: The Shifting Rhetoric of Forties Female Representation." *Quarterly Review of Film and Video* 11 (1989): 1–21.

Rich, B. Ruby. *Chick Flicks: Theories and Memories of the Feminist Film Movement*. Durham, NC: Duke University Press, 1998.

Rios Bustamante, Antonio. "Latino Participation in the Hollywood Film Industry, 1911–1945." In *Chicanos and Film*. Ed. Chon Noriega. Minneapolis: University of Minnesota Press, 1992: 141–167

Rivière, Joan. "Womanliness as a Masquerade." In *Formations of Fantasy*. Ed. Victor Burgin, James Donald and Cora Kaplan. New York: Methuen, 1986: 35–44.

Rogers, Mary F. *Barbie Culture*. London: Sage, 1999.

Roiphe, Katie. *The Morning After: Sex, Fear, and Feminism on Campus*. Boston: Little, Brown, 1993.

Romney, Jonathan and Adrian Wooton (eds). *Celluloid Jukebox: Popular Music and the Movies since the Fifties*. London: BFI, 1995.

Ross, Steven J. *Working Class Hollywood: Silent Films and the Shaping of Class in America*. Princeton, NJ: Princeton University Press, 1999.

Rowe, Kathleen. *The Unruly Woman: Gender and the Genres of Laughter*. Austin: University of Texas Press, 1995.

Rowe-Finkbeiner, Kristin. *The F-Word: Feminism in Jeopardy: Women, Politics, and the Future*. Emeryville, CA: Seal, 2004.

Silverman, Kaja. *The Acoustic Mirror*. Bloomington: Indiana University Press, 1992.

Smith, Jeff. *The Sounds of Commerce: Marketing Popular Film Music*. New York: Columbia University Press, 1998.

Stacey, Jackie. *Star Gazing: Hollywood Cinema and Female Spectatorship*. London and New York: Routledge, 1994.

Stoddard, Karen M. *Saints and Shrews: Women and Aging in American Popular Film*. Westport, CT: Greenwood, 1983.

Stoller, Debbie. "Feminists Fatale: BUSTing the Beauty Myth." In *The* BUST *Guide to the New Girl Order*. Ed. Marcella Karp and Debbie Stoller. New York: Penguin, 1999: 42–47.

Streeby, Shelley. *American Sensations: Class, Empire, and the Production of Popular Culture*. Berkeley: University of California Press, 2002.

Tasker, Yvonne. *Working Girls: Gender and Sexuality in Popular Cinema*. New York: Routledge, 1998.

Tasker, Yvonne and Diane Negra (eds). "In Focus: Postfeminism and Contemporary Media Studies." *Cinema Journal* 44.2 (Winter 2005): 107–33.

Troost, Linda and Sayre Greenfield (eds). *Jane Austen in Hollywood*. 1998. 2nd ed. Lexington: University Press of Kentucky, 2001.

Turim, Maureen Cheryn. *Flashbacks in Film: Memory & History*. New York: Routledge, 1989.

——"High Angles on Shoes: Cinema, Gender and Footwear." In *Footnotes: On Shoes*. Ed. Shari Benstock and Suzanne Ferriss. New Brunswick, NJ: Rutgers University Press, 2001: 58–90.

——"Seduction and Elegance: The New Woman of Fashion in Silent Cinema." In *On Fashion*. Ed. Shari Benstock and Suzanne Ferriss. New Brunswick, NJ: Rutgers University Press, 1994: 14–58.

Valdivia, Angharad. *A Latina in the Land of Hollywood*. Tucson: University of Arizona Press, 2000.

Walsh, Andrea S. *Women's Film and Female Experience, 1940–1950*. New York: Praeger, 1984.

White, Patricia. *unInvited: Classical Hollywood Cinema and Lesbian Representability*. Bloomington and Indianapolis: Indiana University Press, 1999.

Williams, Linda (ed.). *Viewing Positions: Ways of Seeing Film*. New Brunswick: Rutgers University Press, 1994.

Willis, Susan. *High Contrast: Race and Gender in Contemporary Hollywood Film*. Durham, NC: Duke University Press, 1997.

Wojcik, Pamela Robertson and Arthur Knight (eds). *Soundtrack Available: Essays on Film and Popular Music*. Durham, NC: Duke University Press, 2001.

Wolf, Naomi. *Fire with Fire: The New Female Power and How It Will Change the 21st Century*. New York: Random, 1993.

Wyatt, Justin. *High Concept: Movies and Marketing in Hollywood*. Austin: University of Texas Press, 1994.

# Contributors

Deborah Barker is an associate professor of English at the University of Mississippi. Her first book, *Aesthetics and Gender in American Literature: The Portrait of the Woman Artist* (Bucknell University Press, 2000), delineated the aesthetic debates surrounding the fictional image of the woman artist. Her current book project, entitled *The Rape of the South*, explores the uses of sexual and racial violence in the cinematic South.

Carol M. Dole is professor of English at Ursinus College, where she teaches both British literature and film courses. Her publications on the portrayal of women in film include an article on female law enforcement officers in *Reel Knockouts: Violent Women in the Movies* (University of Texas Press, 2001). She is currently studying the evolution of film adaptation practices.

Suzanne Ferriss is professor of English at Nova Southeastern University. She has co-edited two volumes on the cultural study of fashion: *On Fashion* (1994) and *Footnotes: On Shoes* (2001), which was nominated for the Popular Culture Association's Susan Koppelman award. She is also co-author of *A Handbook of Literary Feminisms* (Oxford University Press, 2002). Most recently, she co-edited *Chick Lit: The New Woman's Fiction* (Routledge, 2005) with Mallory Young.

Holly Hassel is assistant professor of English at University of Wisconsin-Marathon County. She received her Ph.D. from the University of Nebraska-Lincoln in 2002, focusing on alcohol and gender in twentieth-century American women's fiction. Her current research and teaching interests include feminist film studies, and the scholarship of teaching and learning in literary studies.

Lisa Henderson is associate professor of communication at the University of Massachusetts, Amherst, where she teaches media and cultural studies. She is the author of numerous essays on cultural production and sexual representation, as well as a book in progress titled *Love and Money: Queers, Class, and Cultural Production*.

Karen Hollinger is professor of film and literature at Armstrong Atlantic State University. She is the author of *The Actress: Hollywood Acting and the Female Star* (2006) and *In the Company of Women: Contemporary Female Friendship Films* (1998).

Myra Mendible is associate professor in the Humanities division at Florida Gulf Coast University, where she teaches for the English department and the Interdisciplinary Studies program. She has published articles in a variety of peer-reviewed journals, including *Feminist Media Studies; Genders: Innovative Work in the Arts, Humanities and Social Theories; Critique: Studies in Contemporary Fiction;* and the *Journal of American Culture*. Recently, she edited the anthology *From Bananas to Buttocks: The Latina Body in Popular Culture* (University of Texas Press, 2007).

Lisa M. Rüll is an Academic Support tutor at the University of Nottingham and has lectured in Further and Higher Education across the UK. She completed her Ph.D. on the art collector Peggy Guggenheim at the School of American and Canadian Studies at the University of Nottingham. Her publications include exhibition catalogues on Surrealism and contemporary art, as well as reviews for *Scope: An Online Film Journal, The European Journal of American Culture,* and *Cercles*.

Margaret Tally is associate professor of Sociology at Empire State College of the State University of New York. She is the author of *Television Culture and Women's Lives: Thirtysomething and the Contradictions of Gender* (University of Pennsylvania Press, 1995) and has published articles in *Women's Studies, Studies in Popular Culture* and *Journal of Social Forces*. She is currently working on a book exploring how motherhood is represented in contemporary popular films.

Maureen Turim is professor of English and film studies at the University of Florida. She is author of *Abstraction in Avant-Garde Films* (1989), *Flashbacks in Film: Memory and History* (1989), and *The Films of Oshima Nagisa: Images of a Japanese Iconoclast*. She has published over fifty essays in anthologies and journals on a wide range of theoretical, historical and aesthetic issues in cinema and video, art, cultural studies, feminist and psychoanalytic theory, and comparative literature. Several of these essays have appeared in translation in French and German. She has also written catalogue essays for museum exhibitions. Her current book project is entitled *Desire and Its Ends: The Driving Forces of Recent Cinema, Literature, and Art*.

Kate Waites is professor of English and Gender Studies at Nova Southeastern University. She has published articles on women's life writing and images of women in popular culture in the *College English*

*Association, Auto/Biography, Literature/Film Quarterly,* and *The Journal of Popular Culture.* She is also the author of a work of creative non-fiction, *Particular Friendships: A Convent Memoir* (2006).

**Mallory Young** is professor of English and French at Tarleton State University. She has published on a variety of topics, from the *Odyssey* to Texas women's literature and, with Suzanne Ferriss, has co-authored several articles on chick culture. She and Ferriss co-edited *Chick Lit: The New Woman's Fiction* (Routledge, 2005).

# Index